Duncan J. D. Smith

ONLY IN
VIENNA

A Guide to Unique Locations,
Hidden Corners and Unusual Objects

—

Photographs by
Duncan J. D. Smith
except where stated otherwise

**The
Urban
Explorer**

A Nazi-era anti-aircraft tower (Flakturm) in the Augarten (see no. 63)

Contents

Introduction

Most visitors would agree with the words of Karl Kraus, the renowned Austrian writer and satirist. Vienna is indeed one of Europe's most culture-rich capital cities. It is also one of the easiest to navigate. The many available guidebooks offer the casual visitor a fabulous array of museums and galleries, churches and palaces, reflecting the history of the city from Roman times via the Habsburg Empire up to the present day. However, for those with a little more time on their hands and a desire to discover something of the place for themselves, this guidebook has been expressly written.

Based on personal experience walking all twenty-three of the city's districts (*Bezirke*), the author points the city explorer in new and unusual directions. It only takes a few minutes of planning, and a glance at a decent street map, to escape the crowds and the orchestrated tours and discover a rather different city**. This is the Vienna of hidden courtyards and subterranean surprises, coffeehouse culture and sacred spaces, quirky museums and forgotten cemeteries. It is also Vienna with a dark and sinister past, its unkempt Jewish cemeteries and Third Reich anti-aircraft towers bearing grim witness to terrible times.

As would perhaps be expected, many of these locations are to be found within the narrow streets of the city centre, Vienna's 1st District known variously by locals as the *Innere-* or *Altstadt*. On streets that trace medieval thoroughfares and Roman ones before them lurk atmospheric church crypts, converted medieval wine cellars and many of the last city's last old fashioned shops.

An equal number of locations, however, lie outside the footprint of the old city walls, marked today by the grand *Ringstrasse* boulevard. The Inner Suburbs (*Vorstädte*), for example, consisting of the 2nd and 3rd to 9th Districts laid out during the 18th century, contain the bones of composer Vivaldi, a little-visited Armenian Monastery and the so-called Fool's Tower. The Outer Suburbs (*Vororte*) comprising the 10th to 23rd Districts, meanwhile, beyond the *Gürtel* ring road and the Danube, are home to artist Gustav Klimt's last studio, a converted gasometer and an emperor's private railway station.

Using Vienna's exemplary transport network of trams (*Strassenbahn*), underground trains (*U-Bahn*) and buses (*Autobus*), the explorer can easily and often quickly reach all these places and that's without detracting whatsoever from the sense of personal discovery that each has to offer. Indeed, directions have been kept to a minimum so as to leave readers free to find their own particular path.

Whether strolling in the Vienna Woods where Sigmund Freud pondered the meaning of dreams, relaxing in a tranquil Japanese garden in a quiet suburb, or gazing at what was once proffered as Montezuma's headdress in the heart of the city, the reader will hopefully take away with them a more indelible memory.

In embarking on these mini-odysseys, the author would only remind readers that telephones be switched off in places of worship, which should not be visited during services, and that due respect be shown in the peaceful city courtyards that are home and workplace to many Viennese. Other than that, treat Vienna as a giant oyster containing many precious pearls. I just hope you enjoy finding them as much as I did.

Duncan J. D. Smith, Vienna

* The dates given after the names of Austria's monarchs are the actual years they reigned for, whereas those given after non-royal personalities relate to their birth and death.

** The author is a great believer in traditional folding paper maps, which he believes still offer a unique and intriguing overview of a city. Plenty are still available, with the larger ones covering all 23 districts of the city, including tram, bus and rail routes.

After each entry there is a selection of others within walking distance.
An alphabetical gazetteer of opening times of places mentioned in the text can be found at the back of the book together with suggestions for further reading.

A bird's eye view of Vienna from the north-west around the time of the Second Turkish Siege (1683)

1 On Beethoven's Bastion

1st District (Innere Stadt), a tour of the Mölker-Bastei and surroundings; take U-2 to Schottentor

For all its charm and magnificence there are times when the centre of Vienna is too busy. Fortunately, the 1st District also contains a number of quiet corners awaiting discovery. One of the best is Mölker-Bastei, just a stone's throw away from Schottentor and the bustling Ringstrasse.

To visit Mölker-Bastei is to step back in time. The journey begins at the bottom of a flight of steps, opposite an entrance to the former Palais Ephrussi (recently made famous in Edmund de Waal's popular book *The Hare with Amber Eyes*). The steps rise steeply, culminating in a cul de sac of smart eighteenth century town houses. The presence of the hillock on which the houses stand seems a mystery in a relatively flat city like Vienna, until one learns this is one of the last remaining bastions of Vienna's Renaissance city wall.

Erected between 1531 and 1566 to protect Vienna against the Ottoman Turks, the wall was a colossal construction. Eight metres high and twenty metres wide it was punctuated by gates and towers, and ran along the course of today's Ringstrasse. Vienna's famously grand boulevard was laid out soon after the walls were demolished in the 1850s, for fear they might be used to harbour homegrown revolutionaries as had happened in 1848.

Quite why the Mölker-Bastei escaped demolition is a mystery, although it could be something to do with the house at the far end of the row. This is the Pasqualatihaus (named after its onetime owner), where on the fourth floor Ludwig van Beethoven (1770-1827) lived in 1804–08 and again in 1810–14. The composer penned his only opera *Fidelio* here. Peep inside the building's well-preserved courtyard, with its old communal water fountain and roof-winch, to get a feel for Beethoven's world (what was his apartment is now a public museum).

A sharp left turn sees Mölker-Bastei become Schreyvogelgasse, and the houses are suddenly Biedermeier and Baroque. One of them, the Dreimäderlhaus, is where Schubert allegedly wooed three sisters simultaneously through an upstairs window. Whilst this seems unlikely it is documented for certain that in 1853 Emperor Franz Joseph I (1848-1916) was attacked hereabouts by a knife-wielding Hungarian assassin. He was saved by his Irish adjutant, and in thanks ordered the construction of the nearby Votivkirche (see no. 56).

As the street widens another Baroque house appears on the lefthand side, its façade adorned with a golden house ornament in the form of God's all-seeing eye. The unassuming doorway beneath it is where Orson Welles appears for the first time in the 1949 film classic *The Third Man*. The camera crew threw buckets of water over the cobbled street so as to enhance the scene's *film noir* atmosphere (see no. 2).

To the left of Harry's doorway a narrow road leads upwards traversing the full thickness of the old city wall. At the top it descends by means of another staircase into what would have been the city proper. Each brick was made by royal appointment and is stamped with the double eagle of the Austro-Hungarian dual monarchy.

A quiet corner on the Mölker-Bastei

At the bottom is traditional clothiers Tostmann Trachten at Schottengasse 3a. The shop occupies a small part of the so-called Melker-Hof, an imposing Baroque building constructed by the monks of Melk Abbey, who occupied it during their visits to the city (the bastion bears their name, too). From 1629 onwards the monks were permitted to sell their own wine in Vienna, and they stored it in vast cellars beneath the building. These labyrinthine cellars, which served as an air raid shelter during the Second World War, can be visited on request (see no. 6).

Returning to pavement level outside the wall, there are two further points of interest. One is the Trümmerfrauen Denkmal, a memorial recalling those Viennese women who between 1943 and 1954 helped clear the rubble from their ruined city. It has courted controversy because many former Nazis helped clear rubble, and the creation of the monument has long been a pet project of Austria's right-wing Freedom Party. The other is a memorial garden to Vienna-born Joseph Rock (1884–1962), the last of the great plant hunters.

Other places of interest nearby: 2, 53, 56, 57

2 Harry Lime's Doorway

1st District (Innere Stadt), doorway at Schreyvogelgasse 8
on the Mölker-Bastei; take U-2 to Schottentor

With the closing of the Second World War, Austria was for ten long years carved up into four zones by the occupying Allied powers (Great Britain, United States, France and USSR). Although the bombed-out capital found itself deep within the Russian zone, it was decided to make the city an international sector, patrolled by a representative from each of the four powers (the so-called "four men in a jeep" era).

It was against the resulting backdrop of black marketing, espionage and counter-espionage that Sir Carol Reed's classic 1949 film thriller *The Third Man* was set. Based on an idea by Graham Greene, and a resulting film script requested by Sir Alexander Korda, it concerns American writer Holly Martins (played by Joseph Cotten) who visits 1948 Vienna to look up his old friend Harry Lime (Orson Welles). On arrival, however, he witnesses Lime's funeral, having been apparently knocked down outside his apartment (in reality the Baroque Palais Pallavicini in Josefsplatz, well worth glancing at in the evening when its gilded ceilings and chandeliers can be seen from the street). Martins grows suspicious and discovers that Lime has been dealing in sub-standard penicillin resulting in several deaths, and that Lime's demise was merely a stunt to avoid arrest.

Harry Lime's doorway on Schreyvogelgasse

In the 57th minute of the film Harry famously re-appears, very much alive, in the doorway at Schreyvogelgasse 8 on the peaceful Mölker-Bastei, which still looks exactly as it did in the film (see no. 1). After coming clean to Martins in his famous "cuckoo clock" speech below the Ferris wheel *(Riesenrad)* in the Volksprater, Lime is cornered by police in the city's labyrinthine sewer system and shot dead (the police enter via a steel hatch still visible in Friedrichstrasse on Karlsplatz; Reed's film crew actually used a staircase on Lothringerstrasse). Filming took place in the covered section of the River Wien that runs between the Naschmarkt and the Stadtpark, with a tense shootout at the subterranean weir below Friedrichstrasse (see nos. 6 & 96).

Other notable scenes in the film include the Café Marc Aurel, now the Midi restaurant at Hoher Markt 5, Café Mozart, which was mocked-up on Neuer Markt, and the Casanova Revue Theater at Dorotheergasse 6–8, where Martins undertakes his late-night detective work.

In addition to solid supporting roles from Trevor Howard and Alida Valli, and a memorable main theme played on the zither by *Heurige* musician Anton Karas, what makes *The Third Man* so special is author Greene's detailed depiction of post-war Vienna. He was briefed by his MI6 boss Kim Philby, stayed in the British-occupied Hotel Sacher, and was shown around the city by Elizabeth Montagu, sister of England's Lord Montagu of Beaulieu (she also acted as the film's location advisor, English language coach to the Austrian actors, and escort to Mr. Welles, who lodged at the Hotel Orient on Tiefer Graben, a so-called *Stundenhotel*, where rooms rented by the hour are popular with lovers and prostitutes). The only detail Greene didn't get right was Welles's fear of sewer rats!

See the original black and white film in the Burgkino at Opernring 19, where it has been showing since 1980, and experience the sewers first-hand as part of the guided walk *In the Footsteps of the Third Man* (visit www.viennawalks.com). Absolutely essential is the Third Man Museum *(Dritte Mann Museum)* at Pressgasse 25 (4th District), with its posters, photos, and archive documents covering not only the film but also Vienna's history pre- and post-war (see page 231). Pride of place goes to the zither used by musician Anton Karas to record the film's memorable theme tune, actor Trevor Howard's annotated script, and the cap worn in the film by actor Herbert Halbik who played Little Hansel. There is even a jukebox playing several hundred versions of the theme tune and a real gravestone seen in the film acquired from the Central Cemetery. The last resting place of Karas can be found below a zither-shaped headstone in the cemetery at Sievering *(Friedhof Sievering)*.

Other places of interest nearby: 1, 3, 4, 5, 6, 53

3 Turkish Delights

1st District (Innere Stadt), sculpture at the corner of
Freyung and Strauchgasse; take U-3 to Herrengasse

With the fall of Constantinople in 1453, the Byzantine Empire ended
and within forty years the burgeoning Ottoman Empire was expanding
westwards towards the Danube. In 1526, Suleyman the Magnificent
(1494-1566) captured Pest in Hungary (now part of modern Budapest)
and by autumn 1529 he had advanced to the gates of Vienna with

A Turkish horseman with
scimitar on Strauchgasse

300,000 men housed in 25,000 tents. Only the
dogged resistance of the city garrison under
Count Niklas of Salm (his Egyptian marble
tomb is in the Votivkirche at Schottentor),
the early onset of winter and re-supply
problems forced Suleyman to retreat (see the
wall plaque at the corner of Kärntnerstrasse
and Walfischgasse marking the site of the
old Kärntnertor gate, where fierce fighting
took place).

As a result, Ferdinand I (1521–64)
erected new walls around the city and
moved the imperial court permanently in
1533 to the Hofburg. It was at this time that
the famous Swiss Gate *(Schweizertor)* was
built (see no. 26).

Following the death of 50,000 inhabitants from bubonic plague in 1679, it was
a weakened garrison of 10,000 that again
faced Ottoman might during the second
Turkish siege of 1683. This time Grand
Vizier Kara Mustafa arrived with 200,000
men and laid siege to the city, against the
wishes of his Sultan, Mehmet IV, who merely wanted the trade routes
secured. In the meantime, a united Christian army under Duke Charles
of Lorraine and King John III of Poland (Jan Sobieski) was formed and
eventually routed the Turks at the Battle of Kahlenberg. For his diso-
bedience Mustafa was strangled in Belgrade by the Sultan's emissary
(using a cord of black silk), and Vienna was rebuilt in the triumphant
style of the Baroque. A stone from the Löwel-Bastei, where the Turks
very nearly broke through the city's defences, is now displayed in

12   1st District

one of the side wings of the Burgtheater and inscribed with the date '1683'.

Dotted around the city are tangible reminders of these perilous times, such as the carved scimitar-wielding Turkish horseman on Strauchgasse. It is said to commemorate a baker who discovered Turkish tunnellers in a cellar here and alerted the Viennese guard thereby saving the city. Although the story seems unlikely there's no denying the many stone Turkish cannonballs embedded in some of Vienna's old buildings. Examples include one at Sterngasse 3 shot from Leopoldstadt; three found during renovation work in 1963 in the medieval Griechenbeisel inn at Fleischmarkt 11/Griechengasse 9; one at Am Hof

A gilded Turkish cannonball on a wall in Am Hof

11, subsequently gilded and displayed outside an inn; and several embedded in the South Tower and walls of the Stephansdom, one of which can be seen on the middle buttress of the nave wall with "1683" carved below. Also from this period is the Stephansdom's *Pummerin* bell (meaning Boomer!), the second largest free-swinging bell in Europe, cast in 1711 from 180 Turkish cannon of the type which reduced the spire of the Minoritenkirche to its present stumpy form during the first siege.

Other Ottoman-era reminders include the Upper Belvedere Palace, with its skyline resembling Ottoman tents. It was designed by Lukas von Hildebrandt for Prince Eugene of Savoy (1663–1736), who pushed the Turks back to Hungary. And let's not forget the crescent-shaped croissants (*Kipferl*) so beloved of the Viennese (see no. 50). There is also a Turkish map of Vienna, drawn from memory, found in a Grand Vizier's secret archive in Belgrade in 1688, and now amongst other Turkish spoils in the Wien Museum in Karlsplatz. Vienna's Museum of Military History (*Heeresgeschichtliches Museum*) also holds a collection of Turkish trophies worth tracking down (see no. 43).

Formal reconciliation between Vienna and Turkey is celebrated by an ornate, Koran-inscribed fountain at the top of Währing's Türkenschanzpark. Meaning 'Turkish entrenchment', the park marks the site of the Ottoman's final stand during the second siege.

Other places of interest nearby: 2, 4, 5, 6

4   Court of the Babenbergs

1st District (Innere Stadt), a stroll around Am Hof; take U-3 to Herrengasse

Most tourists visiting Vienna's city centre gravitate towards the Hofburg, the Habsburgs' sprawling winter palace, or else the towering Stephansdom, and it's understandable why. There are other locations in the area, however, where Vienna wears its history less obviously. The cobbled square known as Am Hof is a good example.

Unless there's a market being staged or some other celebration, many people use Am Hof only as a means of getting somewhere else. This is a pity since pausing here for just ten minutes is enough to provide a potted history of Vienna courtesy of a handful of intriguing buildings.

First on the scene were the Romans. They selected this spot for their legionary fortress of Vindobona, drawn by a mound of glacial boulders that provided an ideal lookout over the Danube. The remains of an impressive Roman drain have been excavated beneath Am Hof, and the defensive moat protecting the north wall of the fortress is still represented by the street called Tiefer Graben (meaning 'deep ditch').

The name 'Am Hof' means 'at Court' and reflects the fact that the Babenberg Duke, Heinrich II Jasomirgott (1141–77), built his palace here when he chose Vienna as his capital in 1156 (see the wall plaque at Am Hof 2). It was the Babenbergs who upgraded Austria to an independent dukedom in the wake of the collapse of the empire of Charlemagne, and restored Vienna's trade and culture thereby giving it city status. They controlled Vienna until the accession of Rudolf of Habsburg as ruler of Austria in 1276.

The Habsburgs faced many perils until their demise in 1918. The column at the centre of Am Hof, for example, records their gratitude at being delivered from Protestant Swedish Forces during the Thirty Years' War (1618–1648). The cannonball hanging at Am Hof 11 recalls the Second Turkish Siege (1683) during which the Ottomans came close to taking the city before being decisively repulsed.

The defeat of the Turks, as well as that of Protestantism and the plague, saw parts of Vienna rebuilt as a triumphant Baroque city. Witness the lovely Urbanihaus erected in the 1730s at Am Hof 12, with its intricate iron lantern. Next door at Am Hof 13 is the Collalto Palace, where in 1762 the 6-year old Mozart first displayed his prodigious musical talents. And next door again is the Kirche am Hof (or the Church of the Nine Choirs of Angels) from where in 1806 the end of the ailing Holy Roman Empire was announced following the defeat of the Austrian Emperor by Napoleon.

During the revolutions that swept Europe in 1848, in protest against rising unemployment and food prices, the mob stormed the Civilian Arsenal (*Bürgerliches Zeughaus*) at Am Hof 10. After order was restored the building was converted into a fire station, the idea for which was first mooted by Baroque architect Johann Bernhard Fischer von Erlach (1656–1723) as a means of protecting his own work in the area. In 1935 the fire station expanded into the Märklein-isches Haus, a former palace at Am Hof 7 and now houses Vienna's Fire Brigade Museum (*Feuerwehrmuseum*). The narrow red-painted building squeezed between the Arsenal and the fire station was once the sparkling wine factory of Johann Kattus. Founded in 1857, it has since moved out to Döbling, where its extensive cellars can be visited.

The former Civilian Arsenal on Am Hof

This tour concludes at Am Hof 6, a wholly modern building featuring Olafur Eliasson's curious *Yellow Fog* art installation, which emits smoke daily at dusk.

Vienna's innate sense of grandeur extends not only to its fire station but also to other utilitarian buildings. A modern example is Friedrich Hundertwasser's psychedelic municipal incineration plant (*Fernwärme Wien*) at Spittelau. Even the city's oldest preserved secular building, a former watermill concealed in a courtyard at Heumühlgasse 9 (4th District), boasts delicate Gothic windows.

Other places of interest nearby: 3, 5, 6, 8

5 The Lucky Chimney Sweep

1st District (Innere Stadt), effigy of a chimney sweep at Wipplingerstrasse 21; take U-3 to Herrengasse

Effigy of a chimney sweep
on Wipplingerstrasse

On the corner of a building on Wipplingerstrasse, overlooking the Viennese Art Nouveau (*Jugendstil*) Hohe Brücke bridge (1903), is the enormous effigy of a white-capped chimney sweep with his ladder and coiled flue brush. The building he adorns, however, has nothing to do with his profession. It is in fact a lottery establishment – the chimney sweep being seen across Austria as a bringer of good luck.

From medieval times onwards the open fireplace, and later the stove, was at the heart of every Austrian home. The resulting soot-filled chimneys could ignite if not kept clean, posing a serious threat of fire in days when most houses were timber built and thatched. Owners deemed irresponsible in this respect could face the death penalty, and so it brought relief and a feeling of good fortune if a chimney sweep visited one's street. Although children often feared his blackened appearance, it was believed he could deflect the attentions of the devil, thus bringing protection to households against danger and disease.

The connection between chimney sweeps and good luck is celebrated every New Year's Eve (called *Silvester* in Austria, after Pope Silvester I, who died in Rome on December 31st 335AD), when good luck trinkets (*Glücksbringer*) bearing his image (or hers since female sweeps are common today in this respected profession) are exchanged. Shiny chimney sweeps' buttons were once highly prized in this respect and today's trinkets may well be a development of this older custom.

The link with New Year is because sweeps would often render their annual account at this time, and with it a gratuity and New Year's wishes would be exchanged. Even now older Viennese believe that seeing a chimney sweep in the morning will bring the onlooker good fortune for the rest of the day. So much so, that a Chimney Sweeps' Museum (*Rauchfangkehrermuseum*), operated by proud members of the sweeps' guild, has been established at Klagbaumgasse 4 (4th District). Visitors will learn how a sweep cleaning one of the chimneys of the Hofburg overheard and reported a plot to assassinate Empress Maria Theresa. In gratitude sweeps ever since have been allowed to wear belt buckles bearing the Habsburg double eagle.

The Three Kings' initials on a city doorway

Lucky pigs, again in the form of trinkets as well as in edible pink marzipan, are also exchanged at New Year, the pig being the holy animal of the old Germanic gods, as well as the sow being a symbol of prosperity and fertility in many European cultures. In the past when meat was scarce, the man who owned a pig was lucky indeed!

Another unusual New Year custom, observed on January 6th (*Heilige Drei Könige*), is the chalking-up of the initials of the three kings – Caspar, Melchior and Balthazar (*C + M + B*) – on house doors, together with the year, to bring protection and prosperity to Christian households in the coming year. It is often forgotten that the three initials also stand for for *Christus Mansionem Benedicat* (Christ shall bless this house).

New Year good luck tokens including pigs and chimney sweeps

Other places of interest nearby: 4, 8, 9, 10

6 Vienna Subterranea

1st District (Innere Stadt), a tour of subterranean locations including the archaeological remains in Michaelerplatz; take U-3 to Herrengasse

In Middle Eastern archaeology ancient cities are often called *'tell'* sites, that is to say mounds built up over time, layer after layer, on exactly the same spot. To some extent the same can be said of Vienna's 1st District, which today sits on top of a 9 metre-thick layer of cultural debris, including ancient Roman (see no. 13) and Jewish (see no. 9) layers, with those of the medieval and later periods above them. Periodically these layers are brought to light, as during the construction of the U-Bahn, when a medieval chapel was found in Stephansplatz (see no. 22) and an old crypt of the Minoritenkirche revealed off Landhausgasse. Similarly, during the excavation of the Freyung car park, a 12th century cobbled pavement was found and re-laid at present ground level for pedestrians to examine.

Excavations in 1992 in Michaelerplatz *(Archäologisches Grabungsfeld Michaelerplatz)*, which are still visible today, revealed Roman buildings with frescoes and under floor heating (1st–5th centuries AD), medieval houses and a deep well (13th century), walls of the former Imperial pleasure gardens (16th–18th centuries), vaulted cellars (18th– 19th centuries), and part of the Old Burgtheater, demolished in 1888 to make way for the Michaelertrakt (or wing) of the Hofburg. An old doorway from the theatre, where both Mozart's *Le Nozze di Figaro* (1786) and *Così fan Tutte* (1790) were premiered, can be seen inside the Michaelertor on the left-hand side.

Also revealed was a finely-constructed drain made of bricks stamped with the Habsburg double-eagle motif, making up a tiny part of Vienna's labyrinthine sewer system that was made famous by the film *The Third Man* (see no. 2). The city's drainage statistics are incredible – 1,826 kilometres of channels providing a storm sewer system, with house sewers adding an extra 5,063 kilometres of which 182 kilometres are walkable.

Other curious aspects of this subterranean world are crypts (see no. 33) and cellars punched deep into the Viennese clay to gain valuable extra space in the increasingly cramped city. The peculiarity here, of course, is that in those cellars running to several levels (up to five is known), the deepest are the most recent! Tostmann's traditional Austrian outfitters *(Trachten)* at the bottom of the Mölkersteig near

Old cellars revealed by archaeologists in Michaelerplatz

Schottentor has a staircase leading down to an amazingly extensive cellar system that can be visited on request (see no. 1). It may be legend that a woman locked in here in 1940 emerged the next day at the Stephansdom many streets away, but it does demonstrate how the construction of cellars was both uncontrolled as well as uncharted. Below Demel's famous cake shop (*Konditorei*) and café on Kohlmarkt, a cellar was found to be connected to the Hofburg by an ancient tunnel

Mysterious tunnels await discovery beneath Tostmann's shop on Schottengasse

used subsequently by thieves to break into a bank vault half way along – it has now been sealed!

Many of Austria's Baroque monasteries possessed labyrinthine, multi-levelled cellars in Vienna, where they stored wine produced from their own vineyards (e.g. the Zwölfapostelkeller at Sonnenfelsgasse 3, the Heiligenkreuzerhof Monastery at Schönlaterngasse 5 and the Melker Stiftskeller at Schottengasse 3). These sprawling brick-vaulted wine cellars have now become uniquely Viennese taverns that are truly one of Vienna's most unexpected discoveries. A wonderfully atmospheric example well worth visiting is the Piaristenkeller at Piaristengasse 45 (8th district), its 300 year-old cellars housing an opulent restaurant as well as the Emperor Franz Joseph Hat Museum (*Kaiser-Franz-Josef-Hutmuseum*). By appointment the candlelit monastic cellars that once housed the Imperial wine collection (*k.u.k. Weinschatzkammer*) may also be seen.

The deepest wine cellars in Vienna are below the Urbanihaus in Am Hof (see no. 4), whilst just nearby is the cosy vaulted Brezlg'wölb (Pretzel Vault) at Ledererhof 9. The oldest cellar is the Esterházykeller in the bowels of the Esterházy Palais at Haarhof 1, where since 1683 Hungarian wine has been sold from the princely estate of that name. There are many other cellars nearby filling what was once a deep ditch (now called Graben) that ran around the Roman fort (see no. 14).

Not surprisingly, cellars also made ideal air raid shelters in the Second World War, identified by the letters *LSK* (*Luftschutzkeller*) painted on the wall outside. Tragically, a direct hit on the Philipphof in Albertinaplatz, once home to the renowned Jockey Club, killed hundreds when the cellars there gave way – the victims were never recovered and the site is today marked by the Monument against War and Fascism (*Mahnmal gegen Krieg und Faschismus*) created by Austrian sculptor Alfred Hrdlicka (1928-2009) in 1988.

Other places of interest nearby: 3, 4, 7, 8

7   The Sign of the Black Camel

1st District (Innere Stadt), Zum Schwarzen Kameel at
Bognergasse 5; take U-3 to Herrengasse

Until the reign of Empress Maria Theresa (1740–1780), the names
of the streets and squares of Vienna were not officially recorded but
rather recognised only by local names. There were also no official
house numbers, instead domestic dwellings were given either the
name of their owners, or were identified by figurative signs. As many
inhabitants could not read or write, shops were identified by striking
and unambiguous symbols. The Wien Museum (Vienna Museum) in
Karlsplatz contains some fine examples of this early street art, both
from shops (e.g. an eagle carrying an ornate key from a locksmith's
workshop) as well as houses (e.g. a red hedgehog (*Zum roten Igel*)
and the eye of God (*Zum Auge Gottes*)). There is also a beautiful 18th
century wrought-iron lantern, that once hung at Schönlaterngasse 6
(*Zur schönen Laterne*), where a 1971 replica now hangs to remind visitors how the street acquired its name; both were made in the former
Old Smithy – Alte Schmiede – at number 9.

In 1771, a continuous numbering system (*Conscriptionsnum-
mern*) was established in the 1st District.
Running to well over 1000 and used
originally to aid recruitment, it was
not until 1862 that individual streets
were finally numbered, as part of a
system still in use today. Occasionally
an 18th century building can still be
spotted bearing its old continuous house
number, carved or painted onto its lintel,
often side-by-side with the more modern
street number embossed on a metal
plate (e.g. Kleeblattgasse 5, Köllnerhof-
gasse 3, Fleischmarkt 16, Ballgasse 8 and
Kohlmarkt 11, all in the 1st District).

Despite these developments Vienna
has hung on to many of its colourful
house names. These include golden lions
at Wiedner Hauptstrasse 36 (*Zu den
zwei goldenen Löwen*), black ravens
at Rotenturmstrasse 21 (*Zu den drei*

The sign of the Black Camel
on Bognergasse

Raben), a club-wielding caveman at Währinger Strasse 85 (*Zum wilden Mann*), a playful seal at Währinger Strasse 6–8 (*Zur Robbe*), white horses at Josefstädter Strasse 85 (*Sechsschimmelhof*), a spouting whale at both Lerchenfelder Strasse 29 and Piaristengasse 58 (*Zum Walfisch*), the biblical *"Flight from Egypt"* (*"Zur Flucht nach Ägypten"*) at Piaristengasse 56–58, and the mythical basilisk at Schönlaterngasse 7 (*Zum Basilisken*).

Similarly, some commercial establishments retain their symbols, for example a red hand above the old glove-makers (1854) on Schottengasse, a pipe-smoking Turk over the door of tobacco importer Adolf Lichtblau at Hermanngasse 17, innumerable hanging keys denoting locksmiths, and even a pair of wooden Lederhosen outside Grünangergasse 12! A few also retain their old names, such as the Black Camel (*Zum schwarzen Kameel*), founded in 1618 as a spice store at Bognergasse 5 by Johann Baptist Cameel (a relative named the Camelia flower), where both Beethoven and Lord Nelson shopped. Another is the Blue Carp (*Zum blauen Karpfen*), a former Baroque inn at Annagasse 14 founded c.1700 by Georg Kärpf.

In the late-19th century numerous shops revelled in their exclusive appointments to supply the Austrian Imperial Court, hence the *k.k.* (*kaiserlich-königlich*) (imperial-royal) designation still to be seen over their doors. They included J. & L. Lobmeyr (1823) glassmakers at Kärntnerstrasse 26 (1st District), Habig (1867) hat makers at Wiedner Hauptstrasse 15 (4th District) and Ch. Demel's Söhne (1786) confectioners at Kohlmarkt 14 (1st District), supplier of edible decorations for the Imperial Christmas tree. Two final shop-related curiosities are the distinctly non-Austrian crests above Knize's outfitters at Graben 13 (1st District), They hark back to when the store supplied dress uniforms to the Turkish Sultan and the Shah of Iran.

Following the so-called Compromise (*Ausgleich*) of 1867, the Dual Monarchy of Austria-Hungary was established by which Hungary got its own parliament in Budapest and Emperor (Kaiser) Franz Joseph I of Austria was also crowned King (König) of Hungary. Consequently, everything Hungarian was prefaced k. (königlich) (royal), whereas in the rest of the empire the initials k.k. (kaiserlich-königlich) (imperial-royal) were used; meanwhile everything Austro-Hungarian was prefaced k.u.k. (kaiserlich und königlich) (imperial and royal).

Other places of interest nearby: 4, 6, 8, 9

8 The Clockmakers' Quarter

1st District (Innere Stadt), the Clock Museum (*Uhrenmuseum der Stadt Wien*) at Schulhof 2; take U-3 to Herrengasse

The huge church dominating Vienna's Am Hof courtyard (see no. 4) is like the Roman god Janus – it exhibits two very different faces. Known variously as Kirche am Hof, or the more colourful Church of the Nine Choirs of Angels (*Kirche zu den neun Chören der Engel*), its public face fronts the courtyard itself. Italian architect Carlo Carlone added this incredible Baroque façade in 1662, and it was from the balcony in 1782 that Pope Pius VI famously gave benediction. It was here too, on 6th August 1806, that a herald proclaimed the end of the Holy Roman Empire (see no. 68).

However, a short walk through an archway beside the church into Schulhof will reveal the other face of this intriguing building. Suddenly, the original and much older 14th century Gothic stonework appears, like a cake being stripped slowly of its white Baroque icing. Similarly, inside the church, the original Gothic Carmelite fittings have been masked by later Jesuit additions, such as attached pilasters and porticoes (this same effect is visible at St. Michael's Church

A Fiaker passing a watchmaker's shop in Schulhof

(*Michaelerkirche*), where a white-plastered Baroque front, facing the Hofburg, contrasts with older unclad Gothic stonework to the rear).

It is typical of Vienna that in a few paces the informed visitor can escape a bustling courtyard and discover a peaceful back street. Schulhof behind the Kirche am Hof is no exception, where tucked between the church's Gothic buttresses are two tiny former watch-maker's lock-ups reminiscent of medieval times, especially when a horse-drawn *Fiaker* clatters by on the cobbles. *Fiakers* were first licensed in 1693 and named after the *Auberge Saint-fiacre*, a Parisian inn outside which hire carriages had long drawn up. The buttresses have been scooped out to allow carriages to pass more easily down this narrow thoroughfare.

Opposite, at Schulhof 2, in the 300-year old Baroque Obizzi Palace, is the Clock Museum (*Uhrenmuseum*), founded in 1921 and the oldest of its kind. Rudolf Kaftan, an early curator, together with the novelist Marie von Ebner-Eschenbach, accumulated the collection. Among the fascinating exhibits on its three floors are many curiosities, including the world's smallest pendulum clock that fits inside a thimble, as well as clocks that are concealed inside walking sticks and landscape oil paintings. There is also an incredibly complicated astronomical clock, the hands of which take 20,904 years to make one complete revolution! Such novelties make this museum of interest to everyone, and not just the specialist.

The Obizzi Palace itself, named also the Harp House for its harp-shaped plan, has an interesting history. It was once the property of Count Ernst Rüdiger von Starhemberg (1638–1701), defender of Vienna during the Turkish siege of 1683. During the fighting it is said that lead cannonballs were cast in the fireplace. The Baroque façade was added in 1690 by Ferdinand Obizzi, who commanded the city garrison.

Before departing the area be sure to walk just around the corner onto Kurrentgasse, where at number 2 there is a window flanked with cherubs. It illuminates a tiny, frescoed, late-Baroque chapel dedicated to Polish saint Stanislaus-Kostka. It is Vienna's smallest church.

Other places of interest nearby: 4, 5, 7, 9

9 Out of the Depths I Cry to You

1st District (Innere Stadt), the Judenplatz Museum *(Museum Judenplatz)* at Judenplatz 8; take U-3 to Herrengasse

Historical records from Upper Austria reveal a Jewish presence in that part of the country from as early as 903AD. A Jewish community has existed in Vienna since the 12th century and in 1238 they were granted privileges by the last of the Babenberg Dukes, Friedrich II (1230 – 46). As a result Vienna's medieval Jewish Quarter, focussed on the area now known as Judenplatz, began to flourish. It was home to the *Or-Sarua-Synagogue* that contained one of the most important *Talmud* schools in the German-speaking world. Its floor was set a little below ground level in accordance with a Bible verse from Psalms ("Out of the depths I cry to you"). The peaceful conditions offered to Jews in Vienna, whose services were highly valued, even provided a haven to those fleeing from intolerance elsewhere in Europe.

However, in 1421 under the Catholic Habsburg Duke Albrecht V (later Emperor Albrecht II, 1438–39), Jewish property was appropriated to fill the royal coffers in the face of poor harvests and threats from the Protestant Hussites of Bohemia (now the Czech Republic). The result was an atrocious pogrom known as the first Viennese *Geserah*. Albrecht justified it by accusing the community of desecration of the Eucharistic Host, ritual murder and of being in league with the anti-Habsburg Protestants. The Synagogue was burned down, its stones re-used in the city's Old University (*Alte Universität*) and the Jewish community forcibly baptised. Those that refused were

Judenplatz with the Holocaust Memorial (left) and the statue of Lessing (right)

The notorious anti-Semitic inscription at Judenplatz 2

burned alive on the Erdberg, thrown into the Danube, jailed or expelled: many opted for mass suicide.

The anti-Semitic feeling of the time is reflected in a notoriously offensive wall inscription at Judenplatz 2. Called *Zum Grossen Jordan*, the expulsion is gleefully recorded in Latin below a depiction of the baptism of Christ: "By baptism in the River Jordan bodies are cleansed from disease and evil, so all secret sinfulness takes flight. Thus the flame rising furiously through the whole city in 1421 purged the terrible crimes of the Hebrew dogs. As the world was once purged by the flood, so this time it was by fire." History relates how the Jews would eventually re-group in Leopoldstadt in the early 17th century (see no. 65), the location of their final ghetto under the Nazis (see nos. 14 & 59).

It was during the 1990s, whilst sculptress Rachel Whiteread was planning her affecting Holocaust Memorial (*Holocaust Mahnmal*) in Judenplatz, that the charred remains of the original medieval Synagogue were uncovered several metres below present ground level. The city council agreed that such deeply symbolic remains should be made accessible, which they now are via the Judenplatz Museum at number 8, occupying the ground floor of the Misrachi-Haus *Torah* school. This subterranean museum contains an excellent video reconstruction of the walled Jewish Quarter as it appeared in 1400, and of its Synagogue, whose hexagonal *bimah*, where the *Torah* lectern once stood, is marked out in Judenplatz directly above, next to Whiteread's memorial.

To complete the sense of having come full circle, the statue of German playwright Gotthold Ephraim Lessing, a key figure in the 18th century German Enlightenment, whose views on tolerance and humanism prompted the Nazis to pull it down, was re-cast in 1968 by the original sculptor Siegfried Charoux and now dominates Judenplatz once again. By leaving Judenplatz along Parisergasse, one is walking in the footsteps of Vienna's medieval Jews, who would have exited their ghetto by means of a gate here, the remains of which are preserved just inside the restaurant at number 1.

Other places of interest nearby: 5, 7, 8, 10

10 The Danube Boatmen's Church

1st District (Innere Stadt), the Church of Maria am Gestade, at Salvatorgasse 12; take U-3 to Herrengasse

Of the many churches within the 1st District, that of Maria am Gestade (translated variously as "St. Mary on the Riverbank" or "Virgin on the Shore") is curious for a number of reasons. Together with the Stephansdom, it is one of the few Gothic churches not to have been altered in the subsequent Baroque period, retaining its delicate vaults, tracery and buttresses from the late-14th century. It can be identified from afar, especially when illuminated at night, by its unusual seven-sided filigree tower rising 56 metres into the air. Incredibly it escaped later demolition only because a contractor could not be found who would take away the rubble!

Also unusual is the fact that the nave (the main seating area at the west end) and the chancel (the area directly in front of the altar to the east) are of equal length (the former is usually longer), and the nave is narrower and built slightly askew. This is due to the steep and restricted terrain here on the edge of a natural plateau, used as a defence in both the medieval town and the Roman fort, walls of which were found below the church (see no. 13). Of great interest are the surviving fragments of medieval painted glass incorporated into the beautiful windows behind the High Altar. More would have survived had Napoleon's troops not used the church as an arsenal and stables during their occupation of Vienna in 1809 (see no. 68).

The filigree tower of Maria am Gestade Church from Salvatorgasse

A sculpture on the Fischerstiege depicting Danube fisherfolk

In addition there is a side-chapel containing the mortal remains of Klemens Maria-Hofbauer (1751–1820), named the "Apostle of Vienna" by Pope Pius VII. A trained baker and a founder of the Austrian Congregation of the Most Holy Redeemer, Hofbauer also cared for the Czech community, whose church this has been since 1912.

Outside the main west door, sometimes compared to the prow of a ship, is a flight of stairs. Until the 16th century, the stairs descended steeply to the Alserbach stream, which once formed part of the town moat (and now the street called Tiefer Graben, meaning 'deep ditch'). This accounts for the popular name of *Mariastiegenkirche* (The Church of Our Lady the Steps), as well as the building's age-old connection with the Danube raftsmen and bargees, who once passed so close with their cargoes. Over the porch of a nearby modern building is a very effective sculpture of the boatmen themselves, who would once have used the church.

The nearby Fischerstiege (Fishermen's Steps) also lead down to the riverside and feature a sculpture of fish traders, a reminder that their docks and warehouses would once have been here, too. Similarly, on Vorlaufstrasse there is a sculpted salt merchant, whose salt barge landing would also have occupied part of the riverbank. This accounts for the streets called Salzgries and Salztorgasse, the Salztorbrücke bridge, and also for the presence of the nearby 12th century Romanesque church of St. Ruprecht (Vienna's oldest), Rupert being patron saint of salt miners and first Bishop of Salzburg, whence the valuable commodity originally came. His statue, hidden amongst trees behind the church, can be seen clutching a barrel of salt.

Anyone visiting the Fischerstiege should peep through the glass doors at number 7. In the courtyard beyond are a jumble of ruins, one of the city centre's few unrestored examples of bomb damage from the Second World War.

Other places of interest nearby: 5, 9, 11, 14

11 The Fountains of Vienna

1st District (Innere Stadt), a tour of fountains beginning with
the Andromeda Fountain *(Andromedabrunnen)* in the courtyard
of the Old Town Hall *(Altes Rathaus)* at Wipplingerstrasse 8;
take U-3 to Herrengasse

Lovers of classical music will no doubt be aware of the colourful tone
poem *The Fountains of Rome* by Italian composer Ottorino Respighi,
brilliantly evoking the city where he settled in 1913. Like Rome,
Vienna is embellished with a number of fountains (*Brunnen*), but they
have yet to inspire such wonderful music – which is surprising since
they make such an aesthetic and therapeutic contribution to the urban
scene. By undertaking the following fountain-based odyssey, from the
1st District down to Wiedner Hauptstrasse, the explorer will take in
many of the city's major sights *en route*.

First is the Andromedabrunnen (1741) in the courtyard of the
Old Town Hall (*Altes Rathaus*) at Wipplingerstrasse 8, the last work
of distinguished sculptor Georg Raphael Donner (1693-1741), whose
bronzework depicts the rescue of Andromeda by Perseus, son of
Zeus, from a monster (Donner himself is the subject of a bronze on
Schwarzenbergplatz). The Wedding Fountain (*Vermählungsbrunnen*)
(1729) in nearby Hoher Markt replaces a wooden monument erected by
Emperor Leopold I on the safe return of his son from war, and depicts
the fictional marriage of Mary and Joseph. A smaller fountain at the top
of Tuchlauben (1928) depicting a tailor cutting cloth recalls Vienna's
medieval cloth trade (see no. 12). In the Freyung the Austria Fountain
(1846) has allegorical figures representing the rivers of the former empire
(Danube, Po, Elbe and Vistula) and is said to be stuffed with cigars
smuggled in by the sculptor from Munich thereby explaining the brown
stains! The Water Nymph Fountain (*Donaunixenbrunnen*) (1861) in the
nearby Parisian-style Freyung Passage forms part of an eye-catching M.
C. Escher-like courtyard. The fountain's three figures recall the Danube's
old professions, namely that of fishing, shipbuilding and trading.

Moving over to the Volksgarten there is a contemplative memorial
fountain (1907) to Elisabeth (*Sisi*), wife of Emperor Franz Joseph I.
The Pallas Athene Brunnen (1902) outside the Parlament on Dr.-
Karl-Renner-Ring has mermen representing the rivers Danube and
Inn (front), and Elbe and Moldau (back). The Danube Fountain
(*Danubiusbrunnen*) (1869) in Albertinaplatz has figures representing
the rivers Danube and Wien.

Georg Raphael Donner's Andromedabrunnen

The Providentia Fountain (*Donnerbrunnen*) (1739) in Neuer Markt was Vienna's first non-religious public sculpture with figures representing the Danube tributaries Traun, Enn, Ybbs and March. Its naked figures were originally removed by Empress Maria Theresa's Chastity Commission and may now be found in the Baroque Museum (*Barockmuseum*) in the Lower Belvedere.

The fountains in Michaelerplatz (1895–97) symbolise Habsburg might on land and at sea, whilst on the Graben are two fountains with lead figures by Johann Martin Fischer (1804), those on the Josefsbrunnen depicting *The Flight into Egypt* and the others, on the Leopoldsbrunnen, showing *The Discovery of St. Agnes's Veil.*

The Academy of Sciences in Dr-Ignaz-Seipel-Platz is adorned with two graceful wall fountains (1755) by sculptor Franz Josef Lenzbauer, and in the quaint Franziskanerplatz, close to one of Vienna's smallest coffee houses, there is the *Mosesbrunnen* (1798).

The Stadtpark on Parkring contains the Danube Sprite Fountain close to the famous golden statue of Johann Strauss, and nearby is the Venetian mosaic *Minervabrunnen* (1873) on Stubenring outside the MAK (*Österreichisches Museum für angewandte Kunst*) it was exhibited originally at the 1873 World Exhibition in the Prater.

The High Jet Fountain (*Hochstrahlbrunnen*) (1873) in Schwarzenberg Platz commemorates Vienna's first alpine spring water pipeline from the Rax and Schneeberg mountains 75 kilometres southwest of the city.

Finally, off Wiedner Hauptstrasse, there is a dragon fountain (1846) on Rilkeplatz, the Viennese Art Nouveau (*Jugendstil*) Mozart Fountain on Mozartgasse, with its figures from *The Magic Flute* (*Die Zauberflöte*), and the *Engelbrunnen* (1860) in a charming square at Wiedner Hauptstrasse 56 – an ideal spot to finish the journey and enjoy some well-deserved refreshment under the trees!

Other places of interest nearby: 9, 10, 12, 13

12 The Summer House Frescoes

1st District (Innere Stadt), the Neidhart Frescoes (Neidhart Festsaal) at Tuchlauben 19; take U-3 to Herrengasse

Hurrying between Hoher Markt and Kohlmarkt pedestrians seem not to notice the little statue on the corner at Tuchlauben 20. It depicts a man in medieval garb, his legs astride a portable brazier deriving welcome respite from the rigours of winter. But why is he here, and what is his connection with Vienna's oldest secular wall paintings, preserved in the building opposite at number 19?

For the answers one must imagine Tuchlauben as it appeared during the fourteenth century. At this time the street was lined with medieval buildings, with ground floor arcades known as *Lauben* where garments and fabrics (*Tuch*) were sold, hence the name Tuchlauben.

The cloth merchants of Tuchlauben were allowed to sell fabrics imported from Flanders and the Rhineland, and it was a lucrative business since high quality fabrics were not manufactured in Vienna. The practice is recalled by the nearby Tuchmacher Brunnen, a fountain depicting a merchant cutting a length of cloth.

By 1415 the house at Tuchlauben 19 is referred to as the Sommerhaus (Summer House), having been purchased in 1398 by Michel Menschein, a successful Styrian fabric merchant who left an indelible impression on the building. He commissioned a cycle of wall paintings in his banqueting hall, the remains of which were revealed during restoration work in 1979. Their survival is remarkable since the original building had been largely demolished before being rebuilt in the early eighteenth century.

Menschein was a wealthy man, and he owned several properties in the area. In 1396, for example, he purchased the house at Tuchlauben 20. He named it the Winterhaus (Winter House) and adorned it with the statue of the man and the brazier. In the same year he purchased Tuchlauben 19, and named it the Sommerhaus (Summer House), to tie them together.

The reason for the house names is explained when one studies the wall paintings preserved at Tuchlauben 19, where the seasons are used to provide a framework for a continual figural narrative designed to entertain and impress Menschein's guests.

The paintings were undertaken *al seco* probably by a local artist working in the Bohemian idiom of illuminated manuscript. The scenes are inspired by the rustic poetry of Neidhart von Reuental

A scene from the Neidhart Frescoes at Tuchlauben 19

(c. 1190–c. 1240), a songwriter (*Minnesänger*) in the court of the Archduke of Austria, which extols the virtues of chivalrous and knightly love, virtues he believed were being eroded by uncouth peasant society.

Menschein's cycle of wall paintings originally ran to thirty metres in length, half of which have been preserved and can be visited. Along the north wall the scenes are related first to Summer and then to Winter. Summer is represented by a Peasant Brawl (in which several men are engaged in unknightly combat with oversized swords), a Ball Game (traditionally a literary convention for the summer season), and the Theft of the Mirror, whereby a peasant gropes beneath a woman's skirt (surely the antithesis of knightly wooing!), and attempts to pilfer a mirror, the symbol of courtly joy. Winter consists of further fighting amongst the peasantry, this time using snowballs for the favours of a peasant girl, and a sleigh ride of the type enjoyed by the well-to-do in medieval Vienna.

Along the south wall the cycle continues with Spring and Autumn. The former begins with the so-called Violet Prank, Neidhart's most popular story, wherein a man has discovered the first violet of spring and has concealed it with his hat in readiness for his noble lady to find it. Unexpectedly a peasant uncovers the flower and defecates on it! Unperturbed the characters move on to a Round Dance celebrating the arrival of spring, and it's worth noting that this is Europe's oldest artistic representation of dancing to music. The cycle finishes with Autumn, and a banquet at which there is much drinking and feasting.

Other places of interest nearby: 9, 10, 11, 13

13 The Ruins of Vindobona

1st District (Innere Stadt), the Roman Museum *(Römermuseum)*
entered via shopping arcade at Hoher Markt 3;
take U-1, U-4 to Schwedenplatz

Although the area around Vienna had been inhabited since prehistoric times, the history of Vienna proper begins in 15BC, when the Romans under Emperor Augustus penetrated Celtic Noricum, thus incorporating the Vienna Basin into their province of Pannonia Superior. In the late-1st century AD they established a defensive line of military encampments along the Danube (known as the *Limes*) as a bulwark against marauding Germanic tribes to the north, as well as providing bases for their fleet along this important trading waterway. The provincial capital of Carnuntum, 40 kilometres to the east of modern Vienna, at the crossroads of the Danube with the amber trade route from the Baltic to the Mediterranean, received extra protection in the form of a garrison fort that the Romans called *Vindobona*.

They chose the so-called City Terrace on which to build the fort, a naturally elevated area of glacial boulders that rises above the Danube's floodplain from Nussdorf in the north to Simmering in the south (see no. 96) – thus was Vienna founded. They built a classic square-planned Roman fort whose walls and ditches have long since been supplanted by modern streets: Rotenturmstrasse, Graben (meaning 'ditch', once the fort's southern moat) and Naglergasse (the curving street facades at either end still following exactly the curved corners of the Roman fortress), Tiefer Graben (meaning 'deep ditch', along which the Alsbach and Ottakringerbach streams once flowed), and Salzgries-Seitenstettengasse (below which an arm of the Danube ran, now the Danube Canal). A walk along these streets permits an appreciation of the ancient topography, as well as the original extent of the fort.

Although nothing Roman remains above ground today, having been built over from medieval times onwards, a few tantalising windows have been opened on this ancient world. Demolition of houses at Sterngasse 5, for example, revealed a Roman bath house, a column of which has been re-erected next to the Theodor-Herzl-Stiege. Below the fire station at Am Hof 7/10 there is a section of terracotta drain *(Römische Baureste Am Hof)* that ran below the *Via Sagularis* and emptied into the Ottakringerbach, part of the fort's elaborate sewerage system. Roman walls were found below the church of Maria am Gestade (see no. 10) and Roman paving slabs found during the construction of the Artis Cinema at Schultergasse 5 are now displayed in the basement. A wall plaque at Naglergasse 2 mentions Roman walls uncovered during house-building in 1901.

Under-floor heating in the Roman ruins below Hoher Markt

There is also tangible evidence for a thriving civilian community that existed *outside* the walls of the Roman fort. During the excavation of an underground car park below the Freyung, for example, remains of buildings were found that once lined part of the main Roman road (*Limesstrasse*) east to Carnuntum (now Herrengasse), a map of which can be seen in the window of Herrengasse 16, and in Michaelerplatz can be seen the walls of Roman houses that lay at an intersection of the main road with another leading down Kohlmarkt to the fort (see nos. 6 & 12). The 13th century Giant's Portal (*Riesentor*) of the Stephansdom has an inscribed Roman gravestone incorporated into its right-hand arch suggesting a deliberate attempt to Christianise a former pagan burial site; and on Rotgasse there is a modern mosaic marking the site of the *Porta Principalis Dextra*, a gateway which opened out onto Wollzeile, that in turn led to a cavalry base east of the fort, fragments of which can be seen on the platforms of the U3 U-Bahn station at Rochusgasse. Of the gate itself several sturdy foundation blocks are preserved in the impressively-vaulted cellars deep beneath a shop at Ertlgasse 4.

Another shop with surprising Roman remains is at Wipplingerstrasse 27, where a complete Roman skeleton is displayed in the basement! The most impressive remains, however, are those in the Roman Museum (Römermuseum) below Hoher Markt, Vienna's oldest square and former fish market, where a pair of Roman houses were found along one of the fort's two major streets, the *Via Principalis* (Hoher Markt–Wipplingerstrasse leading northwest to Comagena, Roman Tulln; the other main street ran along Marcus Aurelius Strasse – Tuchlauben southwards to Aquae, Roman Baden). The remains follow the usual Roman house plan of rooms set around a porticoed atrium with under-floor heating (*hypocaust*). The houses date from a rebuilding of the fort in 180AD by the 10th Legion, the original having been built c. 100AD by the 13th/14th Legions but destroyed by Germanic tribes.

The Jugendstil Ankeruhr clock in a corner of Hoher Markt

Although driven back by Emperor Marcus Aurelius (who died either in Vindobona or Sirmium) thus allowing Roman Vindobona to prosper further and to establish its first vineyards, the tribes later returned precipitating a full Roman withdrawal by c.400AD. In 833AD the name *Wenia* is first mentioned, as part of the Holy Roman Empire founded by Charlemagne, and the old Roman walls and roads would in time provide a foundation for medieval Vienna (see no. 26).

Most visitors go to Hoher Markt to see artist Franz Matsch's Viennese Art Nouveau (*Jugendstil*) clock known as the *Ankeruhr* (1911) with its midday procession of mechanical figures, one of whom is Roman Emperor Marcus Aurelius. Also worth visiting is the Wien Museum (Vienna Museum) in Karlsplatz for its fascinating collection of Roman statues, altars, lamps and frescoes.

Other places of interest nearby: 11, 12, 14, 15

14 An Infamous Address

1st District (Innere Stadt), Morzinplatz;
take U-1, U-4 to Schwedenplatz

Following the first violent expulsion of Vienna's Jews in 1421 (see no. 9) and a second in 1670 (see no. 65), the Jewish community of the early-20th century had become a settled and vital part of Viennese life. A third expulsion seemed unimaginable and yet, between 1907 and 1913, the young Adolf Hitler (1889–1945) was in the city honing his own brand of fanatical anti-Semitism. Like Vienna's Christian Socialist mayor Karl Lueger, whom he greatly admired, he learned quickly that given a suitable scapegoat he could turn the envy and discontent of Vienna's *petit bourgeosie* to his own political advantage.

As a budding artist in 1907-08 Hitler lived in an apartment at Stumpergasse 31 in Mariahilf and then just around the corner at Felberstrasse 22. It was during this time, in between drinking coffee in the Café Sperl, that he was twice rejected as being "inadequate" by the Academy of Fine Arts (*Akademie der bildenden Künste*) on Schillerplatz. Increasingly disgruntled and without money he subsequently occupied a flat on Sechshauser Strasse, a homeless shelter in Meidling and finally a men's hostel called the Männerheim at Meldemannstrasse 25–27 in Brigittenau. In May 1913, Hitler abandoned Vienna altogether in favour of Munich and then Berlin, only to return to the Austrian capital twenty-five years later, in March 1938, as Führer of the German Third Reich. This time he spent the night in the luxurious Hotel Imperial on Kärntner Ring and proclaimed the annexation (*Anschluss*) of Austria from the balcony of the Neue Burg (see no. 63) before flying back to Germany.

Within days Vienna's elegant Hotel Metropole on Morzinplatz was commandeered as the regional headquarters of the Nazi secret police (*Gestapoleitstelle Wien*) and Heinrich Himmler's henchmen began rounding up opponents of National Socialism. This included members of the preceding Austro-fascist Party, Communists and Socialists. Men, women and children were taken to the hotel, via a back entrance at Salztorgasse 6, for interrogation, torture and dispatch to either the Gestapo prison at Berggasse 43 (9th District) or else the concentration camps. Thereafter followed the first wholesale rounding up of the Jewish population, culminating on 9th November with the notorious Night of Broken Glass (*Reichskristallnacht*), a ruthless pogrom during which more than forty synagogues, prayer houses, schools and cemeteries were desecrated. Of the 6,500 Jews arrested 3,700 were sent to the concentration camp at Dachau in Bavaria (see nos. 59 & 65).

Numerous plaques around Vienna's Jewish quarter in the 2nd district of Leopoldstadt record former synagogue and school sites, including Leopoldgasse 13–15 and 29, and Große Schiffgasse 8 (see also Neudeggergasse

This relief on the Leopold-Figl-Hof recalls Nazi horrors

12 in Josefstadt, and Müllnergasse in Alsergrund). A plaque on the wall of Schiffamtsgasse 18–20 marks the home of one Dr. Arnold Deutsch, deemed undesirable by the SS (*Schutzstaffel*) and murdered; whilst another in a pretty schoolyard at Kleine Sperlgasse 2a marks the spot where 40,000 Jews were rounded up between October 1941 and March 1943. A total of 65,000 would eventually be murdered, as recorded on the recently-erected Shoah Wall of Names Memorial (Shoah Namensmauern Gedenkstätte) at the bottom of Alser Strasse (9th District). Only the City Synagogue (*Stadttempel*) at Seitenstettengasse 2–4 in the 1st District survived, due in part to its facade being concealed from the street and because torching it would have threatened neighbouring buildings (see no. 15). The Vienna Wiesenthal Institute for Holocaust Studies (Wiener Wiesenthal Institut für Holocaust-Studien) at the bottom of the street tells the full story.

Needless to say the world's first Jewish Museum (1895) was also destroyed, although today there is a new one (*Jüdisches Museum*) at Dorotheergasse 11. It contains a poignant collection of charred ceremonial objects retrieved from the rubble of Vienna's synagogues.

Not far away, a plaque at Neutorgasse 8 commemorates Dr. Hans Zimmerl, a member of the Austrian Freedom Movement (see no. 19). He was beheaded in 1944, along with a thousand others, on a guillotine referred to chillingly as "Instrument F". It was in Vienna's oldest criminal court, the Landesgericht, at Landesgerichtsstrasse 11 in Josefstadt (the oppressive tiled chamber that witnessed the executions is preserved but only open to victims' families).

In the face of such horrors it came as some relief when the Hotel Metropole was razed by allied bombing in the last weeks of the war (a similar fate awaited Adolf Eichmann's Central Office for Jewish Emigration at Prinz-Eugen-Strasse 20–22, formerly the Palais Rothschild, from where the Nazis orchestrated their "final solution" for Vienna's Jews). One building to survive was the Viennese Nazi Party's

A wall plaque recalling Stalin's stay in Vienna

'Brown House' at Hirschengasse 25 (6th District), which serves today as a youth hostel. Meanwhile, the Metropole site is now occupied by the Leopold Figl Hof, named after Austria's post-war Chancellor (1945–1953), who himself survived the Dachau concentration camp. Notice the relief on the front of the building depicting a noose and a guillotine either side of a figure slumped across barbed wire. The hotel's notorious former back entrance now leads to a memorial for members of the Austrian Resistance Movement (*Gedenkstätte für die Opfer des österreichischen Freiheitskampfes*), whilst in front of the building is a Monument to the Victims of Fascism.

It is made of granite boulders from the quarry at Mauthausen concentration camp near Linz in Upper Austria, where prisoners hacked out stone for the cobbles of Vienna's streets. On it are carved the words *"Niemals vergessen!"* ("Never forget!").

A further poignant memorial to the victims of the camps are the three black paving slabs to be found on Lothringerstrasse, carved impeccably by Jewish prisoners and brought recently to Vienna from a former Nazi-era political building in Nuremberg.

Quite rightly there are no wall plaques recording the numerous places Hitler stayed during his time in Vienna and they should not be treated in any way as tourist destinations: the history books serve well enough to remember his appalling "achievements" in the city. However, it is worth noting here that just prior to Hitler's departure for Munich in 1913 his future adversary Josef Stalin arrived in Vienna. The young, up-and-coming Bolshevik stayed at Schönbrunner Schlossstrasse 30 where he wrote his paper *Marxism and the National Question*, before returning to St. Petersburg. A wall plaque of questionable taste still hangs there today, erected in 1949 when Vienna was in Russian hands and Stalin was still alive. Even more chilling is the fact that Hitler the artist is known to have visited the park at nearby Schloss Schönbrunn to paint. Is it just possible that two of the twentieth century's greatest monsters passed each other on the street without ever realising it?

Terror revisited Morzinplatz in November 2020, when a lone Islamist gunman shot and killed four civilians and wounded twenty three others. A memorial on nearby Desider-Friedmann-Platz recalls the incident.

Other places of interest nearby: 11, 13, 15, 16

15 Refuge for an Architect

1st District (Innere Stadt), the Kornhäusel Tower *(Kornhäuselturm)* at Judengasse 14 between Friedmannplatz and the end of Fleischmarkt; take U-1, U-4 to Schwedenplatz

Sandwiched between Vienna's magnificent Baroque/Rococo architecture of the 17th–18th centuries and the retrospective pomp of late-19th century Historicism (Ringstrasse Style), is the so-called *Biedermeier* period. The era it covers, between the Congress of Vienna in 1814–15 and the 1848 Revolution, saw Austrian Chancellor Prince Clemens von Metternich impose autocratic rule that effectively excluded the middle classes from political life. As a result they retreated into a cosy world of artistic and leisurely pursuits – Neo-classical architecture (see nos. 52 & 82), furniture (see nos. 18 & 48), decorated Christmas trees, Schubert and Waltzing. These privileged yet politically apathetic *bourgeosie* were satirised by a German author in the form of a fictional character called "Herr Biedermeier", after whom the era and its decorative arts are named (*Bieder* = respectable/ naïve; *Meier* = a common German surname).

The star architect of the period was undoubtedly Josef Georg Kornhäusel (1782–1860), remembered for his unobtrusively elegant neo-classical buildings. In 1826–32 he redesigned Vienna's Schottenkloster (Monastery of the Scots) at Freyung 6, notable for its stretched-out classical pediment. In 1822 Kornhäusel remodelled the Josefstadt Theatre (*Theater in der Josefstadt*), Vienna's oldest (1788), whose doors have kept open continuously ever since. The occasion prompted an especially composed overture by none other than Ludwig van Beethoven.

A very different commission was the design of the City Synagogue (*Stadttempel*) in 1824–26 at Seitenstettengasse 2–4. Curiously, it does not look like a synagogue from the outside because Emperor Joseph II's Edict of Tolerance (*Toleranzpatent*) (1781) forbade such non-Catholic buildings from betraying their function (see no. 17). This may account for it being the only one of Vienna's many synagogues to escape Nazi torching in 1938, although in part this was due to the building's close proximity to other buildings within the 1st District, which would also have caught fire (see no. 65).

Just around the corner, next to the Jerusalemstiege, erected to celebrate 3000 years of that city's history, is the unusual Kornhäusel Tower (*Kornhäuselturm*). Allegedly this huge tower house-cum-

The so-called Kornhäusel Tower on Judengasse

studio was designed by the architect as a refuge from his nagging wife, having a retractable iron staircase from the first floor rather than a conventional doorway at street level!

For more of Kornhäusel's well-proportioned and elegant work catch the blue tram (*Lokalbahn*) from outside the State Opera (*Staatsoper*) and travel to the delightful *Biedermeier* spa town of Baden. Set romantically at the edge of the Vienna woods, many of its public buildings, including the town hall, were designed by Kornhäusel. There is also the little-known Kornhäusl-Villa (or Villa Jenamy), at the corner of Ottakringer Strasse and Maroltingergasse (16th District), one of Vienna's oldest villas.

When he died Kornhäusel was first buried in the *Biedermeier* Cemetery of St. Marx's (see no. 42) but was later reinterred in the Central Cemetery (*Zentralfriedhof*) in Simmering (see no. 70). Kornhäusel outlived the *Biedermeier* era itself by a dozen years, the period having been brought to an abrupt end by the March 1848 Revolution (as a result of which the *Biedermeier* is sometimes referred to as the *Vormärz* or pre-March period). With Paris (and soon Italy and Hungary) in revolution, Viennese students and workers met outside the Lower Austrian Landhaus at Herrengasse 13 to oust the arch-conservative Metternich, free the Press and address Vienna's problem of overcrowding, disease and food shortages. A crowd gathered and shots were fired (despite a plaque of 1571 warning visitors not to fight!) sparking not only a revolution and the resignation of Metternich but also the meeting of Austria's first democratically elected assembly (see no. 80). It also prompted the abdication of Emperor Ferdinand I (1835–48) in favour of his nephew the 18-year old Franz Joseph I (1848–1916).

Other places of interest nearby: 13, 14, 16, 17

16 The Story of Coffee

1st District (Innere Stadt), the former Julius Meinl building at Fleischmarkt 7; take U-1, U-4 to Schwedenplatz

One of the most enduring Viennese urban legends concerns the city's addiction to coffee (on average over half a litre, per person, per day). It was for many years recounted how bags of curious green beans were found amongst the abandoned possessions of retreating Turkish troops after their second siege of Vienna in 1683. Thought only to be camel fodder they were claimed by a Polish adventurer called Georg Franz Kolschitzky (1640–94) in return for having penetrated enemy lines and bringing back word of Vienna's impending relief. The reward seemed paltry but clever Kolschitzky knew he could roast and brew the beans to make coffee – and make a fortune in the process. His statue dressed in Turkish garb and wielding an oriental coffee pot can be seen at the corner of Favoritenstrasse and Kolschitzkygasse in the 4th district of Wieden.

The Meinl Moor on the front of Meinl's Graben shop

However, whilst it is true that coffee has been served in Vienna since the late-17th century, its beginnings were rather more prosaic. The world's first coffee house appeared in Istanbul in 1554 followed by Europe's first in Venice (1647), then London (1652), Paris (1660), and Hamburg (1677). Not until 1685 did Emperor Leopold I (1658–1705) grant a license to sell coffee and tea in Vienna, to an Armenian trader called Johannes Deodatus (his original premises are marked by a plaque at Rotenturmstrasse 14).

Despite this late start, it was the Viennese who elevated coffee drinking into a fine art, creating the thirty or so variations available in the city's myriad coffee houses today. From the original sweet *Türkische* served in its individual copper pot to the frothy milky *Mélange*, there's a coffee, and a coffee house (*Kaffeehaus*), to suit all moods (see no. 29).

A name now synonymous with coffee in Vienna is that of Julius Meinl, purveyor of green and then roasted coffee since 1862. In 1891 he built a specialised roasting plant on the very site where the Turkish Grand Vizier Kara Mustafa had abandoned his camp back in 1683 (see no. 3). At Fleischmarkt 7 can be seen the company's former

Façade of the former Julius Meinl Coffee Imports office on Fleischmarkt

office built in 1899, its facade boasting proudly *"Julius Meinl's Kaffee Imports"*. The accompanying reliefs depict somewhat romanticised scenes of coffee being grown, harvested and transported by ship to Europe, accompanied by swooping seagulls. The three coats of arms are those of the great trading ports of Hamburg, Trieste and London.

By 1939 there were a thousand Meinl stores, all identified by the fez-wearing coffee boy logo (*Meinl Moor*), symbolising quality and excellence. Today Meinl still imports and roasts many types of coffee, which it sells in its bazaar-like gourmet store on the Graben (or visit *www.meinl.com*). A carving of the Meinl Moor can be seen outside the store at number 16, though for some reason he is painted entirely white.

Before leaving Fleischmarkt 7 notice the plaque in the entrance stating that Billy Wilder (1906–2002) lived here as a schoolboy. He went on to become a director and screenplay writer in America, famous for *The Seven Year Itch*, *Double Indemnity*, *Sunset Boulevard* and, of course, *Some Like it Hot* starring Marilyn Monroe.

Julius Meinl is not the only coffee brand associated with Vienna. Another is Naber, whose former premises at Wiedner Hauptstrasse 40 (4th District), now Schönbergers Caffè, retain their original wooden fittings and decorative tiled facades. Real coffee fanatics might also enjoy the Coffeemuseum (Kaffeemuseum) at Vogelsanggasse 36 (5th District).

Other places of interest nearby: 14, 15, 17, 18

17 Pedestrians Beware!

1st District (Innere Stadt), a walk along Fleischmarkt and Griechengasse; take U-1, U-4 to Schwedenplatz

Fleischmarkt is an ancient street first documented in 1220. The name recalls the city's butchers who had their guildhall here. Although Fleischmarkt finds its origins in the meat trade it has more recent connections with coffee. At Fleischmarkt 7 stand the original premises of coffee importer Julius Meinl. In business since 1862, the successful company put up this grand building in 1899. A lively frieze along the façade depicts the story of the coffee bean from harvesting to drinking. Hollywood filmmaker Billy Wilder was born in the same building and one wonders if the familiar smell of coffee encouraged him later to take an office over a café in Beverley Hills?

Dropping down from Fleischmarkt towards the Danube Canal is the charming and ever so photogenic Griechengasse. This medieval alley is lined with stone bollards designed to protect the walls from damage by passing carts. At either end hangs a sign from 1912 requiring that "Pedestrians beware of traffic! Drive slowly! Coachmen with heavy vehicles must lead their horses or send an adult escort ahead to warn pedestrians."

To one side stands the Griechenbeisl, an inn dating back to 1447. During the Turkish siege of 1529 it was the Yellow Eagle Inn standing hard against the Babenberg city wall. Cannonballs inside the entrance show it was in the direct line of fire. Later during the plague of 1679 it was the Red Roof Inn. Nearby is where the much-loved ballad singer Augustin was inadvertently buried in a plague pit. His miraculous survival is celebrated by the effigy outside the Griechenbeisl today and the name of the newspaper sold by the city's homeless and poor.

Both Beisl and alley are named after the Greek merchants who gravitated to the area during the 18th century, to orchestrate Vienna's trade with the Balkans and Levant. Theophil Hansen's gilded Church of the Holy Trinity built in the 1850s replaced an earlier Greek church, the construction of which was made possible by Emperor Joseph II's Edict of Tolerance. This 1782 decree is celebrated in an inscription on the house opposite.

At the bottom of Griechengasse is a house with a Madonna and a Rococo lantern. If the door is open peep inside at the old water pump and the mysetrious wood panels inscribed with verses from the Holy Koran.

Cobbled Griechengasse exudes bygone charm

In the courtyard beyond is a 13th century Babenberg-era watchtower. Used subsequently as living quarters it appears in the earliest depiction of Vienna – the Babenberg family tree of 1490 at Klosterneuburg – and is the city's oldest house.

Griechengasse now opens out onto a terrace used formerly as a meeting point by the city militia. The discreet whitewashed building beyond is a second Greek church. Unlike Hansen's flamboyant work, the older Church of St. George still abides by a tenet of the emperor's edict forbidding non-Catholic places of worship from betraying their function externally.

The walk concludes with the Steyrerhof at Griechengasse 4. Incorporated into the walls of this former inn is stonework documenting Vienna's architectural development from the 13th to 17th centuries. Note the spyhole over the doorway. The restored paintwork reveals how colourful medieval Vienna must once have looked.

Other places of interest nearby: 14, 15, 16, 18

18 A Renaissance Rarity

1st District (Innere Stadt), the courtyard at Bäckerstrasse 7;
take U-1, U-4 to Schwedenplatz

One of the great joys of discovering Vienna's 1st District on foot is
stumbling across its many fascinating courtyards (*Innenhöfe*) and
quiet squares (*Plätze*), often quite by accident (see no. 31). Most were
built during the Baroque and *Biedermeier* periods (17th–19th centuries)
but there is one courtyard at Bäckerstrasse 7 that dates right back to
1587 and the century of the Italian Renaissance.

It is curious because there is so little architecture from this period
to be found in Vienna. The reason for this is thought to have been
the huge expense incurred by the building of the city walls following
the first Turkish siege in 1529 (see no. 26). Additionally, no Emperor
lived permanently in Vienna until after 1683, Maximilian I (1493–1519)
spending his money on Innsbruck and Rudolf II (1576–1612) spending
his time in Prague, both being places where many wealthy nobles also
gravitated together with their potential architectural commissions. The
few important Renaissance buildings in Vienna include the Maximilian
Palace erected by Emperor Ferdinand I (1556–64) for his son Archduke
Maximilian (now stables (*Stallburg*) for the Spanish Riding School's
Lipizzaners) (*Spanische Reitschule*), the Hofburg's Amalientrakt and
Schweizertor (the latter still with its original drawbridge mechanism
and moat), the graceful cupola atop the Stephansdom's unfinished
North Tower, the façade of the Franziskanerkirche (see no. 32),
and the Neugebäude hunting palace built for Emperor Maximilian II
(1564–76). The latter was a unique pleasure ground whose crenellated
garden walls now enclose the crematorium across the road from the
Central Cemetery (*Zentralfriedhof*) in Simmering (see no. 70).

Returning to the house in Bäckerstrasse (known as the *Schwanfeld-
sche Haus*), the Renaissance entrance portal opens onto a small but
perfectly-proportioned courtyard, which still retains its Tuscan balus-
traded balconies, albeit now blocked up. Behind the plain supporting
columns are the original stables complete with stone troughs, iron hay
basket, and even a harness hanging on the back wall. Added charm
is given by the canopied Madonna and the old signboards for Franz
Nemetschke's first floor piano workshop. On the opposite side are
later balconies with iron railings. Displayed along one of the walls
is the decorative ironwork collection of *Biedermeier* portrait artist
Friedrich von Amerling (1803–87), famous for his portraits evoking

the idealised family life of the Viennese bourgeosie during the early 19th century. Amerling occupied a charming *Biedermeier* courtyard residence at Stiftgasse 8 in the 7th district of Neubau.

Balconies in the Renaissance courtyard at Bäckerstrasse 7

Other Renaissance houses can be found at Bäckerstrasse 12 and 14, as well as another fine portal just around the corner at Sonnenfelsgasse 15, after which it's probably best to head for Salvatorgasse, where a further architectural gem awaits discovery. Here, the late-13th century Chapel of the Saviour (*Salvatorkapelle*) has Gothic vaults inside, and outside an ornate Renaissance portal dating to c.1520. The chapel's founder, Otto Haymo, famously led a conspiracy to liberate Vienna from Habsburg rule after the murder of King Albrecht I (1298–1308) in 1308, an act for which he was executed. His old house, nearby at Wipplingerstrasse 8, was subsequently given to the City Council who used it as their Town Hall (*Altes Rathaus*) until it was replaced by the new Town Hall on the Ringstrasse.

Other places of interest nearby: 16, 17, 19, 20

19   Cryptic Cathedral Carvings

1st District (Innere Stadt), St. Stephen's Cathedral (*Stephans-dom*), on Stephansplatz; take U-1, U-3 to Stephansplatz

There is no better description of the Stephansdom than as a limestone reef rising above a sea of lesser buildings. Bristling with carved ornament, it was commenced in 1137 and consecrated a century later. Until 1732 a cemetery surrounded it, the gravestones now attached to the building itself. But why build the Stephansdom here in the first place?

The answer lies just inside the main portal on the right-hand side, where a Roman gravestone is just about visible. It is an example of the deliberate inclusion of building elements from an older, pagan site of worship. The cathedral builders were respecting but also neutering the old gods. Rather more prosaic is the meaning behind the iron bars left of the portal. They are official measures, or *Ells*, once used in the cloth and building trades.

Moving round to the north side of the cathedral leaves the crowds behind and evokes a different history. Work on the stumpy North Tower or Adlerturm was halted in 1511 when money and manpower was diverted to the city walls, in preparation for the First Turkish Siege. Local legend, however, insists that Master Mason Hans Puchbaum did a deal with Satan and fell from the scaffolding resulting in the cessation of construction. Opinions also differ over the iron handle at the foot of

The Stephansdom is a soaring masterpiece of Gothic architecture

Old standard measures near the entrance to the Stephansdom

the tower. The local Fiaker drivers might tell you it was a 'sanctuary handle' that afforded protection to minor felons who held it. In reality it was part of a hoist used to haul heavy building elements up to the unfinished tower above.

Beyond, at the north-east corner of the cathedral, two sights are bound by lore more than legend. From the Gothic pulpit Saint John of Capistrano preached a crusade against the Ottomans in 1546, whilst the exit from the cathedral catacombs alongside it is where in 1791 the body of Mozart was dispatched to a pauper's grave.

The cathedral's east end is adorned with more former grave monuments, including a statue of Christ in considerable pain, known as *Jesus of the Toothache*. Less perturbing, on the cathedral's sunny south side, is a tree growing out of the wall. A Chinese Ailanthus, or Tree of Heaven, it recalls when Jesuits attempted to establish a silk industry in the city (a hardy species of silk moth eats Ailanthus leaves).

Skirting the South Tower gaze upwards. In 1683 during the Second Turkish Siege the cathedral was hit by a thousand cannonballs. One of them is still embedded in the middle buttress of the nave with the date inscribed beneath it.

The south side terminates with the Singertor named perhaps after the battered tomb of a court minstrel lying alongside. This entrance was used by men in the days when the nave was segregated, which might explain the surprising carved phallus atop one of the pilasters flanking the main portal: a helpful signpost perhaps when illiteracy was the norm!

Rounding the final corner to regain the main entrance there are several reminders of the Second World War. One is a lantern in memory of the prelate Karl Raphael Dorr, who facilitated the reconstruction of the cathedral after it caught fire in 1945. A blackened stone nearby with a Cyrillic inscription signi-

Secret symbol of the Austrian resistance carved near the entrance to the Stephansdom

fies that Red Army troops secured the cathedral during their liberation of the city. Helping the Allies underground was the Austrian Resistance, whose secret symbol 'O5' (the first two letters of 'Oesterreich' when spelt without an Umlaut, a name forbidden by the Nazis who renamed the country Ostmark) is carved to the right of the entrance. For more details on this subject visit the Documentation Centre for Austrian Resistance *(Dokumentationsarchiv des Österreichischen Widerstandes)* at Wipplingerstrasse 8.

Another, more ancient cryptic carving adorns the red marble tomb of the first Habsburg Holy Roman Emperor, Friedrich III (1440–93), inside the cathedral. The vowels of the Roman alphabet – AEIOU – are said to mean *"Alles Erdreich Ist Österreich Untertan"* (the whole world is subject to Austria) although the fact that Hungarian King Matthias Corvinus drove Friedrich from Vienna in 1485 has led many to interpret them as *"Aller Erst Ist Österreich Verloren"* (in the first place, Austria is lost)!

Elsewhere inside the Stephansdom is the Maria-Pócs Altar, with its miraculous icon of the Virgin Mary that shed tears in 1697 during Prince Eugene of Savoy's decisive Battle of Zenta against the Turks. The nearby Kreuzkapelle contains the remains of the prince, as well as a High Gothic crucifix with a beard of real hair said to still be growing! Before leaving check out the recently-discovered drawing of two female saints on a wall behind the cathedral shop's cash desk. It is possibly by a student of German Renaissance painter Albrecht Dürer (1471–1528).

Other places of interest nearby: 20, 21, 22, 23, 24

20 Mozart Passed this Way

1st District (Innere Stadt), the Chapel of the Cross, outside the northeast wall of St. Stephen's Cathedral (*Stephansdom*), Stephansplatz; take U-1, U-3 to Stephansplatz

Mozart's former home on Domgasse seen from Blutgasse

Arguably the greatest composer to be associated with Vienna was Salzburg-born Wolfgang Amadeus Mozart (1756–91). This is certainly true in terms of his prodigious output (c.626 individual works) across such a broad range of formats, including operas, symphonies and concertos. Having toured much of Europe by the age of eight, the expression "child prodigy" could have been invented for him. Endless volumes have been written about the composer and even today there's no escaping his image, from confectionery (*Mozartkugeln*) to ticket touts dressed in the flamboyant style he would have recognised. One mystery surrounding Mozart is why he is the only major composer (other than Vivaldi, see no. 47) whose final resting place is not exactly known.

Mozart first arrived in Vienna in 1781 to help celebrate the accession to the Habsburg throne of Emperor Joseph II (1765–90) after which he decided to stay on. He experienced his most productive years here and occupied fourteen different addresses across the city, only one of which (the so-called *Mozarthaus* at Domgasse 5) is still standing (this fact alone makes it an extremely popular visitor attraction).

In 1782, Mozart married Constanze Weber in the Stephansdom but, despite being musically productive, he became a compulsive gambler losing large sums at billiards, ninepins and cards. That he had money to gamble, however, dispels the suggestion that he was impoverished, though his income was sporadic and he left Domgasse in 1787 when he was unable to afford the rent.

His last home was the Kleines Kaiserhaus at Rauhensteingasse 8, where he wrote *The Magic Flute* (*Die Zauberflöte*) (it is now the *Steffl* department store, where a bust of Mozart, the very first memorial to the composer in Vienna created in 1849, is displayed at the entrance to the Mythos Mozart immersive museum in the basement).

It was here in the early hours of 5th December 1791 that he died of feverish articular rheumatism. He

The Chapel of the Cross outside the northeast wall of the Stephansdom

had been working on his *Requiem* commissioned anonymously by an "unknown messenger" several months before. The mystery patron was later revealed to be the recently widowed Count Franz Walsegg-Stuppach, who intended to pass the work off as his own.

On December 6th Mozart's body was moved to the Stephansdom, where the coffin received benediction in the tiny Chapel of the Cross, outside the northeast wall where it forms a covered exit from the Cathedral crypts below (see no. 33). Due to bad weather it was a sorry little cortège that made its way from the Cathedral to

A Mozart death memorial in the Michaelerkirche

St. Marx's Cemetery (*St. Marxer Friedhof*) (see no. 42), where Mozart's simple coffin was placed in a common grave. History relates how only the gravediggers were present and that the location was subsequently forgotten.

Some claim that Mozart could have avoided this modest end by a small additional payment, and why this was not forthcoming from family or friends remains a real mystery. His wife's absence from the scene, however, was because she was too upset to attend. It should not, however, be forgotten that at this time burial in a common grave was the norm for all but the very wealthy (by order of Emperor Joseph II), and consequently the tending of individual graves was rare. Additionally, funeral services were restricted to the church and mourners rarely made the journey to the cemetery, where the body could only be taken after nightfall. So perhaps it's not such a mystery after all that Mozart's exact resting place has been lost, marked only approximately by a broken column symbolizing his unfinished life (today grave 179).

Even poor Constanze searched in vain decades later, seemingly unaware that common graves were cleared periodically to make space for new ones. A somewhat grander monument erected in 1859 was later removed to the Central Cemetery (*Zentralfriedhof*) in Simmering, where it stands next to the graves of Beethoven, Brahms, Schubert and the Strausses.

Opposite the rear entrance of the Steffl store is Vienna's masonic lodge, hence the street name Rauensteingasse ('Free Stone Alley'), its doorway adorned with a building block suspended on calipers. Both Mozart, his father Leopold and fellow composer Josef Haydn (1732–1809) were freemasons. Examples of specific musical symbols taken from Masonic rites have been identified in several of Mozart's compositions.

Other places of interest nearby: 18, 19, 21, 22, 24

21 Atlases and Caryatids

Vienna's 1st District contains many city palaces constructed in the Baroque period (mid-17th to mid-18th centuries), when exuberant decoration was the fashion. In order to lend strength and power to these buildings the so-called *atlante* was used. It takes the form of a colossal male statue designed to support portals and balconies above. The word *atlante* comes from the Greek name Atlas, a god of the archaic pantheon and brother of Prometheus. In Greek legend Atlas sided with the Titans in rebelling against Zeus, the father of the gods. Atlas was defeated and his punishment was to be condemned to support the sky on his shoulders for all eternity.

A fine example of the Baroque use of the Atlas figure is in the portals of the former Bohemian Court Chancellery (*Böhmische Hofkanzlei*) built in 1709–14 at Wipplingerstrasse 7/ Judenplatz 11 (1st District). From 1627, the Habsburgs were the rulers of Bohemia (now the Czech Republic) hence this magnificent building designed by the great architect Johann Bernard Fischer von Erlach (1656–1723). The figures themselves are the work of Lorenzo Mattielli, a master of the genre. He is also responsible

Atlas figures in the staircase of Prince Eugene of Savoy's Winter Palace

for the freestanding Atlases supporting the ceiling of the *Sala Terrena* (ground floor room) in Prince Eugene of Savoy's Upper Belvedere Palace (1714–23), designed by that other great Baroque architect, Johann Lukas von Hildebrandt (1668–1745).

Atlas figures also appear on the portal of Hildebrandt's Palais Daun-Kinsky (1713–16) at Freyung 4, as well as on the Stadtpalais Liechtenstein opposite the Minoritenkirche.

Both architects had a hand in Prince Eugene's Winter Palace at Himmelpfortgasse 3 (1695–1724) in which there is a spectacular Grand Staircase held aloft by four freestanding Atlases, part of one of the most magnificent Baroque edifices in all Vienna. These Atlas figures are probably the work of sculptor Giovanni Giuliani, who like Mattielli was also a master of this architectural device. However, the façade itself is devoid of Atlases due to the narrowness of the street, although they re-appear on the front of the nearby Palais Erdödy-Fürstenberg.

Anyone wishing to create a checklist of Atlas figures in Vienna should also head to Schwertgasse (1st District), where at number 3 there is a marvellous Baroque portal that sports not only a pair of fine Atlases but also a decorative stone relief carved with the swords that give the street its unusual name. Another splendid pair grace a lovely Baroque palace at Schulhof 4 (the name refers to a school that until its destruction in 1421 was part of Vienna's medieval Jewish ghetto).

Inevitably, the architecture of the backwards-looking Historicist period (Ringstrasse Style) of the late-19th century picked up on the Atlas figures, (e.g. the doorway of the Van-Swieten-Hof (1896) at Rotenturmstrasse 19 and the old Zentralbad (1887) at Weihburggasse 20). Most popular was the re-interpretation of the device as a scantily clad female as seen on the pilasters of the imposing shop at Graben 20, and the overblown examples next-door on Tuchlauben (see front cover). The latter are sometimes referred to as the "Nymphs of Graben" and are said rather colourfully to represent the prostitutes who once plied their trade here!

Rather more modest are the sculpted females occupying the spandrels on the façade of the famous Musikverein, as well as those in the form of gilded freestanding figures inside. Such freestanding female figures are known as *caryatids* and originate in a device used in Greek temples named after the priestess of Artemis at Caryae.

Either side of the Parliament on Dr.-Karl-Renner-Ring are two grand porches supported by *caryatids* echoing those to be found in the Erechtheion on the ancient Acropolis of Athens. Slightly less impressive but no less important are the quadruple-stacked caryatids at the former Grand Hotel National at Taborstrasse 18 (2nd District), Austria's first luxury hotel. It is the world's only example of such an arrangement.

Graceful too are the ladies on the portal of the Equitable Palais at Stock-im-Eisen Platz 3. This building, erected in the 1890s to house an American insurance company and as grand as anything on the Ringstrasse, is often overlooked because of its proximity to the Stephansdom. Note the American eagles incorporated into the facade, and the ark-like finial on the roof alluding to transatlantic relations. The tiny male figures above the doorway, together with the curious ancient timber in a niche on the corner outside, relate to the building's unusual address (see no. 55).

Caryatids guarding the entrance to the Equitable Palais on Stock-im-Eisen Platz

Even the forward-looking Viennese Art Nouveau (*Jugendstil*) couldn't resist the Atlas figure, rendering it in a very stylised manner on the marble-faced façade at the so-called Artaria-Haus Kohlmarkt 9. Designed by Max Fabiani (1865-1962), the building replaced an earlier house where the composer Frederic Chopin stayed during a visit to Vienna in 1830–31 More Art Nouveau Atlases, this time in the form of pseudo-medieval knights clutching swords, can be found in the former bank building (now a very glitzy supermarket) at Schottengasse 6-8 (1st District).

Other places of interest nearby: 22, 23, 24, 28, 29

22 Secret St. Virgil's Chapel

1st District (Innere Stadt), St. Virgil's Chapel *(Virgilkapelle)* in Stephansplatz U-Bahn-Station); take U-1, U-3 to Stephansplatz

Most visitors to Vienna walk over an important and curious piece of the city's history without ever realising it. Marked out in grey stones on the surface of Stephansplatz (and best viewed from the top of the Stephansdom's lofty South Tower) is the outline of the Chapel of St. Mary Magdalene *(Magdalenenkirchlein)*. It was built in the late 14th century in what at the time was a cemetery surrounding the cathedral. It was used for consecrations and funeral masses until its demolition after a fire in 1781. This destruction in turn caused the abandonment of a subterranean room hidden directly below, whose chance re-discovery was only made in 1973 during excavations for the Stephansplatz U-Bahn station.

On Stephansplatz many pedestrians ignore the outlines of two ancient chapels beneath their feet

The mysterious St. Virgil's Chapel below Stephansplatz

What came to light after being hidden for nearly 200 years were the mysterious remains of St. Virgil's Chapel (*Virgilkapelle*). Its outline is marked on Stephansplatz in white stones. The rectangular room measuring 10.5 metres long and 6 metres wide has a floor lying some 12 metres below the present-day pavement. Ignoring the existing roof vault that was added later, the original roof rose 1.5 metres above ground level giving the building an original height of 13–14 metres. Its walls are 1.5 metres thick and broken up by six recesses. They are covered in white plaster painted with red lines to give a crude impression of fine masonry, and at the top of each recess is a circled cross. The closest parallel for this motif is the Syro-Palestinian region and the art of the early Christian and Byzantine world. Also unusual is the fact that the room only has a clay floor with no evidence of paving and that there is a well with no apparent function. Most mysterious of all, however, is how the building was ever entered – it can only be assumed by means of a trapdoor in the vaulted roof that once projected above Stephansplatz.

Although the room's construction is not mentioned in any documents, the building has been dated stylistically to the reign of the last Babenberg Duke, Friedrich II (1230–46) (commentators point to the original vaulting that resembles that of the dateable Michaelerkirche, and the circular cross motif that is reminiscent of a Late Romanesque rosette in the Stephansdom's West Gallery, built in 1230 and re-discovered in 1945). It is thought that Friedrich II, eager to elevate Vienna to a Bishopric, commissioned the subterranean structure as a potential tomb for St. Koloman, patron saint elect of the new diocese. Koloman was an Irish pilgrim to the Holy Land, revered for his healing powers but hung in error in Lower Austria on suspicion of spying (a stone from the site where he died was incorporated into the Bishop's Portal of the Stephansdom in 1361, though his bones now rest at Melk monastery in the Wachau).

After Friedrich's premature death in 1246 whilst fighting the Hungarians, and the accession of the Habsburgs thirty years later since he left no heirs, Koloman's tomb plan was abandoned. Later, in the early-14th century, the cathedral's charnel house (where exhumed bones were stacked to make space for new burials) was destroyed through the building of a new cathedral chancel. As Friedrich's grand subterranean room now lacked a function its high vaulted roof was removed and a lower one installed, enabling a new charnel house to be constructed above.

The subterranean room then passed to the wealthy Viennese merchant family of Chrannest, who used it as a family burial chamber in c.1340. It was they who added several altars, dedicating one of them to St. Virgil after whom the building is named today. When the Chrannest family died out the chamber became a meeting place during the 16th century for the Brotherhood of Merchants, as well as the newly founded Brotherhood of God's Corpse (Fronleichnamsbruderschaft).

By 1378 a chapel is in existence above the subterranean room is known henceforth as the Chapel of St. Mary Magdalene. The seat of the Association of Notaries (Schreiberzeche), whose seal bore the image of their patron, Saint Mary Magdalene, this is the structure marked out in Stephansplatz today in grey. The function of the charnel house, which it replaced then passed to the Stephansdom's sprawling subterranean crypts, where thousands of bodies were laid to rest in the period up to 1783, just two years after the destruction of the chapel, and with it the mysterious subterranean Chapel of St. Virgil (see no. 33).

Other places of interest nearby: 21, 23, 29, 31

23 The Snake's Tongue Poison Detector

1st District (Innere Stadt), the Treasury of the Order of the Teutonic Knights *(Schatzkammer des Deutschen Ordens)* on the first floor at Singerstrasse 7 (staircase 1); take U-1, U-3 to Stephansplatz

In 1190, during the siege of Acre in the Holy Land, the burghers of Bremen and Lübeck founded the wonderfully named Brethren of the Teutonic House of St. Mary of Jerusalem. Mercifully abbreviated to the Order of the Teutonic Knights (or better still *Deutscher Orden*), it was one of the three main military-religious orders to emerge from the Crusades. Despite military defeat at Tannenberg in 1410, and dissolution under both Napoleon and Hitler, the spiritual branch of the order remains active as a charitable body, tending the sick and assisting the development of former Communist countries, where it maintains a strong presence.

The snakes' tongue poison detector in the Treasury of the Teutonic Knights in Singerstrasse

Its history in Vienna began during the reign of the Babenberg dukes, when in 1222 the knights built for themselves a house, the *Deutschordenshaus*, at Singerstrasse 7. In the late-14th century, a Gothic church (*Deutschordenskirche*) was added in which the knights' coats of arms and memorial slabs can still be seen. By 1633 its treasury boasted an exotic collection of objects assembled by the Order's various Grand Masters (*Hochmeister*), and by the late-18th century the house had assumed its present form.

High dignitaries of the church headed the order for much of its history and when a *Hochmeister* died his possessions fell to the Order. An important part of the resulting collection is the precious tableware, either for practical use or purely decoration.

Pride of place must surely go to the *Natternzungenkredenz*, or snake's tongue salt-cellar, of 1526: a most unusual table decoration by anyone's reckoning! Dangling from a red coral branch are thirteen fossilised shark's teeth, thought originally to be adders', vipers' or even dragons' tongues, which were believed to exude moisture when placed near poisoned food or drink. Clearly although the Grand Masters were powerful men they were also fearful of being murdered by devious means. Only two other examples of such salt cellars are known, one in Dresden and the other in Vienna's Kunsthistorisches Museum.

Also curious is the set of Tiger Shell spoons with curvy silver handles from Goa, a wavy-bladed Malaysian dagger (*kris*) with Rhino horn handle in the form of a Buddha, and from Persia strange stones, called *bezoars*, found in the stomach of the Ibex goat to which supernatural healing powers were once attributed. On display, too, is the ceremonial chain of the Order, made up of eleven shields each bearing the Order's distinctive black cross emblem, and a stunning bejewelled table clock in which the time, date and planetary movements are measured out by a series of tiny human figures.

Before leaving the building be sure to glance at the Sala Terrena (ground floor room), a tiny 50-seat concert hall with Venetian-style Baroque frescoes, providing an intimate venue for Mozart concerts. If closed, take a peep at it through the shuttered windows in the delightful cobbled courtyard, replete with window boxes, glazed loggias and fragments of sculpture, where both Brahms and Mozart lived briefly. The view of the Stephansdom's spire, rising above the steepest red-tiled roof one is ever likely to see, is wonderful. It is also worth noting that part of the building here contains the secretive Gästehaus Deutscher Orden, a modest hotel that offers monastic calm a world away from the bustle of nearby Stephansplatz.

Other places of interest nearby: 19, 20, 21, 24, 28

24   The Knights of Blood Alley

1st District (Innere Stadt), a tour of Blutgasse and the
Fähnrichshof; take U-1, U-3 to Stephansplatz

Concealed inside a courtyard behind the Stephansdom there stands a
venerable Plane tree. Within living memory a sharp piece of iron could be
seen jutting out of it. Enquiries as to how it got there invariably brought
the same response from locals: why, it's the sword of a medieval knight!
In recent years the iron has disappeared, and so perhaps now is the time
to throw some light on one of Vienna's more unusual urban legends.

The Fähnrichshof, perhaps Vienna's most charming courtyard, is
best entered from Singerstrasse 11. Meaning the Ensigns' Court this
is where local residents once assembled around their flag *(Fahne)* in

times of unrest or danger. The present
courtyard dates from the sixteenth
century, when it formed a part of
the nearby nunnery of St. Nikolaus,
of which nothing remains except the
street name Nikolaigasse.

In one corner of the courtyard
stands the Plane tree. Several hundred
years old it was originally protected
from the predations of hungry horses by
an iron fence. As the tree grew thicker
so the fence was broken, and fragments
of it became incorporated into the
trunk. It's a prosaic explanation when
compared with the more fanciful theory
concerning the knight's sword, but like
all good urban myths there is some
historical truth behind the tale.

On the opposite side of nearby
Blutgasse stands the
sprawling
Deutschordenshaus. It is named after
the Roman Catholic Order of Teutonic
Knights, founded in Germany in the
late twelfth century. Like their contem-
poraries, the Knights Templar and the
Knights Hospitaller, they were sworn
to protecting pilgrims on their way to

A Teutonic knight's memorial in the
Deustchordenskirche

the Holy Land, after the Crusaders had captured Jerusalem in 1099. Over the next century the Order also set about subjugating the pagan Baltic tribes of what would become East Prussia, opening the area up to German colonisation.

The Order acquired the Deutschordenshaus around 1200, with the Fähnrichshof perhaps providing a secure refuge. It is possible that the narrow passageway in one corner of the courtyard, which could easily have been defended, could be a remnant of the original structure. Certainly the lingering memory of the knights in this part of Vienna would be enough to give rise to the legend of the knight's sword, plunged deep into the heart of the old Plane tree.

The name Blutgasse – Blood Alley – is another mystery. It is tempting to cite Philip IV of France, who famously suppressed the Templars in 1312 after having racked up a huge debt for their military services, which he was unable to repay. Had the Teutonic knights in Vienna been similarly suppressed resulting in a bloodbath that gave rise to the street name? The truth, however, is rather less colourful. Unlike the Templars, the Teutonic Knights were not supressed until the time of Napoleon and Hitler. Besides, the name Blutgasse only came into use in 1547, when it might well have reflected the presence of a nearby slaughterhouse. More fancifully, the name might derive from the Germanic *Bluot*, meaning a sacrificial offering, suggesting the former presence of a pagan shrine. No-one really knows.

Before leaving take a peek inside the narrow passageway referred to above. It contains a dizzying four-storey light well known as a *Pawlatschen* (from the Czech word *Pavlač* meaning 'open gallery'). It is lined with balconies, which were and still are used not only for access but also for hanging out laundry. Additionally don't miss the knights' Gothic chapel (Deutschordenskirche) on Singerstrasse, ablaze with coats of arms, and windows sporting the black cross that once adorned their white cloaks. The knights' treasury to the rear of the church was established by Grand Master Albert of Prussia in 1525 (see no. 23).

Also on Blutgasse is a Peace Museum (*Friedensmuseum*), which given the apparent violent history of the place seems rather fitting. Part of a worldwide non-profit organisation, it deploys the lives of various heroes – from Indian Yoga pioneer Paramahamsa Yogananda to Pakistani Peace Prize winner Malala Yousafzai – as a means of encouraging visitors to become peace emissaries themselves, making the world a better place through the kind treatment of others.

Other places of interest nearby: 18, 19, 20, 21, 22, 23

25   The World's First Fitted Kitchen

1st District (Innere Stadt), the MAK Museum for Applied Arts
(*MAK Museum für angewandte Kunst*), at Stubenring 55; take
U-3 to Stubentor

The Museum of Applied Arts (*Museum für angewandte Kunst*),
abbreviated simply to the MAK, is one of Vienna's more eclectic
museums, presenting eight centuries worth of design, craftwork,
objets d'art and utilitarian objects. Individual rooms are devoted
to different periods as well as to individual collections, such as
Baroque, Biedermeier and Art Nouveau. Also represented is the
Wiener Werkstätte founded in 1903 and similar to the English Arts
and Crafts Movement, Oriental carpets (including the world's only
16th century Egyptian silk *Mameluke* carpet), and furniture. The
latter includes Michael Thonet's 1856-patented, beech bentwood
chairs, which were produced in their millions and became popular
the world over (see no. 48).

An exhibit well worth tracking down lies at the end of one of the basement study collections and is known as the Frankfurt Kitchen (*Frankfurter
Küche*). It was designed by Margarete Schütte-Lihotzky (1897-2000),
Austria's first female student of architecture, who devoted her long life
to improving the
living conditions
of working women
throughout Europe.
In 1920, whilst
still only in her
early twenties, she
received an award
for an allotment
design that brought
her into contact
with the Viennese
Modernist architect
Adolf Loos (1870–
1933), who was
renowned for his
extreme function-
alism and austere
designs (see nos. 82
& 95).

The celebrated Frankfurt Kitchen in the Museum of Applied Arts
on Stubenring

In 1922, Schütte-Lihotzky worked with Loos on Austria's first public housing scheme for the war-disabled and their friendship endured until his death. The collaboration had a profound impact on her career and led to important developments in the design of houses, *kindergartens* and self-assembly furniture.

During the late-1920s, the German city of Frankfurt embarked on a large-scale housing programme and Schütte-Lihotzky was commissioned to help design an inexpensive, functional yet aesthetic apartment. She approached the task scientifically using the American Taylor System to time individual tasks around the home with a stopwatch and to base her design directly on optimal functional requirements. Only in this way would the working woman be able to gain more time for her family – and for herself!

As a result of her findings, Schütte-Lihotzky came up with a compact single unit comprising a built-in kitchen just 6.5 metres square separated from a living/dining area by a sliding door. The latter enabled a mother to keep an eye on her children whilst working in the kitchen and through which she could walk effortlessly the three metres from stove to dining table. In order to minimise the surfaces that needed cleaning, the kitchen units were placed on concrete plinths and likewise the wall units reached right up to the ceiling. The stove had a special ventilation flue and below the window was a storage cabinet kept cool by means of an outside opening. Hardwearing and stain-resistant beech wood was used for the work surfaces and there was an ingenious slot through which refuse could be swept into a bin below. Other ultra-sensible devices included a foldaway ironing board, moveable ceiling lamp, oak flour bins to deter mealworms and aluminium pullout drawers in which to store dry foodstuffs. The blue paintwork was thought to detract flies!

The overall compactness of the design impressed the Frankfurt City Council, as a result of which they built c.10,000 apartments between 1926 and 1930, each with the compulsory inclusion of what was now referred to as a "Frankfurt Kitchen". The costs of the unit were added to the building costs (which overall were reduced through mass-production) and factored into the rent, a solution acceptable to the tenants, who did not have to furnish the kitchen. The example to be found in the MAK is a replica built from Schütte-Lihotzky's memory.

Schütte-Lihotzky's opposition to the annexation of Austria by Nazi Germany and her subsequent alliance with the Communist party led to her arrest by the Gestapo and subsequent dispatch to a Bavarian prison camp. Thankfully her death sentence was lifted. During the ensuing Cold War she received few commissions because of her politics and it was not until 1980 that Vienna recognised her achievements by presenting her with the Vienna City Prize for Architecture, and in 1988 with the Austrian Honorary Medal for Science and Art. In 1997 she waltzed with Vienna's Mayor during her 100th birthday celebrations and in 1998 one of her last commissions was to oversee a housing project designed for women by women.

The Adolf Loos-designed Knize shop on Graben

To discover more about the life and work of this remarkable woman visit her former apartment, now the Margarete Schütte-Lihotsky Zentrum, at Franzensgasse 16/40 (5th District). The place is a time capsule showcasing the best of her distinctively pared-down and ergonomically-considered furniture and fittings.

The architect Adolf Loos (1870–1933) was responsible for some of the most distinctive Modernist buildings in Vienna's 1st District. Best known is the former Goldman & Salatsch tailor's shop overlooking Michaelerplatz. Notably its windows were shorn entirely of the Historicist decoration favoured by the Habsburgs prompting an enraged Emperor Franz Joseph I to describe them as lacking eyebrows! Other works by Loos are tiny architectural jewels in which every element – from door knobs to light fittings – has been carefully thought out and pre-fabricated. They include the tiny American Bar at Kärntner Durchgang 10, its marbled ceiling and mirrors giving the impression of a much larger space, and the equally compact Knize gents' outfitters at Graben 13 (see no. 30). Adolf Loos influenced other architects too, including the Viennese Paul Engelmann (1891–1965). His Haus Wittgenstein at Parkgasse 18 (3rd District) was built in the 1920s for a sister of philosopher Ludwig Wittgenstein (1889–1951) and exhibits the same spare design.

Other places of interest nearby: 17, 18, 26, 27

26   Last of the Old Walls

1st District (Innere Stadt), the Palais Coburg at the junction of the Coburgbastei and Gartenbaupromenade; take U-3 to Stubentor

The Romans were the first to use Vienna's geography to good effect in determining the placing of the walls of their garrison fort, *Vindobona* (see no. 13). After withdrawing from the city in c.400AD these walls together with their associated roads remained, providing the ground plan for medieval Vienna.

The name *Wenia* first appeared in the Salzburg annals of 881AD as part of the Eastern March (*Ostmark*) of Charlemagne's Franco-German Holy Roman Empire. The word it is thought to derive from the Illyro-Celtic word *Verdunja*, meaning woodland stream.

After the empire's collapse, the Saxon King Otto the Great subdued the German lands and in 976AD his son Otto II bestowed the March on the Bavarian Margraves of Babenberg under Leopold I (976–94). It would be their job to protect this eastern frontier, first as margraves (counts) and later as dukes, and by 996AD the name *Ostarrichi* (Eastern Realm, the origin of Österreich) is mentioned officially for the first time.

The Babenbergs restored Vienna's trade and culture, and by the mid-12th century, under Heinrich II (1141–77), they had upgraded Austria to an independent dukedom, built a ducal palace on Am Hof (see no. 4) and given Vienna city status. Using a ransom raised in 1192 from the capture by Duke Leopold V (1177–94) of the English King, Richard the Lionheart, the Babenbergs built their own city wall. Completed by 1250, these fortifications were 4.5 kilometres long, 10 metres high and 4 metres thick, punctuated by gates and towers. Today, however, they have been largely obliterated by later structures and little remains of them other than the occasional fragment (e.g. in the Heiligen-kreuzerhof, near the third stairwell; the saddle-roofed tower in the tiny courtyard at Griechengasse 9; and the original Stubentor gate, Vienna's oldest (c.1200), outlined in black stones on today's pavement). The rest is marked only by street names (e.g. Salztorgasse, Werdertorgasse, and Schottentor) and wall plaques (e.g. the Katzensteig gate at the bottom of Seitenstettengasse; the Stadttor at the Hohe Brücke on Wipplinger-strasse, and the Roter Turm (Red Tower) on Rotenturmstrasse).

In 1278, the Habsburgs came to the fore under King Rudolf I (1273–91) and they remained monarchs of Austria for the next 640 years. However, despite Vienna going on to become the capital of a wealthy empire, its Babenberg-era fortifications were retained and almost gave way during the first Turkish siege of 1529 (see no. 3). As a direct result, Emperor Ferdinand I (1556–64) ordered the construction of a new wall in their place, as well as the strengthening of the Hofburg, then a moated castle known as the *Alte Burg*, to where he moved his court in 1533. Influenced by the architecture of Italian Renaissance fortresses, the massive new brick walls, erected between 1531 and 1566, were pierced by eight gateways, with numerous towers, as well as stone-clad, star-shaped bastions (*Bastei*), which jutted out into open ground known as the *glacis* (see illustration on page 7). This no-man's land was 570 metres wide and sloped away from the walls affording an attacking army little cover. The huge expense of the walls, however, accounts in part for the paucity of other Renaissance architecture in Vienna (see no. 18).

Though very nearly breached, the walls survived a second Turkish siege in 1683 and remarkably were still more or less intact by the time of the 1848 Revolution (see no. 15). By then, however, the only threat to Vienna was homegrown civil disorder, and it was felt that this could be better controlled not by a circuit wall but by two huge barracks (*Kaserne*), connected by a new broad street occupying the former site of the *glacis* (see no. 58). After all, the revolutionaries of 1848 had used the city walls to protect themselves from approaching imperial troops intent on quelling the unrest.

The remains of the city wall in front of the Palais Coburg

Thus, on 20th December 1857 by decree of Emperor Franz Joseph I (1848–1916) work began on dismantling the Renaissance walls, thus providing the cramped inner city with some much-needed breathing space. The result was the horseshoe-shaped, Parisian-style boulevard called the Ringstrasse. Stretching 4 kilometres in length and up to 60 metres in width, it is lined with grand cultural and political institutions, each of which is rendered in a style reflective of its function: the neo-Gothic Town Hall (*Rathaus*), the neo-Baroque Burgtheater, and the neo-Classical Parliament). It remains the Emperor's greatest architectural legacy.

In several places, however, fragments of the old Renaissance walls linger, notably where they continue to provide the foundations for important buildings above. Thus, at the Mölker-Bastei, named after the Benedictine monastery at Melk that once owned land hereabouts, there is still a high brick bastion supporting a row of late-18th century houses. They include the Pasqualatihaus at number 8, where Beethoven lived in 1804 and 1813–15, and where he composed his only opera *Fidelio* (see no. 1). Around the corner from Mölker-Bastei is a street called Schottenbastei, which also recalls the former presence of the city wall.

Most informative of all is the recently restored Coburgbastei, a wall fragment supporting the huge mid-19th century Palais Coburg. In front of the palace there once stood a projecting bastion, the

The ruined Stubenbastei is preserved in the Stubentor U-Bahn station

so-called Brown Bastion (*Braunbastei*), the stone-faced outer edge of which now stands marooned on the pavement.

Back at the wall supporting the palace, windows at street level allow the passer-by to glimpse at the mighty vaulted casemates (*Kasematten*) running deep within the thickness of the brick walls, once busy with troops and cannon. Inside the palace, now a luxury hotel there is a stunning modern mosaic showing a bird's eye view of the Renaissance city walls.

Finally, not far away at Stubenbastei are the substantial remains of the Stubentor gateway and its 22 metre-high flanking ramparts revealed during excavation work for the U-3 underground in 1985–87. Its plan has been marked out permanently in white stones at street level and there is a fascinating little exhibition in the subway foyer illustrating the gate's history from Babenberg times through to its incorporation into the Renaissance wall and final

An Austro-Fascist eagle on a gateway near the Äusseres Burgtor

demolition. One further piece of wall is the nearby Dominikanerbastei, clad in white plaster to match the Baroque church it supports above.

Nothing at all now remains of the walls that once ran along the Danube Canal although there are a few tantalising sculptured fragments from the so-called Gonzagabastei that once stood here, preserved on the U-Bahn platform at Schwedenplatz.

The so-called *Äusseres Burgtor* next to the Neue Burg is the city wall's only extant gateway although it was inserted into the wall only later, in the 1820s, to commemorate the Battle of Leipzig at which the Austrians and the Prussians defeated Napoleon. It is flanked by two entrances added by the Austro-fascist party in 1934, their oppressive stylised eagles being one of Vienna's few examples of fascist decorative architecture. The gate serves as Vienna's chief memorial to fallen soldiers of the First World War.

Other places of interest nearby: 23, 25, 27, 28

27   The Only City Vineyard

1st District (Innere Stadt), Schwarzenbergplatz 2;
take U-3 to Stadtpark

Tucked into a corner of busy Schwarzenbergplatz, behind a grand stone balustrade, is a tiny vineyard. The only vineyard in the First District, it is cared for by the Mayer am Pfarrplatz winery. They run a successful wine tavern in a fine old Biedermeier house at Pfarrplatz 2 in the suburb of Grinzing, where Beethoven lived for a time, so no doubt the little city vineyard acts as a good advertisement for them.

It was in 280AD by order of the Roman Emperor Marcus Aurelius (121–180AD) that the virgin landscape of the Danube was first planted extensively with vines, although the Celts before them were probably also familiar with the grape. Vienna's short hot summers, lingering humid autumns and long cold winters make it ideal white wine country, manifested in crisp, dry, acidic wines, as well as sweet, late-harvest styles.

Today, Austria has ten wine regions, mainly in the sunny east, of which the Vienna is one of the smallest. Still, with 1,433 acres of vineyards and 145 wineries located uniquely within the city limits, it is the world's largest wine-growing city. Eighty percent of the grapes grown, including Weissburgunder, Grüner Veltliner, Gelber Muskateller, and the local speciality, Gemischter Satz, are pressed for Vienna's typically rustic white wine, with only a minority grown for reds and rosés.

Up until the late-17th century, vineyards still covered much of central Vienna. However, with the successful repulsion of the Turks, and the development of the city suburbs in the ensuing Baroque period, the vineyards were gradually pushed back to the foothills of the Vienna Woods (*Wienerwald*) north of the city.

Drinking wine is now as much a part of Viennese culture as appreciating art and listening to Classical music. In the city it is drunk in smart restaurants, homely traditional restaurants (*Beisl*), and converted monastic cellars (see no. 5). The ultimate wine experience occurs during the summer months, when locals and visitors alike travel out to wine villages such as Grinzing, Nussdorf, Sievering, Strebersdorf and Stammersdorf to visit rustic country taverns known as *Heurigen*. The word *Heuriger* comes from the word *heuer*, meaning 'this year', and refers to the most recent vintage. It was Emperor Joseph II (1765–90) who in 1784 lifted the tax on wine, giving vintners the chance to sell home-grown wines from their own premises for up to 300 days a year. The grapes had to be grown in the Vienna area and could not be supplemented with grapes from elsewhere, and the edict remains in force to this day.

Since medieval times, only an authentic *Heuriger* is allowed to advertise that its wine is available by hanging out a pine branch (*Buschenschank*) together with a placard bearing the

The tiny vineyard in a corner of Schwarzenbergplatz

word *Ausg'steckt* (literally 'hung out). However, it is not until after St. Martin's Day (November 11th) that the wine of the previous year is considered properly aged. Saint Martin of Tours was the first non-martyr to be canonised by public acclamation, with the date of his burial in 397 supplanting the earlier pagan feast day of Bacchus, god of wine. In time November 11th became the traditional day to baptise the young wine, accompanied by roast goose (*Martinigansl*), so plentiful at this time of year during the bird's annual autumn migration.

It is also possible, for a few short weeks following the harvest, to sample the early stages of the new wine. They are *Most* (unfermented), *Sturm* (early fermented) and *Staubiger* (fermented but still cloudy).

To find out more about the history of wine in Vienna visit the Viticulture Museum (*Weinbaumuseum*) in the cellar of the Döbling District Museum at Döblinger Hauptstrasse 96 (19th District).

Of course, as with all good wine regions, there are bad years – and 1450 was just such a year. The vintage was so sour, due to adverse weather conditions, that it was used to slake the lime used in the foundations of the Stephansdom's North Tower producing, it is said, an extraordinarily strong mortar!

Other places of interest nearby: 25, 26, 28, 46

28 Where the Wurst is Best!

**1st District (Innere Stadt), Wiener Würstelstand
on Kupferschmiedgasse off Kärntnerstrasse;
take U-1, U-3 to Stephansplatz**

Modern fast food, whilst very convenient in busy modern times, rarely gives the customer a cultural experience to remember, or the opportunity to converse with a fellow diner. In Vienna, however, that is exactly what is on offer, from mid-morning until dusk and beyond, on many of the city's street corners. The culinary institution that is the *Würstelstand* (sausage stand), often with its colourful retro styling of the 1950s, sliding windows and chrome counter, is a welcome, reassuring and integral part of the modern Viennese cityscape. With 300 or so outlets

A classic Viennese Würstelstand in Kupferschmiedgasse

across the capital, this paean to the humble sausage is undoubtedly Vienna's oldest fast food establishment, with a clientele that transcends economic and social boundaries. Here, the impoverished student and footsore shopper stand cheek-by-jowl with the company manager, office worker, builder and late-night clubber; different genders young and old, all enjoying a hearty snack in harmony together. Of the twenty or so different sausages available, each stand will sell about half a dozen types at any one time, from the familiar (thin pairs of boiled *Frankfurters* – called *Wieners* in Frankfurt! – and fried *Bratwurst*; the latter when boiled are called *Burenwurst*) to the less obvious (plump, cheese-infused pork *Käsekrainer*, thin spicy Hungarian *Debreziner* and smoky *Tirolerwurst*). Additionally, perspiring gently in its own tiny oven is *Leberkäse*, liver cheese, a sort of meat loaf that contains neither liver nor cheese and which is served sliced in a sandwich. Occasionally it is made from horse-meat (*Pferdeleberkäse*) and there is

A selection of different Würstel near Schottentor

a further variation that does include cheese (*Käseleberkäse*). Sausages are traditionally served sliced (*aufg'schnittn*) on a paper tray with a toothpick, together with a roll (*Semmel*) or sliced bread (*Brot*), sweet or sour mustard (*süsser* or *scharfer Senf*) or pickles, and all washed down with a carbonated drink or lager beer. Customers wishing to devour a sausage on the hoof should opt for a sausage hot dog-style, slid inside a baguette suitably lubricated with tomato ketchup and wrapped in a paper serviette.

For a somewhat more refined, but no less Viennese, snacking experience try Trzesniewski's famous buffet at Dorotheergasse 1, where myriad open rye-bread sandwiches are served by uniformed waitresses to standing customers, washed down with a tiny glass (*Pfiff*) of beer. During the increasingly chilly months of autumn and winter Vienna's sausage stands are supplemented by others selling hot chestnuts (*Maroni*), sliced baked potatoes (*Bratkartoffeln*), hot potato patties with garlic (*Kartoffelpuffer*), *Glühwein* (mulled wine spiced with cloves) and *Punsch* (hot tea, dark rum, orange juice and cinnamon with a shot of wine) – the perfect cure for cold noses and frozen fingers! They feature on street corners and in the city's famous Christmas markets (*Christkindlmarkt*) (e.g. Am Hof, Freyung, Rathausplatz, Spittelberg and Schloss Schönbrunn), whose long history can be traced back as far as 1298.

Other places of interest nearby: 21, 23, 29, 33

29 The Comfort of Strangers

1st District (Innere Stadt), the Café Bräunerhof at Stallburg-gasse 2; take U-1, U-3 to Stephansplatz

In 2011, Vienna's traditional coffee house culture was designated 'Intangible Cultural Heritage' by UNESCO. This makes it every bit as important as the Argentine Tango, the Mediterranean diet and the Panama hat. According to the listing the Viennese coffee house is a place "where time and space are consumed, but only the coffee is found on the bill."

The city's coffee house tradition is a venerable one, stretching back to the late-17th century, when an Armenian trader was allowed to roast and sell coffee beans by royal decree. The new beverage was well received and coffee houses sprang up rapidly across the city. In the early days, however, the different varieties of coffee had no official names and so customers made their selection using a colour chart!

These days choosing is done by name, the most common varieties being the ubiquitous *Mélange* (espresso with steamed milk and foam; topped with whipped cream, it is called a *Franziskaner*), *Schwarzer* (single espresso), *Brauner* (single espresso served with a little milk or cream), *Verlängerter* (espresso with added water), *Kapuziner* (double espresso topped with whipped cream), and *Einspänner* (espresso in a glass topped with whipped cream). The latter was traditionally popular with Vienna's fiaker drivers and is said to be named after the one-horse cabs common after the First World War, when fodder was short (the word 'Einspänner' refers to a solitary soul).

The traditional Viennese coffee house has a distinctive atmosphere and a specific protocol dating back to its *fin de siècle* heyday. Against a backdrop of dark wood, cream coloured walls and subdued lighting, coffee is served by waiters dressed in black suits and bow ties (it always arrives on a silver tray accompanied by a glass of water). Customers sit at marble-topped tables on either Thonet bentwood chairs or sturdily-upholstered banquettes. Once settled they can read from a selection of national and international papers for as long as they wish. Indeed if they remain for several hours the chances are that they will take lunch or an evening meal, and probably succumb to a slice of *Apfelstrudel*, *Milchrahmstrudel* or *Gugelhupf* along the way. With only discreet attention from the waiter, it has been said that the Viennese coffee house is the perfect place to be alone whilst enjoying the comfort of strangers.

Vienna's traditional coffee houses may share a particular atmosphere yet each has its own individual charm. The grandest include the Café Central on Herrengasse and Sigmund Freud's beloved Café Landtmann on the Ring, both of which once drew intellectuals and artists with their freewheeling conversation and cosmopolitan air. Meanwhile, tucked away in the backstreets is the disarmingly modest Café Hawelka on Dorotheergasse, where the house speciality is jam-filled *Buchteln* served each evening at 9pm. Out in the suburbs is Café Sperl on Gumpendorferstrasse, once a favourite of Adolf Hitler, Café Goldegg on Argentinierstrasse, with its billiard tables, and Café Weimar on Währinger Strasse, frequented by well-heeled punters from the nearby Volksoper.

Tradition is everything at the Café Bräunerhof

This author's favourite is Café Bräunerhof on Stallburggasse, just behind the stables of the Spanish Riding School. It was writer Thomas Bernhard's favourite, too, and little has changed since his time. Mobile telephones are restricted to a special booth and the toilets are vintage to say the least – and yet it's a delight. Come here on a weekday morning and the atmosphere is almost studious, with just a few customers thumbing the day's papers. Visit on a Saturday and it's riotous by comparison, with a quartet belting out traditional Viennese *Schrammelmusik*.

Other places of interest nearby: 21, 22, 28, 31

30 Vienna Made to Measure

1st District (Innere Stadt), a tour of bespoke shops including Rudolf Scheer & Söhne at Bräunerstrasse 4; take U-1, U-3 to Stephansplatz

Vienna's retail landscape is changing rapidly, especially around Graben, Kohlmarkt, and Kärntnerstrasse. Venerable old stores have been ousted by global brands – but all is not lost. In amongst Gucci, Cartier and H&M there are still some traditional family firms, where for over a century hand-crafted suits, hats and shoes have been made for the sartorially elegant.

A fine example is Knize at Graben 13, which has been tailoring bespoke men's suits for over one hundred and fifty years. The company was established in 1858 by the Czech tailor Josef Knize. In 1913 the present shop was opened, its marble frontage and panelled interior a pristine example of the work of Austrian modernist architect Adolf Loos. The intriguing crests either side of the name recall that Knize once supplied dress uniforms to the Sultan of Turkey and the Shah of Iran. Around a hundred suits come out of Knize each year, using cloth imported from Italy and England. Each takes ten days and seven thousand stitches. A thousand more suits are made-to-measure annually from a standard-sized base pattern.

Around the corner at Bräunerstrasse 4 is one of Vienna's oldest bespoke companies. Rudolf Scheer & Söhne have been making shoes since 1816, and from 1878 onwards some of them were worn by the emperor himself. Such royal and imperial patronage explains why the

The window of Rudolf Scheer & Söhne on Bräunerstrasse

phrase K. u K. Hof-Schuhmacher is proudly displayed in gilt lettering on the frontage. In the window are displayed row upon row of wooden forms known as lasts, around which hand-crafted shoes are created.

The shop appears much as it must have done a hundred years ago, with an elegant ground floor waiting room and a creaking wooden staircase leading up to a first floor fitting room. The shoes are made here, too, mostly from calf leather. Each pair requires three fitting sessions and around sixty hours of labour, much of it done in monastic silence.

Similar production standards are to be found in the Mühlbauer millinery studio at Seilergasse 10. This company may have been making hats the old-fashioned way since 1903 but since 2007 they have been sold in the most modern surroundings. The hats, of which an astonishing thirteen thousand are created each year, are manufactured in a second floor workshop near Schwedenplatz. Here they are made in all shapes and sizes, mostly from rabbit fur felt, using a hundred year-old steaming machine and traditional wooden moulds, over which they are stretched.

Grandest of all, and perhaps the most traditional of Vienna's bespoke family firms, is Wilhelm Jungmann & Neffe at Albertinaplatz 3. The finest suit fabrics have been retailed here since 1881, in an oak-lined room worthy of any country house. Well over a thousand fabrics are available, including not only Harris Tweed and cashmere but also *vicuña* fleece taken from Peruvian llamas!

Jungmann also displays its imperial and royal credentials, and their success accounts for the opulence still in evidence at the shop today. A roundel on the ornate ceiling represents an allegory of the silk trade. Of course the location was all important, and being close to the Hofburg, the State Opera, and the Hotel Sacher (a preferred meeting place for the local aristocracy) was undoubtedly good for business.

Vienna has many more idiosyncratic shops, including the following: the Galleria Febella hat shop at Herrengasse 6–8, with its hats for all occasions and felt berets piled high in all colours; the confectioner Altmann & Kuhne at Graben 30, renowned not only for its tiny handmade sweets but also the tiny handmade boxes in which they are sold; the smoked meat specialist Fleischerei Kröppel at Postgasse 1–3; Reimer's Bonbons on Fleischmarkt, with its tempting trays of chocolates, candies and handmade cake decorations; and the defiantly old-fashioned Acculux Hans Kremser electrical shop at Schultergasse 3. A Viennese speciality is the city's old fashioned pharmacies with their rows of apothecary jars and gilded fittings. Notable examples include the Alte Leopoldsapotheke at Plankengasse 6, with its painted window shutters, the Stadtapotheke zum Goldenen Hirschen on Kohlmarkt, replete with an ancient sit-down weighing scale, the former Hofapotheke at the Spanish Riding School (now a gift ship-cum-café), the Apotheke zum Weissen Storch at Tuchlauben 9 identified by a model of a stork, the Engelapotheke at Bognergasse 9, featuring Jugendstil mosaic angels on its façade, and the Alte Löwenapotheke at Josefstädter Strasse 25, which was Vienna's first gas lit shop.

Other places of interest nearby: 31, 32, 33, 34, 35

31   Vienna at your Convenience

1st District (Innere Stadt), the subterranean public conveniences near Graben 22; take U-1, U-3 to Stephansplatz

Toilets have long been a measure of civilisation. The earliest in the royal palace at Knossos on Crete date back to 1500 BC. Under the Romans there was an explosion in toilet technology and Vindobona (as Vienna was known then) would have been well plumbed. Thereafter toilets disappear and by the Middle Ages the Viennese were emptying their waste directly into the street. It was normal European practice and disease was rife. Something needed to change and so in the mid-eighteenth century central Vienna received Europe's first modern sewer system.

Vienna owes its public conveniences to one man, Wilhelm Beetz (1844-1921), a court official and the son of a dairyman. In 1880 he offered the city a twenty five year contract for public conveniences based on those installed in Berlin. The plan was accepted and by 1910 there were seventy three facilities across the city. Many are still in use and they come in two forms. One is an octagonal pavilion made from prefabricated

iron panels inside which is concealed a gentlemen's urinal. The urinal itself is not porcelain but metal, and is coated in special oil containing disinfectant. No water is used, meaning the facility never freezes, and odours are kept to a minimum. Beetz patented this so-called *oelurinoir* in 1883 and received numerous honours as a result. A fine example from 1903 can be seen on Puchsbaumplatz in Favoriten.

The second form is more elaborate. A roofed rectangular pavilion set on a stone base includes separate entrances for both sexes. Inside there are four cubicles on each side, as well as a heated attendant's office, and the usual urinal for men. A recently restored example stands alongside the MAK on Parkring, replete with a decorative coloured glass border beneath its roofline and price list on the door.

A signpost to the subterranean public conveniences on Graben

Beetz reserved something special for the public conveniences on Graben. Out of discretion he placed the facility underground, advertising its presence by a pair of Jugendstil lanterns, which doubled as ventilation chimneys. Unveiled in 1905 it boasts oak doors and brass washstands but despite such luxury it was always free to use (not so these days). The ladies' side once contained an aquarium as proof of the purity of the water, and over the inevitable waterless urinal in the men's area there hangs a copy of Beetz's patent.

PATENT OEL URINOIR. -OHNE WASSERSPÜLUNG GERUCHLOS-
Ö.P.№45054 U.P.№14701 J.P.№32405 D.RP.№72361 E.P.№16447 F.P.№216247 etc.
WILHELM BEETZ, WIEN, III. ERDBERGSTRASSE 17.
ET UM GRÖSSTE REINLICHKEIT UND ORDNEN DER KLEIDER IN DER

Patent details over the Graben urinal

Novelty is still a feature of toilets in Vienna. Take the Toilet of Modern Art, for instance, in the Hundertwasserhaus at Kegelgasse 36–38 (3rd District), which is decorated with the flamboyant artist's trademark crazed tiles and bold colours. There are also the futuristic conveniences designed by architect Manfred Wolff-Plotegg for the Café Korb (1st District), the doors graphically identified with sans-serif punctuation marks. Slightly less cryptic is Café Ansari at Praterstrasse 15 (2nd District), where the toilets are marked 'K' for Kings and 'Q' for Queens. And let's not forget Café Diglas at Wollzeile 10 (1st District), where the call of nature relies entirely on trust: the clear glass cubicle doors only turn opaque when locked from the inside!

For those who love their toilet history, visit the Sanitation Museum (Sanitärhistorisches Museum) at Mollardgasse 87 (6th District), which details Vienna's treatment of wastewater since the 1880s. Centre stage is the last Otto Wagner toilet from his late-19th century Stadtbahn station at Nussdorfer Strasse.

The Viennese penchant for including French words such as *urinoir* in their vocabulary is longstanding. The early Habsburgs strove to maintain their Spanish court manners and to avoid the rationalist influence of France but from the time of Empress Maria Theresa the influence of Paris grew. The language spoken at court was *Schönbrunner Deutsch*, a nasal upper class mode of speech sprinkled with French expressions. Even today the pavement is referred to as the *Trottoir*, a closet is a *Garderobe*, a milky coffee is a *Mélange* – and of course a gentlemen's urinal is also known as a *Pissoir*!

Other places of interest nearby: 22, 29, 30, 32, 33

32 Some Courtyards and Squares

1st District (Innere Stadt), courtyards and squares including the Grosses Michaelerhaus at Kohlmarkt 11; take U-3 to
Herrengasse

For anyone exploring the Inner City (1st District) there's no greater
sense of discovery than coming across the numerous courtyards
(*Innenhöfe*) and squares (*Plätze*) hidden along Vienna's old back
streets (see nos. 18, 23 & 52). Fortunately, the area has been spared
unsightly high-rise development due to its UNESCO World Heritage
status, which serves to enhance the area's charm. With many
courtyard houses constructed between the Baroque and *Biedermeier*
periods (17th-19th centuries) the visitor has the chance to swap
bustling streets for peaceful, sometimes leafy havens in only a few
short paces.

A fine example is the handsome courtyard of the Grosses Michaelerhaus at Kohlmarkt 11. Built in 1720, it is where the composer Josef
Haydn stayed in an unheated attic in 1749 (see the wall plaque on
Kohlmarkt). The Court Poet Metastasio also died here in 1782 (see a
further plaque on Michaelerplatz) (see no. 33). The courtyard contains
a unique row of barrel-vaulted stables as well as graceful wrought iron
balconies. The latter are often referred to as *Pawlatschen*, from the Czech
word *Pavlač* meaning a balconied or galleried courtyard, common in the
19th century tenements of Prague. They were usualy added to maximise
the existing internal living space by creating individual access to each
apartment from the balcony outside. The balconies also added a social
element to tenement living – as well as somewhere to hang one's
clothes out to dry!

Other examples of hidden courtyards with balconies (as well
as elegant glazed loggias) that are worth getting the map out
for include Habsburgergasse 5, Bräunerstrasse 3, Augustinerstrasse
12 (once occupied by Countess Elizabeth Báthory (1560–1614), the
notorious Hungarian murderess), Weihburggasse 16/21, Singerstrasse
7, 16 & 22, Grünangergasse 1, Ballgasse 4, and Bäckerstrasse 2 and
7 (see nos. 18 & 23). Particularly grand courtyards adorn the Palais
Wilczek at Herrengasse 5 and the Palais Daun-Kinsky at Freyung 4.
An extraordinary example at Bäckerstrasse 16 has been converted into
an alpine climbing wall.

Interesting examples of courtyards *outside* the 1st District can be
found at Margaretenplatz 2 and Schlossgasse 21 in the 5th district of

Looking into the courtyard of the Grosses Michaelerhaus off busy Kohlmarkt

Margareten (the latter being one of Vienna's best preserved *Biedermeier* courtyards), and Neudeggergasse 14 and Langegasse 34 in the 8th district of Josefstadt, the latter dominated by a single huge tree (see no. 52).

Sometimes, during later restoration work, buildings and courtyards in the 1st District were connected together by passageways producing maze-like *Durchhäuser* (literally through-houses) that transport the visitor from one street to another. An enjoyable example is entered at Blutgasse 3, where a narrow passage leads past traditional balconied properties into the monastic calm of the ancient Fähnrichshof courtyard, and out through the other side to Grünangergasse (see no. 24).

Also well worth visiting are three charming city squares. They are Dr.-Ignaz-Seipel-Platz, with its fountains, Old University (*Alte Universität*) founded 1365 and Baroque Jesuit Church; the spacious Heiligenkreuzerhof, a gloriously unspoilt piece of 18th century Vienna belonging to the Cistercian Abbey of the same name, and Franziskanerplatz containing one of Vienna's smallest coffee houses – the Kleines Café – and the city's only church with a Renaissance façade. The latter includes a cloister next-door at number 4, whose exterior wall is dotted with curious roundels that once contained portraits of saints.

Other places of interest nearby: 29, 30, 31, 33, 34

33 Church Crypts and Coffins

1st District (Innere Stadt), the crypt of St. Michael's Church (*Michaelerkirche*) on Michaelerplatz; take U-3 to Herrengasse (note: crypt tours in German only)

It could be said that for each of Vienna's historic landmarks above ground, there is another less well-known one concealed below. These subterranean curiosities fall into two groups, namely those uncovered during excavations, which date from an earlier period of Vienna's history (e.g. the Romans and early Jews, see nos. 9 & 13), and those that were deliberately constructed underground, such as cellars (see no. 6), drains (see nos. 6 & 94) and crypts. To experience the latter, most visitors flock to the labyrinthine catacombs (*Katakomben*), that run to several levels beneath the Stephansdom. The oldest are those in the Ducal Vault, which contains the sarcophagus of Duke Rudolf IV (1358–65), the cathedral's founder, as well as fifteen other tombs. Also to be found here, stored in lateral niches, are 70 copper urns containing the internal organs of the later Habsburgs, as dictated by Viennese court protocol (their hearts and bodies lie elsewhere). Below the Apostles' Choir is a vault for Vienna's bishops and archbishops, whilst running under the Women's Choir is one for the canons. There is also a mass grave for thousands of victims of the 1713 plague, their bodies simply thrown down shafts that were then sealed up. Convicts and monks would

Coffins and bones in the crypt beneath the Michaelerkirche

later be given the unenviable task of sorting the bones into some order.

In 1530, Emperor Ferdinand I (1521–64) prohibited burial in graveyards within the city walls for reasons of hygiene and by 1735 the cemetery that once surrounded the cathedral had been cleared (see no. 22). Many bodies were re-buried under the cathedral, their redundant headstones incorporated into the outer walls.

When the catacombs beneath the Stephansdom were full a new crypt was excavated in 1744 below the Stephansplatz itself, consisting of a series of irregular tunnels that eventually extended

The ornate sarcophagus of Emperor Joseph I in the Kaisergruft

below all of the north and eastern parts of the cathedral's above-ground graveyard. Some 11,000 citizens were buried here during the next 40 years, including the great Baroque architects Johann Bernhard Fischer von Erlach (1656–1723) and Lukas von Hildebrandt (1668–1745).

In 1783, when the smell became too much, Emperor Joseph II (1765–90) ordered the closure of all crypts within the city limits and instigated the opening of suburban cemeteries (see nos. 42 & 59). For years the crypts remained inaccessible until the 1870s, when the human remains were finally walled in, creating over thirty chambers filled to the ceiling with bones.

Unfortunately, in the 1960s parts of the Stephansdom crypt were rather over-restored, and so for something more authentic (and certainly less crowded) head instead for St. Michael's Church (*Michaelerkirche*) at the top of Kohlmarkt. The crypt here is smaller and stretches the length and breadth of the Gothic church above it. First documented in 1267, its salient architectural features were written on the crypt walls long ago to assist orientation in the gloom. Piles of paupers' bones were brought here from the former graveyard which from c.1300, until its closure in 1508, occupied Michaelerplatz outside.

The rows of wooden coffins seen in the crypt today, some of which are painted, represent Vienna's well-to-do middle classes and court aristocrats, interred below the church in which they worshipped from the early 1630s onwards. Many coffins have collapsed over time, their boards stacked neatly in alcoves by the Salvatorian Order that became caretakers of the neglected crypt in 1924. It is worth noting the fine preservation of some of the corpses dating back to the days of Mozart, their clothes, hair and skin preserved by the consistently cool temperature.

As happened at the Stephansdom, the crypt was abandoned in 1783 on the order of Emperor Joseph II (1765–90), by which time 4000 people from all walks of life had been laid to rest here, including Court Poet Pietro Trapassi (known as Metastasio), who lived and died in the house next-door, and from whom Mozart purchased several librettos. Most of the corpses, however, have long since vanished, their crushed bones accounting for the unnaturally high floor level!

Of related interest are the incredible bejewelled skeletons from the catacombs in Rome that can be found in the Peterskirche just off the Graben, and in the Ruprechtskirche on Ruprechtsplatz. Rare for Vienna, this typically Italian custom involves clothed and decorated human remains being placed in glass coffins as reliquaries for worshippers to venerate. Another example is that of the martyr St. Bonatus to be found in the Rochuskirche in the 3rd district of Landstrasse.

Those wishing to pursue further the death rituals of the Habsburgs should visit the Imperial Burial Vaults (*Kaisergruft*) below the Capuchin Church (*Kapuzinerkirche*) at Tegethoffstrasse 2, where 140 of their embalmed bodies dating back to 1633 are displayed in ornate sarcophagi. Their hearts are kept in silver urns in the Little Heart Vault (*Herzgrüftel*) in the Lorettokapelle of the Augustinerkirche and their organs are kept in the Stephansdom catacombs thereby ensuring the dynasty's omnipresence even in death.

Other places of interest nearby: 29, 30, 32, 34, 35

34 A Shrine to Esperanto

1st District (Innere Stadt), the Esperanto Museum (*Esperantomuseum*) in the Palais Mollard at Herrengasse 9; take U-3 to Herrengasse

Vienna is home to around 130 museums and collections, of which the more curious ones are devoted to subjects such as snow globes, shoes, crime, cameras, clowns, baking, coffee, pharmaceuticals, toilets, fishing, markets, money, heating, and funerals (see no. 31, 66, 70). Amongst these the explorer should not overlook the 23 district museums (*Bezirksmuseen*), tucked away in the suburbs and containing unusual collections devoted to glass, phonographs (6th), bricks (14th) and chimney sweeps (4th) (see nos. 5, 75).

One unusual collection that lies in the heart of the city in the Palais Mollard at Herrengasse 9 is the Esperanto Museum (or *Esperanto Muzeo* in Esperanto). Whilst it may sound somewhat dry, and indeed it does lack the visual punch of many museums, it offers those interested an intriguing glimpse into the world of planned languages.

Any visitors making the effort to visit the museum will be made extremely welcome by the enthusiastic Esperanto-fluent curators.

Esperanto is a *planned* language (not an *artificial* one, as the curators will stress) created in 1887 by Polish optician Dr. Ludwik Zamenhof (1859-1917). Between 1886 and 1895 he lived in Vienna at Florianigasse (8th district), and his bust can be found in Karlsplatz.

Although Esperanto never became the *lingua franca* Zamenhof had hoped for – the word *Esperanto* is from the French verb 'to hope' – it did quickly replace the earlier planned language of *Volapük*. Today it has 3 million speakers, a hundred associations and an active publishing programme.

Esperanto was planned as a very regular language, one whose vocabulary is two thirds Latin-based (the

An Esperanto advertisement for the Rüger chocolate brand

rest Germanic), with a largely non-European grammar that has only sixteen basic rules. Together with having easy-to-remember word stems derived from a list of 900 internationally recognised ones, as well as fewer cases, Esperanto should be as easy to learn for everyone regardless of their mother tongue.

The Esperanto Museum was founded by Hugo Steiner in 1927, coming later under the auspices of the Austrian National Library (*Österreichische National Bibliothek*). Today it holds the world's largest archive of inter-linguistic studies and language planning, and includes much research material pertaining to the 500 or so other recognised planned languages. Around the walls are fascinating related exhibits such as examples of Esperanto currency, Zamenhof's first book and a recent Esperanto edition of *Asterix the Gaul*. The library even contains a copy of a Klingon-English dictionary as used in the science fiction series *Star Trek*!

Another curious collection residing in the Palais Mollard is the Globe Museum (*Globenmuseum*). Also a part of the National Library, this fascinating collection illustrates the growth of man's knowledge regarding the continents and seas since the 16th century, and also includes celestial globes depicting the constellations of the night sky. It is the only one of its type in the world and contains more than two hundred globes. Austria's oldest globe is here, manufactured in 1536 by Rainer Gemma Frisius, a medical doctor and cosmographer from Louvain in Belgium. Valuable, too, is the pair of globes (terrestrial and celestial) made in 1541 and 1551 respectively by Gerard Mercator, famous for the Mercator Projection used on maps and globes for centuries thereafter. His terrestrial globe was the first to include the curves (known as loxodromes) that cut across the meridians, which are of great importance to navigators. One of the more novel items in the collection must surely be the 19th century inflatable globe complete with its own set of bellows!

The snow globe (*Schneekugel*) is a Viennese invention inspired by early cobblers' lamps (water-filled glass balls used to magnify candlelight). Surgical instrument maker Erwin Perzy made the first one around 1900 and his family still make them by hand today. Traditionally they feature Viennese landmarks such as the Ferris wheel, cathedral and Rathaus, all in a swirl of artificial snowflakes. To discover the secrets of their manufacture visit the Snow Globe Museum (*Schneekugelmuseum*) at Schumanngasse 87 (17th District).

Other places of interest nearby: 30, 32, 33, 35, 37

35   Legend of the Holy Lance

1st District (Innere Stadt), the Kaiserliche Schatzkammer (Imperial Treasury) in the Schweizerhof of the Hofburg; take U-3 to Herrengasse

At the heart of Vienna's Habsburg city residence, the Hofburg (Court Palace), is the Old Palace (*Alte Burg*), where King Ottokar (1253–1278) of Bohemia built the first fortress in 1275, just prior to the accession of the Habsburgs. Part of the original moat is still visible, as well as a piece of walling from the Widmertor gate that gave access through the original city walls. It is here, in what is today called the Swiss Court (*Schweizerhof*), that the famous Kaiserliche Schatzkammer (Imperial Treasury) can be found, containing the Habsburgs' crown jewels together with other treasures dating from their time as Holy Roman Emperors between 1452 and 1806.

Arousing especial curiosity are the supposed holy relics whose ownership was taken as divine endorsement of rightful earthly rule. The power that such objects had over the minds of both ruler and ruled should not be underestimated.

The Ecclesiastical Treasury (*Geistliche Schatzkammer*) contains many such relics displayed in richly ornamented containers dating to the Counter Reformation and the re-establishment of Catholicism.

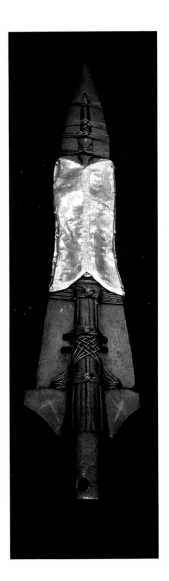

The so-called Holy Lance in the Hofburg's Schatzkammer

Amongst them is a nail from the crucifixion, against which pilgrims once rubbed their rosaries to gain strength, several thorns from Christ's crown of thorns, at least three fragments of the true cross, a piece of Mary's veil, a fragment of Joseph's cloak in which the child Jesus was wrapped, and Veronica's handkerchief soaked in Christ's blood. Further relics, including St. Stephen's cranium and a fragment of St. Andrew's cross, may be found in the Cathedral Museum (*Dom Museum*) at Stephansplatz 6.

Since medieval people viewed the Holy Roman Empire as a continuation of the Roman Empire albeit under the rule of Christ, the Schatzkammer's Secular Treasury (*Weltliche Schatzkammer*) is also weighted with suitably potent religious relics. These include another fragment of the cross, a splinter from Christ's crib, a piece of the Last Supper tablecloth, a horn of the legendary Unicorn (actually that of a Narwhal), and an agate bowl from Constantinople thought once to have been the Holy Grail because Christ's name (*XRISTO*) appears *within* the grain of the stone. Also on display is St. Stephen's Purse said to contain blood-soaked earth from the stoning of Christianity's first martyr in whose name Vienna's Cathedral is consecrated (Austrians remember St. Stephen on December 26th, which is known as *Stefanitag*).

Most curious of all is the Holy Lance (*Heilige Lanze*) reputed to have been used by the Roman soldier Longinus to pierce the side of Christ on the Cross in order to ensure that he was dead. The usual method was to break the victim's legs but the use of the spear fulfilled Old Testament prophecy that not a bone of the true Messiah would be broken. Following this brief appearance in the Bible (John 19 v.31–37) legend takes over in relating how the spear later became the property of St. Maurice and was used by Emperor Constantine the Great to Christianise the Roman Empire in the 4th century. It is then said to have been wielded by Charlemagne to shape the new Holy Roman Empire in the 8th century, finding its way eventually to a Nuremburg church, where it became a revered relic visited by thousands, and finally to the treasury in Vienna. It was here, according to some, that a young Adolf Hitler was inspired to create his Third Reich in the 20th century.

Only recently in 2003 was a thorough scientific and academic analysis of the spear undertaken by an English metallurgist, in order to separate fact from fiction. It transpires that the spear was broken in antiquity and mended with silver wire whose process of manufacture can be dated clearly to c.600AD. The spear itself is stylistically closest to medieval weapons, not Roman ones, also pointing firmly to a date in the 7th century.

That just leaves the curious so-called "nail of the Lord", suspended within the length of the spear. In reality little more than an iron pin or toggle, x-ray evidence, together with three tiny brass pinheads protruding from its surface, suggests that an actual nail may have long ago been forged deep within it. An inscribed silver sheath was added to the spear in 1084AD in order to strengthen this "nail of the Lord" whereas only much later, in the 14th century, was a gold one added that made reference to the "lance of the Lord". It must be concluded therefore that the spear is too young to be that of the soldier Longinus, although it cannot be denied that it has gained enormous legendary status with the passing of time.

The Cathedral Museum (Dom Museum) contains one of the world's first portraits

It is unlikely that the whereabouts of the real spear will ever be known. On the other hand the hidden nail, which would appear to pre-date the spear considerably, remains the real candidate for being a true holy relic of Jesus Christ's brief time on earth. Indeed it is the nail's shadowy existence that could account for the spear's power down through the centuries, setting it quite apart from all other religious relics – a sacred object bound invisibly within a secular one, destined forever to defy man's futile attempts at scientific rationalisation.

The Cathedral Museum also contains a painting of Duke Rudolf IV (1358–65), founder of the cathedral and university, painted in c.1360 and thought to be one of the first attempts at modern full-face portraiture in the history of western art. It is often compared to the portrait of the King of France, John the Good (1319–64), hanging in the Louvre. Also worth looking out for are two precious Syrian glass vessels, once believed to have contained earth from Bethlehem stained with "the blood of the Innocents", as well as the magnificent Persian silk garment used during the burial of Duke Rudolf.

Other places of interest nearby: 33, 34, 36, 37

36   The Emperor's Only Statue

1st District (Innere Stadt), the statue of Emperor
Franz Joseph I in the Burggarten, on the Burgring/Opernring;
take U-5 to Museumsquartier (from 2024 onwards)

A visit to one of Vienna's numerous back street antique shops, for example Alte Kunst at Plankengasse 7 (1st District), shows all too clearly how popular Emperor Franz Joseph I once was with the Austrian people. The shop window is crammed with old postcards, framed portraits and kitsch souvenirs carrying the whiskered image of Europe's longest-serving monarch (1848–1916). His sixty-eight year long reign marked Austria's longest period of relative stability, though it was born out of the violence of the 1848 Revolution (see no. 15), and was brought about in part by his legendary distrust of change and innovation (see no. 80). He loved the pomp and protocol of old Spanish court ceremonial and yet, in his private life, was a man of modest tastes. Describing himself as a self-employed civil servant, he rose at 3.30am until the day he died, and gave audience to his citizens twice weekly. He dressed in a simple lieutenant's uniform, ate boiled beef (*Tafelspitz*) almost daily and slept on a single iron bedstead under a camel skin blanket. He had no time for telephones, cars, electricity or even flushing toilets, and preferred hunting to opera. His difficult marriage to his wife Elisabeth (*Sisi*) (1837–98) only added to his legend in life, as did her assassination in 1898, the romantic suicide of his only son Rudolf at Mayerling in 1887, the execution of his brother Maximilian in Mexico in 1867, and the death of another brother Karl Ludwig in 1896 after drinking contaminated water from the River Jordan. Like England's late Queen Elizabeth II the Emperor shouldered such tragedies stoically ("Nothing has been spared me in this world!" he once said), continuing to serve and govern his empire as he always had done.

Also English in style was his private Imperial Garden (today's Burggarten) with its restrained design and fountain, tucked behind the Neue Burg. Thrown open to the public in 1919, three years after the Emperor's death, it today contains his only public statue. Incredibly, despite his image having once graced the walls of households across the land, no public statue existed in Vienna until this one was erected privately in 1957, on what would have been his birthday, August 18th. This in part reflects his modest character but it also seems that by 1916 the Viennese were growing tired of Habsburg rule, as well as suffering

A pensive statue of Emperor Franz Joseph I in the Burggarten

privations arising from the Great War. It was only a matter of time, and with the conclusion of the war, that the Emperor's successor and great nephew, Emperor Karl I (1916–18), was thrown unceremoniously out of Austria. Forced to renounce any further involvement in Austrian state affairs, though refusing to formally abdicate or renounce his claim to the throne, the last Emperor and his family were forced into

Swiss exile in March 1919, transported in a court-green Gräf & Stift limousine that can still be seen in Schloss Schönbrunn's Carriage Museum (see no. 80). The Habsburg era came to an abrupt and ignominious end and Austria's First Republic (a socialist one under Karl Renner) was declared, albeit briefly; grand Vienna, formerly the centre of an empire of 55 million, became suddenly the capital of a small state with just six and a half million inhabitants.

Within a few years an association was established to finance a Franz Joseph monument and numerous designs were submitted. However, it was not until a competition in 1937 that sculptor Hans Andre and architect Clemens Holzmeister were commissioned officially to undertake the work. The annexation of Austria in 1938 by the Nazis, however, put paid to their plans and resulted in a period of mindless iconoclasm. One monument to suffer was a bronze of the Emperor in pensive mood that had adorned a park in Wiener Neustadt. The work of Josef Tuch, it was a copy of an original in stone sculpted by his mentor Johannes Benk in 1904 for the Infantry Cadet School in Hütteldorfer Strasse (14th District). Tuch's work languished in a Liesing scrap yard for the duration of the war until Hans Lauda, President of the Industrial Association, instigated its re-erection during the 1950s in the now public Burggarten. So it was that some forty years after his death, Vienna finally got its one and only statue of Emperor Franz Joseph.

Although the Habsburgs ruled Austria for 640 years, the first ever public statue of one of them, that of the enlightened Emperor Joseph II (1765–90), was only unveiled in 1807 in Josefsplatz. Equestrian in style, the statue occupies what was once the enclosed training ground of the Spanish Riding School. It was typical of the reform-mad Emperor Joseph that he opened up the area as a public square. In deference to the man who had attempted to create a centralised state open to modernisation, the later Emperor Franz added Joseph to his Christian name, hence Franz Joseph I. To find out more about his famous wife, Sisi, visit the Sisi Museum and Imperial Apartments (Kaiserappartements) in the Hofburg, the sprawling Habsburg city palace on nearby Michaelerplatz. Its many wings, courtyards and architectural styles reflect the 636 years the family ruled Austria as emperors and empresses, dukes and duchesses, archdukes and archduchesses, between 1282 and 1918.

Other places of interest nearby: 33, 35, 37, 38

37 Montezuma's Headdress?

1st District (Innere Stadt), the Weltmuseum Wien in the Neue Burg on Heldenplatz; take U-5 to Museumsquartier (from 2024 onwards)

Amongst the Eskimo anoraks, Easter Island canoe paddles and Shinto toilet deities of the Weltmuseum Wien on Heldenplatz is a single exhibit both curious and controversial. Beautifully lit in a case all its own is an Aztec headdress. It is made from 459 shimmering blue and green tail feathers of the male Quetzal bird. This is the world's only surviving feather headdress from pre-Hispanic Mexico and one of only six remaining examples of ancient Mexican feather work. Representations of Aztec deities suggest that such headdresses were considered part of the garments of the gods, and were worn by priests during temple rituals.

Around the turn of the 20th century, the so-called Vienna headdress was bundled together with other suitably exotic-looking objects, and quite incorrectly exhibited as 'Montezuma's Treasures' (see no. 39). Until quite recently guidebooks were still linking these

A magnificent Aztec feather headdress in the Weltmuseum

objects to the famous Aztec emperor, insisting that he gave them as presents to the Spanish conquistador Hernán Cortés, who then sent them back to his Emperor Charles V (1519–56). However, any gifts Cortes possessed were lost irretrievably in the mêlée that followed his unnecessary and fatal imprisonment of the emperor. Moreover, existing inventories of an earlier consignment of gifts made prior to the arrival of Cortés make no mention whatsoever of a feather headdress. Thus, the Vienna headdress is unlikely ever to have had any direct connection with Montezuma.

Cortés eventually conquered Tenochtitlán (now Mexico City) and in the following decades shiploads of precious Mexican artefacts were sent back to Europe as gifts and trophies. Amongst them were hundreds of delicate feather headdresses, one of which ended up in the art collection of Count Ulrich of Montfort-Tettnang in Upper Swabia, in whose inventory it appears in 1575. In 1590 the Habsburg Archduke Ferdinand of Tyrol purchased the headdress for his famous Chamber of Art and Marvels (*Kunstkammer*) at Ambras Castle, near Innsbruck. The headdress then found its way to Vienna, where it was displayed in the Habsburg's Lower Belvedere Palace. Some 300 years later, by which time it had become a very rare artefact indeed, the Vienna headdress was "re-discovered" having been stored away in a cupboard and forgotten. It was at this time that the headdress was linked incorrectly to the Cortés-Montezuma story.

It is this author's view that it is best to regard unique and sensitive artworks such as the Vienna headdress as "cultural refugees", displayed somewhere other than their place of origin. It is the job of the country fortunate enough to possess them not only to acknowledge their true history and provenance but also to protect them for world posterity.

The Neue Burg in which the Weltmuseum is located is also home to the Imperial Armoury (Hofjagd- und Rüstkammer), the Collection of Historical Musical Instruments (Sammlung für Musikinstrumente), the House of Austrian History (Haus der Geschichte Österreich), and the Ephesos Museum. The latter contains tantalising fragments from the Heroon of Trysa, a 4th century BC Lycian tomb transported by Austrian archaeologists all the way from south-west Turkey. It will soon be displayed in its entirety.

Other places of interest nearby: 35, 36, 38, 39

38 A Mysterious Egyptian

1st District (Innere Stadt), the Kunsthistorisches Museum in Maria-Theresien-Platz at Burgring 5; take U-5 to Museumsquartier (from 2024 onwards)

The beautiful Egyptian reserve head in the Kunsthistorisches Museum

Without a doubt one of Vienna's most important museums is the Kunsthistorisches Museum, housed in a custom-made Ringstrasse building in the neo-Renaissance style and opened by Emperor Franz Joseph I (1848–1916) in 1891. The art collection is considered one of the world's finest and exists thanks to the wealth and artistic interests of the Habsburg dynasty.

It was instigated by Emperor Rudolf II (1576–1612) and added to by a succession of others (including, for example, Archduke Leopold Wilhelm during the Baroque period), each with individual tastes, resulting in a staggering collection of 15th–18th century paintings. Included are works by Titian (court painter to Emperor Karl V), Bruegel (acquired through family connections in the Low Countries) and Velásquez (through the Spanish Habsburgs). Empress Maria Theresa's son, Emperor Joseph II (1765–90), was responsible for opening up the Imperial Collection to the public and it still forms the core of the present museum.

Most visitors are drawn immediately by the picture gallery (*Gemäldegalerie*), with its world famous Old Masters, as well as the fantastical Chamber of Wonders (*Kunstkammer*), which contains a display of natural and manmade curiosities assembled by generations of Habsburgs. Fewer make it to the Coin Collection (*Münzkabinett*) in which can be found the curious stone currency of the Micronesian Island of Yap or the Collection of Classical Antiquities (*Antikensammlung*), with its fragment of the Parthenon. But one should be sure not to miss the Egyptian and near Eastern Collection (*Ägyptische-Orientalische Sammlung*), where amongst the pink granite temple columns from Aswan and the painted mummy cases something very unusual can be found.

Known as the Reserve or Substitute Head (*Ersatzkopf*), this limestone sculpture 27 centimetres high was found by Austrian archaeologists early in the 20th century in a cemetery on the Giza Plain, west of the great pyramid of Cheops. To be precise it was found in *Mastaba G*, a *mastaba* being a flat-topped stone or mudbrick structure marking the tomb of a wealthy individual or family. A chamber for statues of the deceased is usually incorporated into the *mastaba* and a vertical shaft leads down into the actual rock-cut burial chamber below.

The head has been dated to the 4th Dynasty of the Old Kingdom, that is to say c.2500BC and the reign of the Pharaoh Khufu (known as Cheops by the Greeks). Despite the head's incredible antiquity, the unknown artist has imbued it not only with humanity but also an otherworldly serenity and self-assuredness. Yet unlike most Egyptian funerary sculptures, which archaeologists expect to find in the above ground statuary chamber, the Reserve Head was found buried deliberately at the entrance to the burial chamber. As a result its original purpose is hotly disputed, although the consensus amongst experts is that in the period before mummification, the Egyptian soul (or *ka*) could be guaranteed a place in the afterlife by including such a Reserve Head in the tomb. Although some thirty other such heads have been found in ancient Egypt, the Vienna example is by far the most beautiful – and its beguiling and timeless visage may never give up its true purpose. The fact that each of the heads found so far have unique features suggests that they are idealised representations of the tomb owners themselves and as such are amongst the earliest portraits ever made.

The museum's Egyptian collection also contains a clay model of a hippopotamus from the Middle Kingdom (c.2000BC), its blue-glazed body adorned with lotus blossoms and papyrus leaves. The inclusion of such a statue in Middle Kingdom tombs is not surprising since hippopotamus hunting was a royal privilege granted to those citizens who won favour with the pharaoh.

The fascinating Papyrus Collection (Papyrus-Sammlung) in the nearby Neue Burg on Heldenplatz contains painted mummy masks, Coptic textiles, and even a prescription for pharaonic toothpaste!

Other places of interest nearby: 36, 37, 39, 49

39 A Cabinet of Curiosities

1st District (Innere Stadt), the Natural History Museum (*Naturhistorisches Museum*) on Maria-Theresien-Platz at Burgring 5; take U-2 to Volkstheater; take U-3, U-5 to Volktheater (from 2024 onwards)

For some visitors, Vienna's Natural History Museum (Naturhistorisches Museum) on Maria-Theresien-Platz might seem a somewhat dusty and old fashioned place, with few of the hi-tech displays that most major museums have installed in recent years. Its cabinets are antiques in themselves and the labelling sometimes still refers to long-vanished provinces once part of the old Austro-Hungarian Empire (e.g. Illyria on the eastern Adriatic coast and Galicia, now part of Poland and Ukraine). For the explorer interested in the unusual, however, this museum provides a wonderfully rich hunting ground containing a bewildering array of strange objects from the natural world.

Opened in 1889, the building was erected by order of Emperor Franz Joseph I (1848–1916), the core of the collection having belonged to Emperor Franz I (1745–65), husband of Empress Maria Theresa (1740–80). In 1748 he had bought the world's largest natural history collection from Johann Ritter von Baillou (1684–1758), a Florentine scholar, to which exten-

The Natural History Museum in winter

sive and important additions were made subsequently as a result of Imperial expeditions, diplomatic gifts, acquisitions and bequests. This author found the following unusual items particularly worthy of tracking down, displayed as they are in rooms beautifully decorated to reflect the different collections they contain.

The geological and mineralogical rooms are an Aladdin's cave, including a huge split amethyst geode at the entrance, and a one-piece crystal obelisk weighing in at 1,680 kilos. Staying with the geological theme, don't miss the magnificent Colombian emerald once wrongly attributed to the Aztec emperor Montezuma (see no. 37). Rather less colourful but no less fascinating is the world's finest collection of meteorites.

Few will be able to resist the extensive palaeontological holdings, including the world's largest fossilised spider from Argentina's tropical swamps and measuring a frightening half a metre in length. There is also the world's largest fossilised tortoise, the leg of a 70-ton Ultrasaurus and a replica of the first nearly complete Diplodocus skeleton found in Sheep Creek, Wyoming, and sent by American industrialist Andrew Carnegie to Emperor Franz Joseph in 1909. Also gifted to the emperor, only this time by the Meiji Emperor of Japan, is a pair of fearsome giant Spider Crabs.

Quite different is the tiny but famous 25,000-year-old limestone figure of a fertility goddess known as the Venus of Willendorf. It is

A giant Spider Crab awaits visitors

displayed in its own darkened room alongside another figure, the Fanny of Galgenberg, which is named after an Austrian ballerina. At 32,000 years old, it is one of the world's oldest figurative sculptures.

Elsewhere visitors will find a unique study collection of Polyps and Medusas rendered in glass by Rudolf Blaschka (1857–1939) of Dresden, as well as work by the world's first underwater painter produced in a primitive diving bell off the coast of Sri Lanka. An entire room is given over to sharks, including the corpse of a Great

See the world's best preserved remains of a Dodo

White alongside the shoe of an Austrian sailor found in its stomach.

Other curiosities include a pair of stuffed eagles shot in 1889 by Crown Prince Rudolf (1858–1889) just before his suicide at Mayerling, a bizarre collection of tapeworms, including one from the intestines of a Munich doctor measuring almost two metres in length, the remains of New Zealand's extinct Giant Moa together with its equally giant egg, and the world's best-preserved remains of the extinct Dodo. Specimens of less well-known extinct species include the Thylacine, Great Auk, Stellar's Sea Cow and White Swamphen.

Finally, sitting in the corner of one of the enormous taxidermy cabinets is Honzo the chimpanzee, brought from Cameroon by Austrian explorer Ernst Zwilling (1904-1990) to the zoo at Schönbrunn, and infamous for his bad temper and love of beer and cigarettes!

40 Honouring the Plague Saint

3rd District (Landstrasse), the Karl Borromäus Fountain
(*Borromäusbrunnen*) on Karl-Borromäus-Platz;
take U-3 to Rochusgasse

It is often said that city-dwellers rarely visit places of interest lying on their own doorstep, and that it is visitors who become better acquainted with them. One location that disproves this theory is Vienna's mighty Karlskirche in Karlsplatz (4th District). Dedicated to Saint Carlo Borromeo (1538–84), it is well known to tourists and inhabitants alike. Also dedicated to the Italian saint, however, is a little-known fountain in nearby Landstrasse (3rd District). Its presence also disproves the theory but in a different way since not even the tourists seem to know of it!

The Karlskirche is Vienna's finest Baroque church, erected by Emperor Karl VI (1711–40) in gratitude for Vienna having survived

∧ detail of one of the columns
outside the Karlskirche

the plague of 1713. It is difficult not to think that Karl's dedication of the church to Saint Carlo, canonized for his efforts during the 1576 plague of Milan where he was archbishop, was in part because they both shared the same name. Consequently both could be glorified by this magnificent building designed by Johann Bernhard Fischer von Erlach (1656–1723).

Borromeo's life is illustrated in the ribbon-like reliefs of the two 33 metre-high columns in front of the church. They resemble the "double column and scroll" motif of the Spanish Habsburgs, from whom Karl was descended, and from where the dollar sign ($) is thought to have originated. The saint also appears over the pedimented doorway, as well as in the frescoed dome and over the high altar.

Leaving such grandeur behind, the life of Borromeo is taken up in the more modest and intimate setting of Landstrasse's Borromäusplatz. This uniquely beautiful fountain known as the Borromäusbrunnen

The little-known Borromäus Fountain in Landstrasse

(Borromäus Fountain) was created in 1909 by sculptor Josef Engelhart (a member of Gustav Klimt's Secession movement) and Slovenian architect Jože Plečnik, who would later design Vienna's first concrete church (see no. 87). Set in a sunken square surrounded by benches, the fountain takes the form of a simple obelisk surrounded by a clover-shaped basin alive with sculpted frogs and lizards. Beneath a frieze of vine leaves and grapes are dancing cherubs whilst above are three groups of figures acting out the saint's life. This is a surprisingly peaceful place to while away ten minutes musing on how fortunate one is not to have lived in the days of the plague, or for that matter in the early-20th century, when anti-semitism was rife in Vienna, promoted by then mayor Karl Lueger (1844–1910) for whom the fountain was originally created. Lueger got his comeuppance recently when part of the Ringstrasse named in his honour was renamed Universitätsring and his statue at Stubentor was daubed in graffiti.

Plague columns (*Pestsäulen*) celebrating Vienna's deliverance from various pandemics can be found around old Vienna. They include a famous gilded one on Graben (1679), as well as more modest examples outside Josefstadt's Piaristenkirche (1713), the Maria Geburt Church (1730) in Hietzing, and St. Ulrich's Church in Neubau.

Other places of interest nearby: 41

41 A Little Piece of Russia

3rd District (Landstrasse), the Russian Orthodox Cathedral of St. Nicholas *(Kathedrale zum Heiligen Nikolaus)* at Jaurès-gasse 2; take U-3 to Rochusgasse

For many the only tangible sign of a Russian presence in Vienna is the huge Russian Heroes' Monument (*Russisches Heldendenkmal*) in Schwarzenbergplatz. Soviet troops had wrested the city from the Nazis after bloody street fighting in April 1945 and erected the monument shortly afterwards. Below the statue of a heroically posed unknown Soviet soldier are the names of the fallen together with the words of Stalin. It is an unfortunate truth that some older Austrians still recall the brutality of their Russian "liberators", as well as the hardships endured by those living in the Russian controlled zone between 1945 and 1955, when Molotov finally signed the Austrian State Treaty (*Staatsvertrag*) heralding the Second Republic.

Despite this, Austria is legally obliged to maintain the monument, including a controversial, state-funded makeover in 2007 in honour

of a visit by Russian President Vladimir Putin (b. 1952). Since then the monument has been repeatedly attacked by political activists, notably in 2017 when the colours of the Ukrainian flag were painted across it.

For a different take on Russian culture one should head for Vienna's 3rd district of Landstrasse and its glorious Russian Orthodox Cathedral of St. Nicholas (Kathedrale zum Heiligen Nikolaus). Luigi Giacomelli designed the church in 1893–99 for the

The Russian Orthodox Church of St. Nicholas in Landstrasse

Russian embassy, after a plan by St. Petersburg architect Grigorij Iwanowitsch Kotov. If the visitor is fortunate enough to witness a service here they will be rewarded with a glimpse of the incredible candle-lit and gilded interior brimming with painted icons. The air is filled with the fragrance of burning incense, and the glorious unaccompanied *a capella* singing that has been the central form of worship in Russian churches for a thousand years. The exterior of the church is magical, too, with walls of white stone and red brick, broken by oriental-type arched windows obscured by iron grilles. Below the typically Russian onion-domed roof is a beautiful frieze of coloured glazed tiles lending a late-Byzantine feel to the proceedings.

The Russian Orthodox chapel of remembrance in the Central Cemetery

On the subject of tiling it's worth a stroll to nearby Ungargasse. At 59-61 stands the Portois & Fix building, erected in 1900 in the Viennese Art Nouveau (*Jugendstil*) style with an abstract façade of tiles in muted shades of green and brown. The company was commissioned by the Emperor's wife Elisabeth (*Sisi*) (1837–98) to re-decorate her rooms at Schloss Schönbrunn.

Returning to things Russian, don't forget the tiny Orthodox chapel of remembrance at Simmering's Central Cemetery (*Zentralfriedhof*), just inside Gate 2 on the left-hand side (see no. 70). Constructed in 1894 it is surrounded by the graves of some of Vienna's Russian inhabitants.

Being a truly cosmopolitan city, Vienna has numerous other places of worship erected and used by varying denominations and faiths. These include a splendid Buddhist Stupa on the banks of the Danube in the Prater, erected in 1983 to celebrate Austria becoming the first European country to officially recognise Buddhism, and a mosque with a 32 metre-high minaret (*Islamisches Centrum*) at Hubertusdamm 17, next to the Neue Donau U-Bahn station.

Other places of interest nearby: 40

42 Among Lilacs and Birdsong

3rd District (Landstrasse), St. Marx Cemetery (St. Marxer Friedhof) at Leberstrasse 6–8; take Tram 71 from Schwarzenbergplatz (near U-Bahn Karlsplatz U-1/U-2/U-4)

St. Marx Cemetery (St. Marxer Friedhof) in Landstrasse, now hemmed in on three sides by busy roads, is known mainly for the wintry night in December 1791, when Mozart's body was placed in a mass grave here and subsequently lost (see no. 20). Not surprisingly this accounts for the majority of visitors to this leafy oasis, filled with butterflies and birdsong, including the occasional distinctive call of the Nightingale.

St. Marx's, together with Vienna's four other municipal suburban cemeteries, was closed down in 1873, the business of burying the city's dead being transferred to the huge new Central Cemetery (*Zentralfriedhof*) opened in Simmering in 1874 (see no. 70). While the other cemeteries were converted into parks in the 1920s (see no. 59), the Cemetery of St. Marx was simply abandoned to nature. Despite some later restoration, its mourners in time dwindled away to nothing. This very fact, however, makes a visit here such an unforgettable experience.

Established in 1783, and known subsequently as the *Biedermeier* Cemetery, St. Marx's was the first graveyard to be created outside the *Linienwall* ramparts (today's Gürtel ringroad), following Emperor Joseph II's (1765–90) Funeral Edict that same year (see no. 33). This dissolved all crypts within the Gürtel on health grounds (burial in graveyards had already been outlawed) dictating that they be "relocated to the free and excellently ventilated periphery". At first, mass burials were the norm (as was the case with Mozart) and it was only later, in the mid-19th century, that family vaults became commonplace.

A series of overgrown tracks lead off the cemetery's main gravel paths, lined with row-upon-row of weathered and crumbling headstones. It is a peaceful and melancholic place. Crosses, urns and angels jostle for space amongst the overgrown lilacs, their blooms and scent overwhelming in April and May. Some plants having become so large are now engulfing the very tombs they were intended to adorn.

A stroll along the main path up beyond the Mozart grave (number 179) and around the cemetery perimeters gives one the feeling of visiting an archaeological site. There is a plan of the cemetery's six thousand graves at the entrance though most of the well-known names, including *Biedermeier* architect Josef Kornhäusel (see no.

15) and Suez Canal engineer Alois Negrelli were later reinterred in the Central Cemetery (*Zentralfriedhof*) in Simmering (see no. 70). Grave 7 in the 4th row on the right, for example, is the original grave of Josef Strauss (1827–76), second son of Johann Strauss the Elder, moved later to Grave 44 in group 32A of the Central Cemetery.

Look out also for the unusual sarcophagus-style tomb at the back of the cemetery against the right-hand wall. It is inscribed in English to the memory of a British Brigadier General who was military commissioner to the Austrian army and died in Vienna in 1854. These days, other than the occasional groundsman sweeping the paths and watering the grass, the Cemetery of St. Marx is peopled more by ghosts from the past than visitors from the present.

An abandoned gravestone amongst trees in the Cemetery of St. Marx.

Not far from St. Marx's is Vienna's former cattle market (*Zentral-Viehmarkt*) opened in 1883 on Viehmarktgasse, its gate adorned with a pair of mighty stone cows; it has recently been re-developed as a media and technology centre. Also in the neighbourhood is the *Jugendstil* Villa Mautner-Jäger at Landstrasse Hauptstrasse 140. It was built in 1902 for society lady, Hertha Jäger, whose sister married Secession artist Koloman Moser (1868-1918). He had a hand in designing the villa's well-preserved interior.

Another Biedermeier cemetery can be found in the woods towards the top of Kahlenberger Strasse (*Friedhof Kahlenberg*) in the 19th district of Döbling. Containing only 130 bodies, its most famous occupant is Karoline Traunwieser who died aged just 21 and who was said to have been the most beautiful girl in Vienna. Also here is the tomb of Charles-Josef de Ligne (1735-1814), an Austrian statesman of Wallonian descent. He died during the Congress of Vienna (1814–15) after catching a cold outside his house at Mölker-Bastei 10 in the 1st District, where he was awaiting his mistress.

43   The Mortar of Belgrade

3rd District (Landstrasse), the Museum of Military History *(Heeresgeschichtliches Museum)* im Objekt 18 of the Arsenal off Arsenalstrasse; take Tram D from Schwarzenbergplatz (near U-Bahn Karlsplatz U-1/U-2/U-4) to Hauptbahnhof and walk through the Schweizergarten

In the wake of Vienna's 1848 Revolution (see no. 15), four vast fortress-like barracks were erected at strategic points around the city (see no. 58). One of these, the so-called Arsenal completed in 1856, was built on a high point in the 3rd district of Landstrasse. Constructed of red brick, it was designed by future Ringstrasse architect Theophil Hansen, together with Ludwig Förster, in a heady synthesis of Byzantine, Hispano-Moorish, and late-medieval Italian (neo-Gothic) styles. Emperor Franz Joseph I (1848–1916) decreed that one of the Arsenal's buildings known as 'Objekt 18' be earmarked as Vienna's first purpose-built museum, to glorify the Imperial Army.

The interior of the Museum of Military History *(Heeresgeschichtliches Museum)* continues the feeling of a Byzantine church or Moorish palace, such exoticism providing a peculiarly fitting backdrop to the collection of spoils and trophies from the Turkish Wars to be found on the first floor (see no. 3). These include the Great Seal of Sultan Mustafa II, removed from the neck of his Grand Vizier by Prince Eugene of Savoy (1663–1736) at the Battle of Zenta (1697), so winning back Hungary for the Habsburgs. There is also the huge tent of Grand Vizier Damad Ali Pasha that the Prince acquired at the Battle of Peterwardein (1716). In 1717, a single shot from the so-called Mortar of Belgrade (exhibited nearby) hit a Turkish powder magazine killing 3,000 Ottoman troops. This single action assisted greatly Eugene's capture of Belgrade and helped facilitate the eventual securing of Western Europe against the Ottoman threat.

As light relief, in the west wing of the ground floor, look at the incredible array of uniforms worn by the armies of the Crown Lands following the establishment of the Austro-Hungarian Dual Monarchy in 1867. Despite having suffered numerous defeats in the 19th century, the Austrian army won a prize for most elegant outfit at the 1900 Paris Exhibition!

The adjoining First World War section begins with the event that started it all – the assassination of Emperor Franz Joseph I's nephew and heir, Archduke Franz Ferdinand (1863-1914), by Bosnian Serb nationalist Gavrilo Princip in Sarajevo on 28th June 1914. It is sobering to compare the tiny bullet-hole in the door of the Archduke's car with the massive destruction wrought by artillery displayed nearby, designed to expedite the appalling war that followed. On the wall is Albin Egger-Lienz's painting *To the Unknown Soldier* whose image of advancing infantry was a symbol of the type of mass warfare that would by 1918 have claimed eight million lives.

Archduke Franz Ferdinand was assassinated in this car by Serb nationalist Gavrilo Princip

Also on the ground floor, is the couch on which Austro-fascist Chancellor Engelbert Dollfuss (1892-1934) died after being shot by the Nazis during their abortive coup on July 25th 1934. Although German annexation of Austria did not follow until 1938, this incident was a part of the grim chain of events that led to the Second World War in 1939.

Finally, and somewhat surprisingly, there is a section devoted to the naval power of land-locked Austria. Of course during the Habsburg era Austria controlled the Adriatic port of Trieste, although it is still a surprise to learn that the Austro-Hungarian fleet was once the sixth largest in the world! On display is the barnacle-encrusted conning tower of Imperial submarine U20, raised from the seabed, as well as memorabilia relating to submariner Captain Georg von Trapp of *The Sound of Music* fame. There is also a model of the Austrian expedition ship *Admiral Tegethoff* that set out in 1872 to find a northeast passage, via Arctic waters north of Russia, to the Pacific. Icebound the vessel drifted north through the Barents Sea, where an archipelago was discovered and named Franz-Josefs-Land.

The crew abandoned ship in 1874 and returned to civilisation, an arduous journey illustrated by artist Julius von Payer, whose paintings are on display and who is buried in Simmering's Central Cemetery (*Zentralfriedhof*) (see no. 70).

On leaving the museum be sure not to miss Europe's largest collection of gun barrels exhibited in one of the outside pavilions.

The Arsenal is not just about war since a surprisingly cosy traditional restaurant (*Beisl*) can be found in one of the courtyards, and a medieval-themed market takes place in the grounds at Christmas.

The infamous Mortar of Belgrade

For a world-class display of court arms and armour visit the Imperial Armoury (Hofjagd-und Rüstkammer) in the Neue Burg on Heldenplatz (1st District). Highlights include the Cuirassier Armour by Lorenz Helmschmid made for Emperor Maximilian I and the Boy's Folded Skirt Armour by Konrad Seusenhofer for the future Emperor Charles V. Those who fancy firing a weapon for themselves should visit Joh. Springers Erben at Josefsgasse 10 (8th District). Established in 1836 and purveyor to the Imperial Court, the company makes new guns and sells second-hand ones, too. There is a working rifle range in the cellar.

44 A Ballroom Reborn

3rd District (Landstrasse), the Sofiensäle at Marxergasse 17; take U-3 to Rochusgasse

On 16th August 2001 a fire broke out on Marxergasse in Vienna's 3rd District. Allegedly caused by a careless workman, the flames raged for eight hours. Only when the smoke cleared could the damage be assessed. The legendary Sofiensäle, once Vienna's most beloved ballroom, was a smouldering ruin.

The story of the Sofiensäle is a very Viennese one. It begins with a child of empire, the Bohemian Franz Morawetz (1789–1868), who came to Marxergasse after his wealthy wife bought him a textile business there. In 1838, after the venture had failed, Morawetz instead built a Russian steam bath (*Banya*), at the suggestion of a visiting Russian soldier. One of his first visitors was the chambermaid of Archduchess Sophie, the emperor's mother, who came looking for a cure for joint pain. So impressed was she that the archduchess followed suit. The establishment was named Sofienbad in her honour.

Success came quickly for Morawetz and in 1846 he was able to extend his operation. His chosen architects, Eduard van der Nüll and August Sicard von Sicardsburg, designed for him one of Vienna's first steel-framed public buildings. With the inclusion of a ballroom-cum-concert hall the Sofienbad became the Sofiensäle, and in 1848 Johann Strauss the Elder (1804-1849) conducted at the opening ball.

The Sofiensäle held almost 3,000 people and offered year-round entertainment, with bathing during the summer months and concerts and balls in winter. Thousands of Viennese learned to waltz here under the reliable baton of the Strausses. From the turn of the century the main hall (*Großer Saal*) also served as a lecture venue, and in 1912 the author of *Winnetou*, Karl May, came to speak. In the audience were two very different onlookers: Nobel Peace Prize winner Bertha von Suttner and unemployed artist Adolf Hitler.

During the First World War the Sofiensäle doubled as a convalescent home for wounded soldiers, and in 1926 it witnessed the founding assembly of the nascent Austrian Nazi Party. The ignominy continued in the 1930s, when the building was used as a collection point for Jews awaiting deportation.

After the Second World War the Sofiensäle returned to its peaceful ways, and in 1946 it played host to the Austrian premiere of Fred Raymond's operetta *Maske in Blau*. The vaulted ceiling of the *Großer*

After many ups and downs the Sofien Säle are born again

Saal guaranteed excellent acoustics prompting Decca Records to adopt it in 1950 as its principal European recording venue. Notable works included the first complete studio recording of Wagner's *Ring Cycle* conducted by Georg Solti. After Decca's departure in the mid-1980s the Sofiensäle was reinvented once again, this time as Vienna's biggest clubbing venue.

When eventually the increasingly tatty premises burned down it seemed to be the end of the line for the Sofiensäle. The once grand *Großer Saal* was a roofless shell, its boxes with their red velvet seats now open to the elements. Demolition seemed inevitable. That the ornately plastered façade and *Großer Saal* had listed status, however, saved the day.

After several years of litigation the ruins were acquired in 2006 by the IFA (a part of the Soravia real estate group), who announced a rebuild costing 50 million Euros. The old façade has subsequently been restored and now gives access to a brand new multi-functional structure beyond, containing sixty eight apartments, a hotel and restaurant, various studios, and a fitness centre. And at the heart of it all is a re-roofed and revitalised *Großer Saal* that will function as an events venue. The new Sofiensäle is thus set to welcome a new generation of pleasure seekers.

Other places of interest nearby: 40

45   The Bones of Antonio Vivaldi

4th District (Wieden), the grave of Antonio Vivaldi at the Vienna Technical University (Technische Universität Wien) on Argentinierstrasse; take U-1, U-2, U-5 to Karlsplatz (from 2024 onwards)

One of the most recognisable pieces of classical music is the first violin concerto of Antonio Vivaldi's *Four Seasons (Le quattro stagioni)* evoking the unfettered joys of spring. Although Vivaldi ranks today among the most widely recorded of Baroque composers few people know that he lies buried in Vienna.

Antonio Lucio Vivaldi was born in Venice on 4th March 1678, inheriting two distinctive traits from his father: a talent for playing the violin and red hair! Indeed, after being ordained in 1703 Vivaldi was referred to affectionately as *il Prete Rosso* or the Red Priest.

An anonymous portrait of composer and priest Antonio Vivaldi

In his mid-twenties Vivaldi became *maestro di violino* in the *Ospedale della Pietà*, an orphanage in which boys learned a trade and girls were given a musical education. The most talented girls stayed on and became members of the renowned *Ospedale* orchestra and choir. Whilst playing the violin Vivaldi was often accompanied by the angelic voices of the orphan girls, and over the next thirty years he would compose many of his instrumental concertos and sacred choral works in this way.

Vivaldi's reputation as an international composer came in 1711, with the publication of his *L'Estro Armonico* concertos. Despite their success he increasingly devoted his time to opera, the most popular entertainment in eighteenth century Venice. In 1718 he worked as *Maestro di Capella* in Mantua, where the surrounding countryside inspired the writing of his *Four Seasons*. He then toured Italy and accepted a personal invitation from Pope Benedict XIII to play in Rome. By the time Vivaldi returned to Venice in 1725 he had become a Baroque superstar.

It was during his time in Mantua that Vivaldi became acquainted with an aspiring young soprano called Anna Giro, who accompanied him on his tours. Inevitably rumours of a relationship surfaced but Vivaldi

Only a wall plaque marks the grave of Antonio Vivaldi

denied any wrongdoing. Some commentators have claimed that such rumours made it difficult for Vivaldi to remain in his native Venice, forcing him to flee to Vienna in 1740. It seems more likely that he relocated to seek imperial patronage at the court of Emperor Charles VI (1711-1740).

Vivaldi occupied an apartment in a house above the Kärntnertor, one of eight gateways that pierced Vienna's Renaissance city wall. Now long demolished, the house stood approximately where the Hotel Sacher now stands. Also gone is the Kärntnertor Theatre that stood nearby. It seems logical that Vivaldi chose this area so as to be near a theatre that could stage his operas.

Like other composers of his day, however, Vivaldi had no reliable income and often sold his manuscripts at paltry one-off prices. When the emperor died not long after, any hopes Vivaldi may have had of currying royal favour were dashed. Vivaldi himself died on 28th July 1741, a pauper in a rented apartment.

The funeral service was held in St. Stephen's Cathedral and was attended by six choristers, one of whom was the nine-year old Josef Haydn (1732-1809). Vivaldi's remains were then placed in a simple grave in the Armensünder-Gottesacker, a cemetery located outside the Kärntnertor gate (cemeteries *inside* the city wall had been closed on health grounds in 1530). In 1789 this cemetery too was abandoned, by order of Emperor Joseph II (1780-1790), who decreed that new cemeteries be opened *outside* the Linienwall (today's Gürtel). Vivaldi's remains were never retrieved or relocated. Later still, between 1815 and 1818, Vienna's Polytechnicum (later Technische Universität) was built on the former site of the cemetery, where today only a simple wall plaque marks the approximate spot.

The home of composer Josef Haydn is still preserved at Haydngasse 16 (6th District). Occupied by Haydn for the last dozen years of his life, it contains the clavichord on which he composed *Die Schöpfung* (The Creation), as well as a surprisingly bucolic inner courtyard.

Other places of interest nearby: 25, 43

46 A Perfect Pair of Pavilions

4th District (Wieden), the Otto Wagner Pavilions on Karlsplatz; take U-1/U-2/U-5 to Karlsplatz (from 2024 onwards)

By the 1890s, the rapidly growing city of Vienna had been freed from its old circuit walls, and its suburbs were being urbanised. In 1893, work began on the construction of the *Stadtbahn*, the city's first public transport system independent of roads. As with the Paris Metro, it was decided that the architectural elements of the system would have a corporate appearance, one in tune with the very latest European design ideals.

The architect chosen to supervise the building of the thirty or so stations, bridges, tunnels and other facilities along the proposed 40 kilometre-long stretch of railway was Otto Wagner (1841–1918) (see nos. 80, 84, 85). He was the perfect choice bearing in mind that in 1897 he co-founded Vienna's Secession Movement with Gustav Klimt (1862–1918). Between them they pioneered the Viennese Art Nouveau (*Jugendstil*) in which functionality and aesthetics became perfectly fused. Wagner believed that the new railway, which ran

One of a pair of Jugendstil former railway pavilions on Karlplatz

predominantly overland, was vital to the creation of a modern city (his visionary plans for an exclusively underground system went unheeded at the time).

Travelling on today's electrified U-Bahn, which in 1925 replaced the steam-powered railway of Wagner's day, it is easy to recognise his idiosyncratic style, which rebelled against the backwards-looking Historicist style favoured by the Habsburgs. Typical is his use of elegant cut masonry, *Jugendstil* motifs such as sunflower-rosettes, wreathes, stylised lettering, and everywhere green metalwork – from balustrades and lanterns to window frames and door grilles. The stations at Stadtpark, Kettenbrückengasse, Hietzing and Rossauer Lände on what is today's U-4 line are fine examples.

Known originally as the Wien Valley Line, it followed the course of the Wien River, which was partially culverted at the same time and in the same style (see no. 96). Look out for the spectacular triple-span viaduct that crosses both river and road at Sechshauser Gürtel, and the technically impressive Zollamtssteg footbridge further downstream, beneath which rail and river run diagonally to each other.

The jewel in the crown, however, is the pair of pavilions facing each other across Karlsplatz. Erected in 1899, and located originally either side of Akademiestrasse, they were designed to provide entrances to the railway, one for each platform, and to represent *Jugendstil* architecture at its most refined. Unlike the railway's other stations, which were built from stone and plaster, the pavilions were made of pre-fabricated metal frameworks on which panels of white Carrara marble were suspended. They were topped with a novel roof of corrugated copper, oxidised to Wagner's trademark green. The *Jugendstil* decoration consists of golden sunflowers stamped onto the marble, with a gold vegetal trim running around the roof. The result is still surprisingly fresh thanks to Wagner insisting that the pavilions' construction and components be visible to onlookers unlike the plastered brick of Vienna's Historicist buildings that still fool many visitors into thinking they are real stone. Today, the pavilions have lost their original function, although one of them does at least provide access to the U-4 U-Bahn, whilst the other serves as a café.

It should not be forgotten that Otto Wagner also designed the line servicing Vienna's western districts along what is now the U-6 line. The stretch between Spittelau and Margaretengürtel follows the path of the old *Linienwall*, an earthen embankment built in 1704 to protect Vienna's vulnerable inner suburbs or *Vorstädte* (3rd–9th Districts) from attack. It mainly comprises an elevated track supported by a graceful series of brick-built railway arches (*Stadtbahnbogen*), most of which have since been infilled with shops, warehouses, restaurants, and bars. Particularly elegant is the monumental bridge at Währinger Strasse-Fuchsthallergasse alongside which stands Wagner's little chapel to St. Johannes Nepomuk, patron saint of bridges. Unfortunately, Wagner's dream of making the Gürtel ring road along which the U-6 runs into another Ringstrasse never came to fruition and his railway is today one of the few redeeming architectural features of this now busy thoroughfare.

One of many vintage trams at the Tramway Museum

To see the sort of carriages that were originally used on Otto Wagner's railway visit Vienna's superb Tramway Museum (*Strassenbahnmuseum*). Suitably housed in a former tram depot at Ludwig-Koessler-Platz (3rd district), the museum contains many examples of trams and U-Bahn trains, as well as all the equipment to go with them, including signs, lights, rails and control desks. There are also examples of early horse-drawn trams, which appear remarkably flimsy compared with the sturdy albeit lightweight vehicles used today. The museum regularly sends its working trams out onto the network for use by tourists and for private events.

Vienna has a museum for most things in life but it lacks an aircraft museum despite a modest history of flight and aeroplane manufacture. The city's international airport is at Schwechat, where a recently-erected memorial by local artist Arik Brauer (1929–2021) recalls those forced by the Nazis to build aircraft during the Second World War at what was then the Schwechat-Heidfeld military air base. It depicts a skeletal man struggling to carry a bent propeller, one that comes from an actual German aircraft downed in the Baltic.

Other places of interest nearby: 27, 45, 47

47 The Composers' Quarter

4th District (Wieden), Wiedner Hauptstrasse 7;
take U-1, U-2, U-5 to Karlsplatz (from 2024 onwards)

Vienna is often referred to as the "City of Music" and walking around the city certainly bears this out. It sometimes feels as though every street bears a plaque to one composer or another, invariably Mozart (1756–91), Beethoven (1770–1827), Schubert (1797–1828) or Haydn (1732–1809). They are all associated with Vienna having either been born here (Schubert was born at Nussdorfer Strasse 54 in the 9th District), found their first audience here (Mozart first performed in the Palais Collalto on Am Hof in the 1st District), composed here (Haydn wrote his *Die Schöpfung* (The Creation) at Haydngasse 16 in the 6th District) or died here (Beethoven expired at what is now Schwarzspanierstrasse 15, also in the 9th).

Although the mainstream guidebooks cover these well-known characters in great detail, the explorer can still discover locations that escape most visitors. An example of this is at Währinger Strasse 26, where an old and ornate marble plaque identifies a former garden house in which Mozart penned his three great symphonies in *E major*, *G minor* and *Jupiter* in *C major*, as well as the opera *Così fan tutte*.

As an antidote to the great composers it makes for an enjoyable walk to follow in the footsteps of some less obvious ones in the 4th district of Wieden, south of the famous Musikverein. Beginning at Wiedner Hauptstrasse 7 can be found the former *Hotel Goldenes Lamm* (Golden Lamb Hotel), where the Czech composer Antonín Dvořák (1841–1904) occasionally stayed. He is famous for his symphonies, concertos and chamber music, as well as his ever-popular *Slavonic Dances*. Around the corner at Karlsgasse 4 is the former home of German-born Johannes Brahms (1833–97) who liked Vienna's provincial feel, referring to it as "the village". One-time Musikverein director, his romantic chamber and piano music appeals to both laymen and academics alike. His statue adorns nearby Ressel Park, close to the Technical University (*Technische Universität*), where the Strauss brothers once studied and where Italian Baroque composer Antonio Vivaldi (1678–1741), the so-called Red Priest, was buried (see no. 45).

Farther along Wiedner Hauptstrasse at number 32 is the house where Christoph Willibald Gluck (1714–87) died on 15th November 1787. He is best known for being in charge of Empress Maria Theresa's court orchestra and for his opera *Orfeo ed Euridice*, the first to subordinate its music to dramatic action. Nearby at Waaggasse 1 is a plaque to Finnish composer Jean Sibelius (1865–1957) who lived here during a study trip in 1890–91. Despite gaining inspiration from Vienna-based composer Bruckner for his tone poem *Kullervo*, which would in time lead to his seven magnificently moving symphonies, and clearly loving the ambience of Vienna, as seen in the quotation on the plaque, Sibelius failed an audition as violinist for the Vienna Philharmonic Orchestra.

Wall plaque to Finnish composer Jean Sibelius

Not far away at Mozartgasse 4 is the building where Richard Strauss (1864–1949) lived between 1919 and 1925. Unconnected to Vienna's waltzing Strauss dynasty, he is remembered for his symphonic poems *Also sprach Zarathustra* (*Thus spake Zarathustra*) and *Till Eulenspiegel*, the opera *Der Rosenkavalier* and the moving *Vier Letzte Lieder* (*Four Last Songs*).

Finally, at Johann Strauss Gasse 4 is the site of the last home of Waltz King Johann Strauss (see no. 64). Although the building was destroyed in the war, the opening bars of his famous *An der Schönen blauen Donau* (*The Blue Danube Waltz*) can be seen inscribed on the wall of number 10 farther up the street. Wieden also contains the last home of Franz Schubert (1797–1828) at Kettenbrückengasse 6, where the young composer succumbed to typhus. Now a museum (*Schubert-Sterbewohnung*) it contains the last letter and silver toothpick of the man responsible for many symphonies, string quartets as well as this author's favourite, the tender song *Ständchen* (*Serenade*), written in 1826 at what is now Kutschkergasse 44 in the 18th district of Währing.

Not far from the start of Wiedner Hauptstrasse is the Wienzeile, an extended pedestrianised zone that sits over both the U-4 U-Bahn and the culverted River Wien, part of the architect Otto Wagner's ambitious scheme to prevent flooding and improve the city's transport infrastructure. At pavement level is the Naschmarkt, a lively 1.5 kilometre long market selling food and drink from around the world. Look out for the sauerkraut seller, the old market traders' café Zur Eisenen Zeit and the tiny Naschmarkt Museum in the market's former chapel.

Other places of interest nearby: 45, 46

48 Commodes and Candelabra

7th District (Neubau), the Möbelmuseum Wien at Mariahil-ferstrasse 88 & Andreasgasse 7; take U-3 to Zieglergasse

"Bizarre, sensuous, eccentric and precious" is how the myriad objects to be found in the Möbelmuseum Wien have been described. This criminally overlooked museum contains unique and fascinating everyday objects once used by the Habsburgs, as well a collection of objects reflecting the continuing development of Viennese furniture-making and interior design.

Founded by Empress Maria Theresa (1740–80) in 1747 as the Kaiserliches Hofmobiliendepot, the Imperial Depot of Court Movables was responsible for the upkeep and storage of surplus and outmoded furnishings from the numerous Habsburg properties. It also facilitated the annual move of the imperial household to its various summer and winter residences, in the days before these properties were permanently furnished. In 1901 Emperor Franz Joseph I (1848–1916) commissioned the present storage facility at Mariahilferstrasse 88 and in 1924, several years after the fall of the monarchy, its doors were opened to an intrigued Viennese public.

Not to be missed is the incredible Egyptian Room originally installed in the Hofburg in 1810 by the third wife of Emperor Franz II (I) (1792–1835). Equally stunning is the so-called Heritage – a room crammed with surplus and unwanted candelabra, picture frames, vases and prayer stools illustrating how tastes changed as each new monarch came to the throne.

The Habsburg Hall has an intimate collection of objects relating to individual personalities such as the weighing scales of Elisabeth (*Sisi*), wife of Emperor Franz Joseph I, Crown Prince Rudolf's cradle and Emperor Franz II (I)'s personal garden tools, as well as his Brazilian canaries *Bibi* and *Büberl* – stuffed of course! Also here is the lead coffin in which the executed Emperor Maximilian of Mexico, brother of Emperor Franz Joseph I (1848–1916), was returned to Vienna in 1867. Most exotic is Prince Eugene of Savoy's (1663–1736) Indian chintz wall hangings from his hunting lodge in the Marchfeld, whilst in the Emperor Franz Joseph Hall can be found Crown Prince Rudolf's Turkish Room with its colourful carpets and divans, assembled after his journey to the Orient in 1881.

Beyond the Habsburg collections there follows a lovely series of 19th century *Biedermeier* and Historicist alcoves depicting the styles favoured by the bourgeoisie during that century. Look out for the red salon with its tiger skin rug from the 1920s, said to have been a man-eater shot in India by Count Louis Esterházy and presented to Emperor Franz Joseph I as a gift. Thereafter may be found a collection of commodes (the predecessor to the flushing lavatory) and spittoons (for spitting chewed tobacco into), as well as the museum's current furniture depot brimming with pieces from the various state holdings. There is also the world's most comprehensive display of chairs, including examples of Michael Thonet's mass-produced, beech bentwood chairs, patented in

A reconstructed 1830s Biedermeier room in the Möbelmuseum Wien

1856 and a fixture of Viennese coffeehouses. Also worth finding is Ernst Plischke's supremely comfortable reclining easy chair in the apartment he designed in 1928 for the ceramic artist Lucy Rie.

The collection concludes with the innocent-looking neo-Rococo table at which the Austrian State Treaty (*Staatsvertrag*) was signed in the Upper Belvedere Palace on May 15th 1955, heralding the final withdrawal from Austria of the four allied powers who had controlled the country since the closing of the Second World War. From this date onwards, Austria would be free, independent and neutral.

To acquire one's own Habsburg-era furniture visit the Dorotheum at Dorotheergasse 17 (1st District). Established in 1707, and one of the world's oldest auction houses, it is named after the Dorotheerkloster, a convent that originally stood on the site. This explains the fragmentary gravestones embedded in the building's courtyard walls.

Other places of interest nearby: 49, 50, 86

49 In an Armenian Monastery

7th District (Neubau), the Mekhitarist Monastery (*Mekhi-taristenkloster*) at Mechitaristengasse 4; take U-2, U-5 to Rathaus (from 2024 onwards) (note: monastery tours by appointment only)

Mechitaristengasse (7th District) is curious for two things: its unusual name, and the coat of arms over the door at number 4, which includes a bishop's mitre. It marks the entrance to the Armenian Mekhitarist Monastery (*Mekhitaristenkloster*), one of Vienna's least-known places of worship.

To explore this intriguing place book a monastery tour. First stop is the magnificent church built in 1874 and atypically orientated north-wards so as to fit into the pre-existing monastery complex. Its design and magnificent paintings are the work of Viennese architect Camillo Sitte (1843–1903). Over the altar is a huge depiction of the Virgin Mary protecting the land of Armenia, with Noah's ark to the left, perched on top of Mount Ararat. The Armenian sung liturgy is performed here every Sunday at 11am.

The Mekhitarist Order was founded in Constantinople in 1701 by an Armenian Catholic monk, Mekhitar 'The Consoler'. Having converted from Eastern Orthodoxy to the Benedictine Rule, he set about training monks to serve the spiritual and educational needs of his fellow Armenians. Fleeing Ottoman persecution, the order relocated in 1715 to the Venetian island of San Lazzaro, with a second monastery built in 1773 in Trieste. When Trieste was occupied in 1797 by Napoleon, the Mekhitarists as Habsburg subjects were granted asylum in Vienna. This, however, was as much an act of goodness on the Habsburgs' part as a commercial ploy since the Mekhitarists were savvy merchants and educated linguists. Yet at that time Armenians in Vienna were often branded as spies, despite an Armenian trader, one Owanes Astouatzatur (Johannes Deodatus), having kick-started the city's coffeehouse revolution in the wake of the Turkish Siege of 1683. The Viennese preferred to bestow that particular honour on the Polish adventurer Jerzy Franciszek Kulczycki, who had helped repel the Ottomans at the city gates.

Next is the monastery proper, an enormous, six-storey structure designed by Vienna's Biedermeier maestro, Josef Kornhäusel (1782–1860) (see no. 15). On the ground floor is the refectory, with its cabinets of fine crockery and large painting of Jesus feeding the five thousand.

The monastery's cultural heart, its museum and library, meanwhile are located on the upper floors. To get there take the lift, which is surely unique in having a mosaic floor again depicting Mount Ararat.

The museum contains everything from collections of seashells and meteorites to an Egyptian mummy and silk vestments from Madras (the latter an example of the extent of the Armenian diaspora). The library is equally impressive in its range of material. One of the world's finest collections of Armenian literature, it includes a copy of the first book printed

This library cabinet in the Mechitaristenkloster honours the Austrian Emperor's Jubilee of 1898

in Armenian, the *Urbatagirk* or Book of Friday (1512). Whenever a manuscript is unfurled there is a distinct aroma because the monks of old used ink mixed with garlic to deter moths!

That the Armenian Church has long condoned dissection, explains in part why the Mechitarists amassed an enviable knowledge of science and medicine, hence the fascinating collection of medical equipment and treatises. The monks published their own books and periodicals, which until twenty years ago were printed in the monastery's printing works. A painted glass advertising board still hangs outside the former works at the top end of Mechitaristengasse, where former Austrian president Franz Jonas (1965–1974) once worked as a typesetter.

Today only a handful of monks occupy the monastery but they keep themselves busy. As well as continuing to preserve Armenian culture and spreading the word with monastery tours, they also distil a herbal liqueur, *Mechitharine*. Based on a secret recipe dating back to 1680 and boasting the inclusion of over forty herbs, fruits, roots and spices, it is available in the monastery shop.

Other places of interest nearby: 38, 39, 50, 52

50 Creation of the Croissant

7th District (Neubau), a former bakery at the corner of Burggasse and Sigmundsgasse; take U-2/U-3 to Volkstheater

Although Vienna is famed for its delicious pastries and cakes, notably *Apfelstrudel* and *Sachertorte*, available in the city's coffee houses and cake shops (*Konditorei*), the less grandiose products of the humble baker should not be overlooked. Many bakers (*Bäckerei*) still produce a wide range of different rolls, buns and croissants, and black and white breads, including the basic wheat and rye loaf known as *Hausbrot* (house bread). One traditional Viennese bakery well worth a visit is Arthur Grimm's at Kurrentgasse 10 in the 1st District – worth it just for a look in the window!

Such old-style bakeries often had lovely gold-on-black glass signboards detailing the various breads available (e.g. Johannesgasse 23 (1st District), which includes a painting of the loaves and rolls themselves). Painted glass shop signs, once commonplace in Vienna, are now rare and considered works of art in themselves (see Thomas Moog's photographic studio on Bognergasse (1st District) and the Golden Lion pharmacy in Josefstadt).

The sign on a former bakery at the corner of Burggasse and Sigmundsgasse in the 7th District (now a cosy bar) makes mention of poppy seeds (*Mohn*), cream cheese (*Topfen*) and croissants (*Beugel*). It is an overlooked fact that Vienna could justifiably be taken as the

An old fashioned baker's signboard

home not only of the croissant but also the bagel. The latter is Jewish in origin but became popular after a Jewish baker presented one to King John III of Poland (Jan Sobieski) who helped repel the Turks during their second siege of Vienna in 1683 (see no. 3). From the same period comes the croissant, its crescent shape said to resemble the half-crescent moon seen on Turkish flags. It found its way to France when Austrian Empress Maria Theresa's daughter Marie

Antoinette married the future French King Louis XVI. In the 1st District at Grünangergasse 8 there is a doorway with bread rolls, croissant and pretzels carved above it belonging to the so-called Kipferlhaus. *Kipferl* is another German word for croissant and legend states that it was here that the first one was baked in 1683.

This relief above a doorway in Grünangergasse depicts various types of bread

Of interest in the 8th district of Josefstadt are two baking-related locations. At Lange Gasse 34 there can be found one of Vienna's oldest bakeries, in business from 1701 until 1963. Located inside a Baroque house built in 1697 and known today as the Alte Backstube it still contains the original ovens. Meanwhile, around the corner at Florianigasse 13 there is the headquarters of the Guild of Viennese bakers, which includes a Bakery Museum (*Bäckermuseum*).

Meanwhile in neighbouring Neubau, there is another historic former bakery at Neustiftgasse 47. Built in 1903, the façade of the Bäckerei Karl Obenaus carries a lively series of reliefs depicting farmers harvesting and bakers baking. Finally, the Brotfabrik at Absberggasse 27 out in Favoriten is a huge former bakery now home to numerous galleries.

The only church outside Vienna's old city walls to survive the second Turkish siege of 1683 was the Servitenkirche at Servitengasse 9 (9th District). As well as boasting some splendid Baroque stucco work, and being the city's first church with an oval nave, it is also home to the magnificent chapel of the Servite St. Peregrine, remembered for giving bread to the poor. So-called *Peregrinikipferl* (Peregrine Rolls) sold in early May at the Café Konditorei Bürger at Servitengasse 12 recall a bygone baker who honoured the saint by distributing bread to the needy. The Servitenviertel itself is well worth visiting for its discreet Jewish history and delightful street cafés and restaurants.

Other places of interest nearby: 38, 49, 52

51 A Library with a View

7th District (Neubau), the Büchereien Wien library on
Urban-Loritz-Platz; take U-6 to Burggasse-Stadthalle

Although central Vienna is built on predominantly level ground, its
buildings have long offered the visitor some striking panoramas. A
climb up 343 steps to the watchman's room of the Stephansdom's
southern tower (*Südturm*), for instance (itself best seen from the
balconies of the nearby Haas-Haus or the Skybar on the top floor of
the Steffl store at Kärntner Strasse 19), affords a wonderful overview
of the rooftops of the 1st District. A similar vista, albeit a lower level
one seen from *outside* the Ringstrasse, is available from the gardens of
the Upper Belvedere Palace.

The eastern districts of the city can be seen from the gondolas
of the Ferris wheel (*Riesenrad*) in the Volksprater, including the
golden chimney of Friedenreich Hundertwasser's colourful Spittelau
municipal incinerator, whereas the western suburbs may be viewed
from Penzing's loftily situated Kirche am Steinhof (see no. 85). A trio
of lookout towers on Vienna's western hilltops also provide some
breathtaking views of this area (see no. 88). A brisk walk up to Schloss
Schönbrunn's *Gloriette* similarly provides a magnificent westwards
overview, as well as northwards to the Kahlenberg and Leopoldsberg
on the edge of the Vienna Woods (*Wienerwald*). From the latter two
natural vantage points may be seen the peaks of the distant Rax and
Schneeberg at the southwestern edge of the Vienna Basin, and the
Hungarian Plains and Carpathian Mountains far away to the east.
For Danube river scenery head to the 252 metre-high Danube Tower
(*Donauturm*), where a viewing terrace offers a panorama from Klosterneuburg all the way to the Hainburg Mountains.

Another less-obvious viewing point can be added to this list, namely
the state-of-the-art library straddling the Burggasse-Stadthalle U-Bahn
station on Urban-Loritz-Platz (7th District). Called the Büchereien
Wien, it contains 240,000 books, 60,000 audiovisual items, 130
computers and 150 studying booths. The library is the work of urban
architect Ernst Mayr, once a self-confessed "second tier architect",
whose anonymously-submitted design was selected out of 120
submissions from across the EU. A highlight for visitors is the broad
stone staircase, made up of 100 stone steps, which climbs up the
building's exterior to a rooftop café and public terrace. Although the
view over to the 1st District is obscured, the viewing balconies afford

an interesting vista both south down the Gürtel ringroad to the Favoriten water tower (see no. 75), as well as north to the astronomical observatory in Sternwartepark (see no. 88), with Kahlenberg and the Vienna Woods beyond. The building makes for a perfect combination of learning and leisure!

For an absolute contrast, but a no less interesting one, visit the *Prunksaal* (Grand Hall) of the National Library on Josefsplatz (1st District). At 77 metres in length, it is the largest Baroque library in Europe. Commissioned as the court library by Emperor Karl VI (1711–40), it was designed by Johann Bernhard Fischer von Erlach in 1723 and contains 200,000 leather-bound volumes, including the private collection of Prince Eugene of Savoy (1663–1736). On the roof is a jumble of statuary dominated by Minerva, goddess of wisdom, flanked by Atlas figures supporting two gilded globes and a clutch of scientific instruments (see no. 21). With its marble columns,

Looking north towards the Kahlenberg from the Büchereien Wien

gilded bookcases, statuary and frescoed dome one couldn't find a better example of how Viennese library architecture has changed from Baroque to modern times.

Taking in the glorious view from Schloss Schönbrunn's Gloriette might be a good time to imagine how the scene looked back in 1945, when the buildings of Vienna suffered considerable damage from allied bombing raids. So successful was the post-war clean-up operation and subsequent re-building helped greatly by the Marshall Plan, that it is difficult today to see where buildings have been patched up. It would be hard to imagine, for example, that the left-hand side of the Gloriette was destroyed were it not for the original bomb-damaged masonry displayed nearby. It is interesting to note that the site of the Gloriette, which was built as a triumphal arch celebrating the victory of Maria Theresa's army over that of Frederick II of Prussia in 1757, was originally meant to be occupied by a palace to rival Versailles: alas it was never realised.

Other places of interest nearby: 49, 50

52   Behind Closed Doors

8ᵗʰ District (Josefstadt), a couple of hidden courtyards on Lange Gasse; take U-2/U-3 to Rathaus and walk up Josefstädter Strasse

Lange Gasse 29 is a modest yet special location that needs little accompanying text since its charm lies in the immediate impact it has on the fortunate city explorer gaining a glimpse beyond its usually-locked wooden doors. Indeed, visitors must only afford themselves a fleeting glance for this is no tourist attraction but rather a place where normal Viennese citizens have lived for the last 250 years.

Situated in the district of Josefstadt, which is named for Emperor Joseph II (1765–90), this is one of Vienna's smallest yet most charming courtyards, created originally for palace servants and labourers in the 18ᵗʰ century. The humble, single-storey row houses have a unique appeal of their own, with washing out to dry and children's toys strewn amongst the pot plants. Should the gates be closed, and no obliging occupant be in sight to afford a peek inside, it is only a short walk to Langegasse 34, where another hidden courtyard awaits. This one, dominated by a single large tree and surrounded by traditional communal balconies, has a tantalising gated garden beyond.

Next, the explorer should head south into the neighbouring 7ᵗʰ district of Neubau and the Spittelberg Pedestrian Area. Remarkably this area was once an island on a Danube tributary, where victims of the 1679 plague were quarantined. Here there is an entire quarter of working class tenements restored recently to their 18ᵗʰ and 19ᵗʰ century condition and complimenting well the houses in Josefstadt. A stroll along the narrow cobbled streets reveals a fine ensemble of buildings, such as Spittelberggasse 9, with its *trompe l'oeil* painted windows, the Baroque houses at 18 and 20, and the pretty *Biedermeier* building at Gutenberggasse 29. It is

The charming hidden courtyard at Lange Gasse 29 in Josefstadt

hard to believe that this stylish area was for years a notorious red light district, where a staggering 58 of the 138 houses were taverns, filled with musicians, prostitutes, textile workers, tramps and, one night in 1778, even Emperor Joseph II himself! To this day the Gasthaus *Witwe Bolte* at Gutenberggasse 13 carries an inscription that states, "Through this door in the arch, Emperor Joseph II fled". It is harder still to think that in 1809 the troops of Napoleon were camped here (see no. 68), as was the Turkish army in 1683 (see no. 3). Indeed the fine Renaissance house at Ulrichsplatz 5 probably only survives today because it was close to where the Grand Vizier Kara Mustafa himself was camped (see the gilded Turkish horseman in a niche on the corner of Kellermanngasse, and the mosaic of Kara Mustafa's tents at Neustiftgasse 43).

On a similar theme is the early-19th century *Biedermeier* passage running through the Sünn-Hof at Landstrasser Hauptstrasse 28 (3rd District). It is wonderfully preserved for its entire length and now contains shops and cafés that spill out onto the street in summer. Such a passageway running between two parallel streets is known as a *Durchgang*. Another lively example is in the Hirschenhof connecting Windmühlgasse 20 with Mariahilfer Strasse 45 in the 6th district of Mariahilf. A wall plaque here records that the famous Viennese *Biedermeier* playwright

A Durchgang between Lerchenfelder Strasse and Neustiftgasse

Ferdinand Raimund (1790–1836) lived here – though it doesn't mention that he committed suicide after being bitten by a rabid dog.

Rather more artsy in feel is the *Durchgang* connecting Lerchenfelder Strasse 13 with Neustiftgasse 16 (7th district of Neubau), its stepped and high-vaulted archways lending an almost Spanish feel. A pristine example in the same district, untainted though by retail development, can be found in the Adlerhof between Burggasse 51 and Siebensterngasse 46.

Finally, a narrow *Durchgang* in the 1st District, filled with shops and restaurants, runs between Lugeck 5 and Wollzeile 5. It is famous for the Figlmüller restaurant that prides itself on serving Vienna's largest *Wiener Schnitzel*!

Other places of interest nearby: 49, 50, 55

53 The Iron Soldier

8th District (Innere Stadt), the Iron Soldier *(Wehrmann in Eisen)* at the corner of Rathausstrasse and Felderstrasse ; take U-2, U-5 to Rathaus (from 2024 onwards)

A longstanding Viennese tradition concerns the tree trunk preserved outside Stock-im-Eisen Platz 3 (1st District). The name of the square – and the lively figures over the building's doorway – recall how Vienna's journeyman locksmiths would hammer nails into a tree trunk for good luck. Soon encrusted with nails it became a venerable symbol of the city's guild of locksmiths (see no. 55).

It is less well known that Vienna's nail-hammering habit manifested itself in a different way during the First World War. Down one side of the Town Hall (Rathaus), at the corner of Rathausstrasse and Felderstrasse (8th District), stands the statue of a knight. Known as the *Wehrmann in Eisen* (Iron Soldier), the knight's armour is made entirely from nail heads.

Inspired by the locksmiths of Vienna, it was one Lieutenant Commander Theodor Graf Hartig who commissioned the wooden statue in 1914. With enthusiastic support from Vienna's city council, it was erected in Schwarzenbergplatz on 6th March 1915. Hartig's idea was that in return for a donation, members of the public would be allowed to drive an iron nail into the statue. The money raised would be used to support those widowed and orphaned by the fighting. Patriotic fervor was whipped up by the authorities during the war years and a visit to the *Wehrmann* was encouraged as a way of registering national pride. It has been estimated that half a million nails were eventually knocked into the statue. The idea of raising public money by hammering nails into sculptures became a craze, spreading not only throughout Vienna but also across the Austro-Hungarian Empire, and more than fifty examples have been documented.

The *Wehrmann* remained in Schwarzenbergplatz until 1919, at which time it was taken to a municipal storage depot, and then to a soldiers' association museum, where it slipped from the public eye. Fast forward to 1934 now and a time when Austria was undergoing another tumultuous chapter in its history, this time at the hands of the Austro-Fascist movement. It was in this year that the Hofburg's Äußeres Burgtor (the only remaining gate of the old city walls) was converted into a memorial for the fallen soldiers of the First World War. This prompted people into remembering the *Wehrmann*, and so

The mysterious Wehrmann in Eisen stands alongside the Rathaus

it was brought out of retirement and set up once again on Schwarzen-bergplatz. As the statue was already covered in nails it was placed on a new wooden pedestal, into which thousands of new nails were hammered to raise funds for the memorial.

Afterwards the Wehrmann was relocated to Felderstrasse, where it has remained ever since. The accompanying marble inscription is suitably patriotic: *"Wehrmann Wiens gemahne an die Zeit, Da uner-schöpflich wie des Krieges Leid Die Liebe war und die Barmherzigkeit!"* (Iron Man of Vienna commemorates the time when suffering brought by war was as great as love and charity!).

Other places of interest nearby: 52, 54, 55

54 Mousetraps and Milking Stools

8th District (Josefstadt), the Folklore Museum Vienna (*Volkskunde Museum Wien*) in the Schönborn-Buchheim Palace at Laudongasse 15–19; take Tram 43/44 from Schottentor U-Bahn and then one stop on Tram 5

The Folklore Museum Vienna (*Volkskunde Museum Wien*) at Laudongasse 15-19 (8th District) houses a collection of objects reflecting everyday life in the Austrian provinces. Founded in 1895, it has been housed since 1917 in the former garden palace of Habsburg imperial vice chancellor Friedrich Karl von Schönborn-Buchheim (1674–1746). The palace was designed by Baroque architect Johann Lucas von Hildebrandt (1668–1745), whose work helped define Habsburg architecture in the 18th century.

The museum is home to an eclectic array of objects from the 16th to 19th centuries, of which the following exhibits particularly caught the author's eye. Pride of place in one room goes to a splendid 18th-century Tyrolean hunting sledge adorned with carved wooden figures. Elsewhere the Tyrolean theme continues with several cheerfully-painted Tyrolean window boxes made in the 1890s by mountain guides, farm hands and shoemakers, and sometimes given as love tokens. Of purely practical use is the one-legged Tyrolean milking stool of a type preferred in central Alpine areas over the more usual three-legged models.

Among the many smaller exhibits are intricately painted Easter eggs dating from the turn of the 20th century (though still exchanged today) from former Crown lands such as Moravia (today the Czech Republic) and Galicia (now part of Poland and Ukraine). Look out, too, for the ingenious Moravian trap designed to catch three mice in one night, the magnificent iron weathervane (c.1860) depicting the various skills of a village blacksmith, and a collection of cups used by the Imperial family to wash the feet of twenty four elderly poor people on Maundy Thursday. The custom came with the Emperor being crowned King of Jerusalem and pictures of Emperor Franz Joseph I and his wife Elisabeth in action can be found in the Habsburg's Silver Collection (*Silberkammer*) in the Hofburg.

The museum also contains various items of traditional folk dress, including a wonderful Slovenian/Croatian grass rain cloak common in southern Alpine regions until the 20th century, as well as winter shoes made of straw and a birch fungus cap. To go with the costumes are any number of colourfully-decorated trunks and wardrobes.

This brief selection concludes with three special objects. The first is a Moravian beehive or *Klotzbeute* (*or Klotzstülper*) made from a tree trunk and carved with the Habsburg double eagle. Second is a splendid glazed ceramic oven in the form of a rotund peasant lady whose inflated skirt ensured the maximum radiation of heat from within. She stood originally in the Korninger Inn in Münzbach bei Perg in Upper Austria and was nicknamed Annamirl by the locals. Best of all, is an intricate wooden mechanical orchestra made in Vienna in 1850, with a video screen alongside it showing it in action.

A model mechanical fairground orchestra made in Vienna in 1850

In recent years the museum has made itself more contemporary by reflecting the plight of refugees in Austria. Their quotes, observations and even personal effects are appended to certain exhibits, providing a refreshing take on what is essentially a very traditional folk museum. A good example of how effective this can be is an unknown refugee's bag retrieved from the Turkish coast and displayed alongside the museum's fine collection of 18th- and 19th-century painted chests and cupboards.

Another lovely former Baroque garden palace, and one similar to the Schönborn-Buchheim Palace in that it is today surrounded by modern buildings, is the Starhemberg-Schönburg Palace. Located at the junction of Schaumburgergasse and Rainergasse in the 4th district of Wieden, it was built for the finanzier Gundaker Thomas Starhemberg (1664–1745) and later occupied by the Schönburg-Hartensteins. Recently restored as an events' venue, its rooftop statues looking down on a garden filled with mistletoe-bedecked trees, suburban Vienna rarely gets more romantic.

Other places of interest nearby: 52, 55

55 In the Locksmiths' Square

8th District (Josefstadt) monument in Schlosserplatzl
at junction of Tulpengasse and Wickenburggasse; take U-2 to
Rathaus ; take U-2, U-5 to Rathaus (from 2024 onwards)

The small geographic area occupying the space between Stephansplatz, Graben and Kärntnerstrasse revels in the unusual name of Stock-im-Eisen Platz. Meaning literally "Stick in Iron Square" it relates to the nail-studded piece of timber that can be seen behind glass on the corner of the grand Palais Equitable building at number 3 (see no. 21). The lively group of figures over the building's doorway throws some light on this curiosity for it depicts a group of young men hammering nails into a log. Viennese tradition stretching back to 1533 relates that a larch tree was felled here in c.1440 and declared by locksmiths to be a symbol of their guild. Thereafter, it became the custom for apprentice and journeying locksmiths to hammer a nail into the trunk for good luck and to guarantee a safe return home. By the 19th century the trunk had acquired such legendary status that even Hans Christian Andersen wrote of it, believing the myth that it was a remnant of

The Palais Equitable building in Stock-im-Eisen-Platz

The little-known locksmiths' monument behind the Rathaus

a primeval forest that once covered central Vienna. It is even said that labourers excavating the Stephansplatz U-Bahn station in 1973 knocked the occasional nail into the ancient trunk for good measure!

At this point the explorer should escape the relentless bustle of Stephansplatz and head instead for the quiet and little-visited Schlosserplatzl (Little Locksmiths' Square) behind the Town Hall (*Rathaus*). Here, in the centre of a rose-filled square is a contemporary *Stock-im-Eisen*, complete with hundreds of modern nails knocked into it. It was erected in 1988 to celebrate the 700th anniversary of the Vienna Guild of Locksmiths. Their offices can be found in the fine balconied building on one side of the square, bearing pertinent carvings on its door as well as a huge wrought iron key hanging on the corner.

Scenes from the locksmiths' story, together with other Viennese legends, can be found painted inside the arcade fronting the Vogelweidhof (1926) at Wurzbachgasse 2–8, a Red Vienna apartment block in the 15th district of Rudolfsheim-Fünfhaus (see no. 95).

Other places of interest nearby: 52, 53, 54

56 The Church of Deliverance

9th District (Alsergrund), the Votivkirche on Rooseveltplatz;
take U-2 or Trams 1, D to Schottenring

On 18th February 1853, on the city walls at Mölker-Bastei (9th District), a Hungarian tailor named János Libényi lay in wait for the Austrian Emperor Franz Joseph I (1848–1916) (see no. 1). Libényi was a fervent Hungarian nationalist opposed to Austria's domination of his homeland. The tailor lunged at the unsuspecting emperor with a knife but was wrestled to the ground by royal adjutant Max O'Donnell. O'Donnell was one of several Irish soldiers known as the "Wild Geese", who had fled religious persecution in Ireland to work for Europe's Catholic monarchs (see no. 90).

So grateful was the emperor at being delivered from a premature death that he ordered a church be built close to the spot. The emperor's brother Archduke Ferdinand Maximilian set about raising funds, and a competition was held to procure a suitable architect.

So it was that Heinrich Ferstel, then only twenty six years of age, came to design what is known as the Votivkirche, the word "votive" meaning an offering given in thanks for deliverance from an unfortunate predicament. Ferstel combined all the classic elements of Gothic architecture in his plan, overseeing personally the building's lengthy construction, from the laying of its corner stone on April 24th 1856 (the second wedding anniversary of the emperor and his wife Elisabeth) to its dedication twenty three years later (the imperial couple's Silver Wedding anniversary).

The Votivkirche on Rooseveltplatz
is not nearly as old as it looks

By this time the city walls had been demolished and the Ringstrasse constructed, punctuated at the northern end by the mighty Rossauer Barracks. The soldiers based there used the Votivkirche as a garrison church, which explains why the church originally lacked its own parish, and why it remains devoid of the usual treasures found in Vienna's other churches.

Despite this the Votivkirche has much to offer visitors. Most obvious is the profusion of superb stonework on its exterior, from the crown-topped twin spires to the carvings of Christ, the prophets, Apostles, and imperial patron saints adorning the main doorway. Picking up on the dedication of the building as a church of deliverance, the central portal focuses on Christ and his redemptive work.

Another delight is the spectacular stained glass, although much of it was blown out during the Second World War. The Emperor's Window in the north transept, for example, represents the deliverance of the

One of the glories of the Votivkirche is its stained glass seen here reflected on the walls

emperor by means of a depiction of a dragon being slain by Saint Michael. The young emperor can be seen on his knees giving thanks. The replacement windows depict more recent history, including the infamous quarry at the Mauthausen concentration camp.

The church also contains several unusual objects, including a chunk of Second World War shrapnel embedded in the right-hand front door, the marble tomb of Count Nicholas of Salm (1459-1530), saviour of the city during the first Turkish siege in 1529, an unusual altar made from artillery shells, and a four metre high candle donated in 1930 in memory of the fallen of the First World War. Were it to be lit its 1,660-thread wick would burn for a hundred years!

Other places of interest nearby: 1, 2, 53, 57, 58

57 A Cloister for Academics

9th District (Alsergrund), the University of Vienna (Universität Wien) at Universitätsring 1; take U-2 or Trams 1, D to Schottenring

The University of Vienna (*Universität Wien)* was founded on 12th March 1365 by Rudolf IV, Habsburg Duke of Austria (1339–1365). This accounts for its its additional name *Alma Mater Rudolfina*. Being married to a daughter of Holy Roman Emperor Charles IV (1316–1378) encouraged Rudolf to elevate Vienna to that of the emperor's birthplace city of Prague, home to Central Europe's oldest university.

Rudolf initially established his university on Dr. Ignaz Seipel-Platz in the city centre, in a building used today by the Austrian Academy of Sciences (*Österreichische Akademie der Wissenschaften*). The library was housed in the students' infirmary before being moved to an extension on Postgasse in the 1820s.

With the demolition of Vienna's old city walls and the subsequent construction of the Ringstrasse, the university moved out to new premises at Universitätsring 1. The building was executed in neo-Renaissance style to a design by the architect Heinrich von Ferstel (1828–1883). Construction commenced in 1873 and the finished building was unveiled by Emperor Franz Joseph I in 1884. As with other grand buildings on the Ring, the chosen architectural style reflected the origin of the institution within.

The imposing façade carries nameplates along its roofline inscribed with renowned academic luminaries, such as economist Adam Smith, jurist Friedrich Carl von Savigny, philologist Friedrich Christian Diez, and the decipherer of Egyptian hieroglyphs, Jean-François Champollion. The same device is used on other buildings on the Ringstrasse, including the Burgtheater and the Kunsthistorisches Museum. No women are mentioned, however, since females were not admitted as full students until 1897, and even then their studies were limited to philosophy only.

Much of the university is open today not only to students but also to members of the public. The first port of call is the bustling main entrance, where a series of red marble wall panels detail all the university's chancellors since 1365. Alongside is an exhibition celebrating Nobel Prize Laureates associated with the university, including Julius Wagner-Jauregg (1927, Medicine) and Elias Canetti (1981, Literature).

The so-called Arkadenhof lies at the heart of the University of Vienna

To the left are the lecture halls and Small Ceremonial Chamber *(Kleiner Festsaal)*, ranged around a grand staircase *(Feststiege)* with a stuccoed ceiling, lorded over by Emperor Franz Joseph I looking somewhat unfamiliar in academic garb. To the right is a matching staircase giving access to the Main Ceremonial Chamber *(Großer Festsaal)*, with reproductions of Gustav Klimt's so-called Faculty Paintings destroyed in 1945. Also here is the Great Reading Room, its sturdy wooden bookcases, old fashioned balconies, and individual green-glass reading lamps imbuing it with considerable charm.

Directly beyond the entrance hall is the Arcade Court *(Arkadenhof)*. Resembling a monastic cloister it is the spiritual heart of the place. The court contains more than one hundred and fifty busts, recalling many of those who have taught at the university. They include Ignaz Semmelweis, remembered as "the saviour of mothers" for his pioneering work with antiseptic procedures, Ludwig Boltzmann, an early advocate of atomic theory, and, of course, Sigmund Freud, whose famous practice is just around the corner on Berggasse (see no. 97). There is also a wall memorial recalling those academics persecuted and murdered after the annexation of Austria by Nazi Germany in 1938. Notable amongst them was Elise Richter, who became the university's first female assistant professor in 1907; being Jewish she was dismissed from her post and deported to the Theresienstadt concentration camp, where she died in 1943.

Approximately eighty six thousand students are currently enrolled at the university, shepherded by a staff of 8,900, of whom more than 6,700 are scientists of one sort or another. The academic facilities now occupy more than sixty locations across the city, and the library, together with fifty departmental brances, houses more than six and a half million books. Little wonder it remains the largest teaching and research institution in Austria.

Other places of interest nearby: 1, 2, 53, 56, 58

58 Vienna's First Skyscrapers

9th District (Alsergrund), a pair of skyscrapers including the Ringturm seen from Deutschmeisterplatz on Schottenring; take Tram D to Börsegasse

At Herrengasse 6–8 (1st District) it's easy to miss a wall plaque recording a long-lost concert hall where Franz Liszt (1811-1886) once performed. It closed in 1913 so the valuable land could be better exploited – but not until 1932 was the new build revealed. The 16-storey, 50-metre high Hochhaus designed by Siegfried Theiss and Hans Jaksch was Vienna's first skyscraper.

The Hochhaus is best viewed from Michaelerplatz, where the inevitable controversy surrounding its construction can be appreciated. Detractors feared a structure out of all proportion with its surroundings. The architects avoided this, however, by cleverly stepping the four uppermost storeys backwards. Once completed the building was quickly accepted and brought kudos to the Christian Social Party that promoted its construction.

The Hochhaus was Vienna's first true skyscraper

With its American flair and state-of-the-art infrastructure – central heating, electric ovens, and prototype tumble dryers – the Hochhaus soon became an address of choice, especially for the actors of the nearby Burgtheater. Glitzy residents in the 224 apartments included Curd Jürgens, Paula Wessely, and Gusti Wolf.

Today it's not possible to ascend to the top of the Hochaus to view the former rooftop restaurant, its sliding windows once opening out onto an *al fresco* dancing area. A hint of glamour remains, however, at Unger und Klein, a tiny street level café that served originally as a milk bar. Trumping the Kleines Café as Vienna's smallest coffeehouse this seductive venue is a jewel of curved glass and polished chrome.

In 1955 the Hochhaus relinquished its vertiginous crown to the Ringturm at the northern end of the Ringstrasse. This skyscraper is best viewed from

Deutschmeisterplatz on Schotten-ring (behind is the mighty Rossauer Barracks erected in the wake of the 1848 Revolution). Occupying the site of a building destroyed in the Second World War, the Ringturm makes no effort to disguise itself. Still the tallest secular building in the 1st District, it was designed by Erich Boltenstern, with 20 storeys rising sheer to a height of 70 metres. Novel for the time, the tower's grand opening prompted a contemporary newsreel to boast "This is not America, this is Austria".

The man behind the building was Norbert Liebermann, general manager of insurance giant Wiener Städtische, which still occupies the building. Having spent his war years in America,

The Ringturm has a weather mast on its roof

Liebermann appreciated the benefits of modern office space and was undeterred when offered the cramped Ringstrasse plot for his company's new headquarters. "We are going to build a high rise," he boasted, creating a symbol of Austria's economic rebirth in the process. This time it was the Social Democrats who took credit for the building of a skyscraper.

A visit to the Ringturm today reveals more than just a landmark workplace. Since 1998 the building's foyer has been home to the acclaimed "Architektur im Ringturm" exhibition series, showcasing architecture past and present from across Central and Eastern Europe. Free entry means a visit is always well worth the journey.

Only at night time does the Ringturm reveal a unique feature: a 20-metre high weather mast adorned with more than a hundred coloured lights. Linked to the computer system of the Central Institute of Meteorology and Geodynamics on the Hohe Warte, the blinking bulbs give the forecast for the following day: ascending/descending red for temperature, ascending/descending green for general conditions, and flashing white for snow and ice. How useful it would have been to the rooftop dancers on the Hochhaus!

Other places of interest nearby: 1, 2, 56, 57, 60, 61

59 An Old Jewish Cemetery

9th District (Alsergrund), the Rossau Jewish Cemetery
(Friedhof Rossau) behind the retirement home at Seegasse
9–11; take Tram D to Porzellangasse. The cemetery may
be visited at any reasonable time by informing a member
of staff in the foyer and then proceeding to the viewing
balcony at the back of the building

The Jews have long had a sizeable and important presence in Vienna, initially in the 1st District (see no. 9) and latterly the 2nd district of Leopoldstadt (see no. 65). For a thousand years they have lived here, numbering 180,000 by 1910 though this number was reduced drastically by the Nazis between 1933 and 1945.

In 1874, the huge Central Cemetery (*Zentralfriedhof*) in Simmering (3rd District) was laid out and for the first time Vienna's Jews were buried alongside Catholics and Protestants, though admittedly in distinct zones. Prior to this the Jews had their own cemeteries of which several survive, albeit under somewhat controversial circumstances.

Vienna's oldest Jewish cemetery, and indeed one of Europe's oldest, is the Rossau Cemetery (*Friedhof Rossau*) in the 9th district of Alsergrund. Its 900 original headstones date as far back as 1450 and continue up to 1783 when the cemetery was closed together with other burial grounds within the *Linienwall* (today's Gürtel ringroad) by Emperor Joseph II (1765–90). Today it languishes somewhat behind a modern retirement home, itself built on the site of an old Jewish hospital demolished in 1972. Amongst the tall grass, and even taller trees, are the 280 headstones that were identified and re-erected after the Nazis desecrated the site in 1938 (see no. 14). However, many still remain cracked and dislodged, and it was not until 1984 that the cemetery was consecrated. Orthodox Jews can still sometimes be seen here reciting the 'Mourner's Kaddish' over certain graves.

A notable grave is that of banker Samuel Oppenheimer of Heidelberg (1630–1703). He was one of the first so-called Court Jews to be protected by Imperial Letter and enticed back to Vienna after the expulsions of 1699 under Emperor Leopold I (1658–1705). Most significantly he organised the financing of Prince Eugene of Savoy's (1663–1736) campaigns against the Turks in the 1680s, as well as the wars with the French, though the Habsburgs never settled their debts with him thereby forcing the Oppenheimer dynasty into eventual bankruptcy. Nearby is the grave of his son-in-law, Samson Werthcimer

(1658–1724), who was financial administrator to no less than three successive Habsburg emperors.

After the cemetery's eventual closure in 1783, Jewish burials were made in a new graveyard appended to Währing's municipal cemetery (*Währinger Friedhof*) opening the same year on Semperstrasse (18th District) just outside the Gürtel ring road. As with

Broken headstones in one of Europe's oldest Jewish cemeteries on Seegasse

other suburban cemeteries it was largely cleared and made into a park in the 1920s, having been made redundant by the new Central Cemetery (*Zentralfriedhof*) opened in Simmering in 1874 (see no. 70). The Jewish part, however, remains to this day, albeit overgrown and unkempt. Surrounded by high walls and presently closed for security reasons, its half-buried and toppled stones, many of whose name plaques were torn off long ago, recall Prague's old Jewish cemetery (note also the charming winged egg-timer carved over the entrance at Schrottenbachgasse 3). Amongst the 10,000 closely packed graves from the late-18th to 19th centuries are those of influential bankers, industrialists and railway engineers. Notables include members of the Fürth family from Bohemia, who built what is now the American Consulate, Israel Hönig von Hönigsberg, the first Jewish Imperial official to be ennobled, the Epstein family, who were also ennobled by the Emperor (hence the coat of arms on their tomb), and Bernhard Pollack, an art collector, whose tomb was later dug out by optimistic treasure hunters in the mistaken belief that it was filled with valuables.

In 1941, the cemetery was commandeered by the Nazis in order to excavate part of it as a fire reservoir. It fell to the area's already traumatised Jewish community to exhume as many bodies as possible. As if that weren't enough, many of the skulls and other bones were then spirited away by Nazi operatives to Vienna's Natural History Museum for insensitive and unecessary measurement and cataloguing. Just over 200 skeletons were eventually returned in 1947 for the city's few remaining Jews to re-bury in what was left of their now vandalised cemetery.

Snowfall adds atmosphere to Währing's Old Jewish Cemetery

Arguably Europe's most important Jewish cemetery, its current lamentable condition, like that of Friedhof Rossau, is due in part to the fact that the families of those interred simply no longer exist. That and the fact that it is normal Jewish burial practice not to reuse graves nor to cut back vegetation unless absolutely necessary.

Both these explanations are graphically reinforced when one visits the old Jewish section, inside Gate 1, of Simmering's Central Cemetery. Its bullet-strafed and tumbling headstones, once as grand as anything in the well-maintained Catholic section next-door, are now largely abandoned to the ravages of untamed vegetation and subsidence (see no. 70). Even the graves of novelist Arthur Schnitzler (Group 6, Row 0, Grave 4), Sigmund Freud's parents, Jacob and Amalia (Group 50, Row 4, Grave 53), and the Austrian branch of the powerful Rothschild family (Group 6, Row 29, Grave 49/051) look a little unkempt, the only evidence of visitors being the rows of tiny pebbles ('Memory Stones') left behind. Nowhere is the tragic destiny of Vienna's pre-war Jewish community more poignantly emphasised.

Another Viennese Jewish cemetery can be found at Ruthnergasse 28 in the 21st District of Floridsdorf. Its rows of headstones give details not only of what those interred did in life (e.g. a rabbi as signified by a carved pair of hands) and what their particular talents were (e.g. a cedar tree representing great wisdom) but also how they died (e.g. a grave from 1928 carrying a carving of a motorcycle).

Other places of interest nearby: 58, 60, 63

60 The Strudlhof Steps

9th District (Alsergrund), the Strudlhof Steps (*Strudlhof-stiege*) on Strudlhofgasse; take Tram D to Porzellangasse

A striking yet curiously-named staircase is tucked away in the 9th district of Alsergrund. The Strudlhof Steps (*Strudlhofstiege*) were constructed in 1910 to a design by the architect Johann Theodor Jager (1874–1943). Their purpose is to connect the former water meadows of Liechtensteinstrasse, through which a Danube tributary once ran, with Strudlhofgasse above, the two areas lying at different levels due to a geological fault.

The steps are named in honour of the sculptor and architect Peter Strudl (c. 1660–1714), founder of the Academy of Fine Arts (*Akademie der bildenden Künste*), Central Europe's first art academy. Before its move to its present location on Schillerplatz (1st District), it was housed in the eponymous Strudlhof at what is now Strudlhofgasse 10. Strudl was responsible, together with his brother Paul, for the fine statues in the Hofburg's Baroque library (*Prunksaal*).

The Strudlhof Steps are an unmissable example of Viennese Art Nouveau (*Jugendstil*). Sweeping stone balustrades, fountains, and standard lamps painted green to resemble verdigrised copper make for an elegant ensemble. It is little wonder that they inspired local writer Franz Karl Heimito von Doderer (1896–1966) when he wrote his career-defining novel *Die Strudlhofstiege, oder Melzer und die Tiefe der Jahre* (The Strudlhof Steps – The Depth of the Years)

Born in Weidlingau bei Wien, Doderer was the sixth and final child of a wealthy Viennese architect and building contractor, related by marriage to leading Ringstrasse architect Heinrich von Ferstel. A cavalry officer during the Great War, he spent 1916–1920 in a Russian prisoner of war camp in Siberia. It was during these years that he decided his life's calling was to be a writer.

After the war, Doderer studied history and psychology and wrote essays, poems and other pieces for various Viennese news-

The first English-language translation of *The Strudlhof Steps*

Jugendstil lamps on the way up the Strudlhof Steps

papers. It was not until 1941, however, that he began work on *The Strudlhof Steps*. He also joined the Nazi party although this was thought to be less about ideology and more about gaining access to the Association of Writers. In 1942, he went to the Russian front winding up again as a prisoner of war, this time in Norway.

After the Second World War, although initially banned from working in publishing because of his Nazi affiliation, Doderer sought spiritual refuge in Catholicism and was soon working again as a freelance writer. The publication of *The Strudlhof Steps* in 1951 quickly made him Vienna's most famous post-war writer. Following publication in 1956 of his other great novel, *Die Dämonen* (*The Demons*), he received the Austrian State Prize for Literature. The reason he still remains largely unknown outside Austria, however, is because the world he reveals is uniquely Viennese - and his books are enormously long!

The Strudlhof Steps transports the reader back to *fin de siècle* Vienna as seen through the eyes of schoolboy Rene Stangeler (Doderer himself). He observes how his parents, sisters, house guests and other middle class characters commute between the oppressive heat of the Viennese summer and the cool, refined rusticity of the Rax, Schneeberg and Semmering mountains. The various strands of the story all eventually come together at the Strudlhof Steps.

Doderer continues the theme in *The Demons*, which he penned in his favourite tavern *Zur Stadt Paris* at Josefstädter Strasse 4 (8th District). This time, however, behind the charming 1920s tea parties and tennis games there runs insecurity, political instability and sexual dissoluteness as Vienna slides towards the civil war of 1934. Both books have a strong storyline running in tandem with a series of philosophical reflections that attempt to understand the mannered, melancholic yet hedonistic Viennese soul.

Doderer died in 1966 and is buried in the cemetery at Grinzing (*Grinzinger Friedhof*) in the 19th district of Dobling. The author's effects, including pictures and furniture from his study, can be found today in the Alsergrund District Museum's Heimito von Doderer-Sammlung at Wahringer Strasse 43, just a stone's throw away from the steps and Doderer's former home at number 50.

To discover more about Heimito von Doderer, as well as a host of other Austrian literary luminaries such as Thomas Bernhard, Stefan Zweig and Joseph Roth, visit the Austrian National Library's Literature Museum at Johannesgasse 6 (1st District). Housed in an impressive Biedermeier building once used for the Royal and Imperial Court Chamber archive, its antique shelves contrast strikingly with today's exhibitions.

An old engraving of the Palais Liechtenstein

The former site of the original Strudlhof at Strudlhofgasse 9 is now occupied by the Palais Strudlhof hotel. Once home to Austrian Foreign Minister Leopold Graf Berchtold (1863–1942), it was here in July 1914 that the ultimatum to Serbia was drafted, which in turn triggered the First World War. It is also where in 1970, the SALT 1 disarmament talks between the USSR and USA took place. Not far from the bottom of the steps is the Palais Liechtenstein, the Baroque summer palace of the princely family of the same name. Completed around 1700, it features glorious painted interiors and stucco work commissioned from an army of Italian craftsmen. The art gallery here is open for special exhibitions and the lovely gardens are free for all.

Other places of interest nearby: 58, 59, 61, 62

61 The Fool's Tower

9th District (Alsergrund), the Narrenturm in courtyard 13 of the Altes Allgemeines Krankenhaus off Spitalgasse; take Tram 40/41/42 from U-Bahn station Schottentor (U-2)

The 9th district of Alsergrund is home to Vienna's New General Hospital (*Neues Allgemeines Krankenhaus* or *AKH*) famous for being Europe's largest. Nearby, on the suitably named Spitalgasse, is its even more famous predecessor, the Old General Hospital (*Altes Allgemeines Krankenhaus*), founded by the enlightened Emperor Joseph II (1765–90) in 1784. In its day the hospital was one of the world's most modern and boasted 2000 beds. Many world famous doctors and surgeons passed through its doors, including psychiatrist Julius Wagner-Jauregg (1857–1940), a 1927 Nobel Prize for Medicine winner for his *Discovery of the Therapeutic Importance of the Malaria Vaccination in Progressive Paralysis*.

Although the hospital's old courtyards are now home to a busy university campus, one of them retains a historic curiosity known as the Narrenturm, or Fools' Tower. Constructed in 1784 to a design by court architect Isidor Canevale (1730–1786), the cylindrical tower was designed as a purpose-built asylum and despite its insentive nickname

The Narrenturm, or Fools' Tower, in the grounds of the Old General Hospital

represented the first time that patients with mental infirmities were housed and treated, rather than being publicly displayed and humiliated. The tower has five floors, each with 28 centrally-heated cells running off a central courtyard, from where a member of staff could easily supervise the patients. Some onlookers nicknamed it the *Guglhupf* after a famous Austrian cake of a similar shape! However, not all the tower's occupants were suffering legitimate mental infirmity as highlighted by the case of one Count Seilern, who was disciplined by the Emperor himself for committing his son to the tower on the grounds that he wished to marry a girl deemed unsuitable!

Disused since 1866, the *Narrenturm* is now home to the Pathological–Anatomical Collection (*Pathologisch-anatomische Sammlung*), which comprises a somewhat grisly collection of c.4000 specimens of physical abnormalities and deformities preserved in formaldehyde (including the world's finest display of kidney and gallstones). The collection, founded in 1796 and housed originally in the dissection ward of the Old General Hospital, was supplied from the hundreds of corpses generated by the hospital annually, as well as court-ordered autopsies. The museum also contains over 2,000 replicas of diseased body parts made out of paraffin wax and a reconstruction of Dr. Robert Koch's 1882 discovery of the tuberculosis bacillus.

Alsergrund has numerous other medical associations being home to many university departments, as well as the original practice of Sigmund Freud (see no. 97). Additionally, there is the Josephinum at Währinger Strasse 25. Opened in 1785, it originally housed the Institute of the Military Academy of Medicine and Surgery, founded by Emperor Joseph II (1765–90) for the training of field surgeons and army doctors. Since 1920, the Institute for the History of Medicine has had a museum here (*Medizinhistorisches Museum*) that includes a unique collection of life-size anatomical study models (*Wachspräparate-Sammlung*). They were commissioned by the emperor in 1780, from the Florentine physiologist Felice Fontana and the Tuscan anatomist Paolo Mascagni. For added realism the figures were modelled out of Ukrainian beeswax.

In Courtyard 6 of the Old General Hospital can be found a tiny prayer house once used by Jewish patients and later desecrated by the Nazis. After the war it was used as a power station but has now been restored as a working synagogue and memorial.

Other places of interest nearby: 54, 58, 60, 62

62 007 in Vienna

9th District (Alsergrund), the Confiserie Zum Sussen Eck
sweet shop at Währinger Strasse 65 opposite Volksoper;
take Tram 40/41/42 from U-Bahn station Schottentor (U-2)

The film *A View to a Kill* was the 14th in the long running and lucrative James Bond series, based on the spy novels of Ian Fleming. However, by all accounts the film relied more on its gadgetry and special effects than the panache and daring-do of its ageing star Roger Moore. Wisely Moore sipped his last Vodka Martini and retired to a life devoted to charity work and a well-earned knighthood. Amongst those considered for his replacement were established "action men" Mel Gibson, Tom Selleck and Don Johnson. Somewhat surprisingly it was the relatively unknown Timothy Dalton who clinched the part. Born

in March 1946 in Colwyn Bay, North Wales he had played a variety of roles in films as diverse as *The Lion in Winter*, *Flash Gordon* and *The Doctor and the Devils*. Not being a typecast actor allowed Dalton to play Bond his own way – dark and introspectively.

His first outing was based on Fleming's short story *The Living Daylights* that had appeared in *The Sunday Times* on 4th February 1962. Directed by John Glen the film premiered at the Odeon in London's Leicester Square on 27th June 1987, attended by Prince Charles and his then wife Diana. The Vienna premiere (titled *Der Hauch des Todes*, or *Breath of Death*) followed on August 13th at the Gartenbau Kino.

This film was of special interest to Bond's Austrian fans because much of the first half of the film uses Vienna as a backdrop. The plot dictates that Bond is sent to Bratislava in the old Czechoslovakia to protect a valuable defecting Russian agent and to eliminate a KGB sniper he knows will be waiting there to thwart him. The Russian,

Bond photos in the window of Confiserie Zum Sussen Eck

Koskov, is in a concert hall (Vienna's Volksoper on Währinger Strasse) and Bond takes up position above a nearby bookshop, in reality the wonderfully old fashioned sweet shop Confiserie Zum Sussen Eck at Währinger Strasse 65 (both venues believably set-dressed to resemble Czechoslovakia). The sweet shop window to this day carries photographs of a saturnine-looking Dalton in *de rigueur* tuxedo and bow tie.

Not surprisingly for a 007 movie, the sniper that Bond lines up through the sight of his rifle turns out to be the beautiful Kara (played by Maryam d'Abo) – and of course he deliberately misses his target! Koskov is then grabbed and dispatched speedily to the safety of the West via a gas pipeline. This scene begins at Vienna's

The Volksoper which appeared in the film The Living Daylights

Steinspornbrücke over the New Danube (still dressed up to mimic the Eastern Bloc) and ends at the Gasometer in Simmering (see no. 72), now *officially* in Vienna. Bond and Kara, needless to say are already involved romantically, and remain in "Bratislava" for several street scenes shot along Vienna's number 42 tram route, suitably disguised with Skoda cars and Czechoslovak shop signs (these include the former Währing tram depot and Kara's apartment on Antonigasse). The pair eventually escape in Bond's Aston Martin and finally cross the border into snowbound Austria using Kara's cello as a sledge! After some fairly schmaltzy scenes visiting Vienna's Schönbrunn palace by horse-drawn *Fiaker* and riding gondola number 10 of the Ferris wheel (*Riesenrad*) in the Volksprater (see no. 66), the film shifts location to Oxfordshire, Tangiers, and then finally Afghanistan.

Curiously, few of the Bond biographies, nor indeed many of the city's guidebooks for that matter, make any mention of Vienna as a film location and indeed few visitors are even aware that 007 was ever here. Coincidentally, during the writing of this book a season of Bond films was screened at the aforementioned Gartenbaukino, and again the accompanying promotional material failed to make any reference to the fact that Vienna had provided much of the backdrop for *The Living Daylights*.

Other places of interest nearby: 60, 61

63 Hitler's Monstrous Monuments

2nd District (Leopoldstadt), the Flak towers *(Flaktürme)* in the Augarten; take Tram 31 from U-Bahn Schottenring (U-2/U-4)

On 9th April 1938 Adolf Hitler addressed the people of Vienna. He spoke of their city, so recently absorbed into the Third Reich, as a pearl in need of a worthy setting. Few could have known that setting would be a noose of concrete anti-aircraft towers *(Flaktürme)* - an acronym of *Flugabwehrkanonen* - built during a war that would leave Vienna in ruins.

There is little getting away from the fact that Vienna's *Flaktürme* are still standing. Two of them dominate the Augarten, looming up at the intersection of tree-lined promenades along which Baroque-era pleasure-seekers once strolled. Looking up at them the contrast is stark, the reminder immutable.

Sealed since the war it takes a while to circumnavigate the base of the huge towers – but it's grimly fascinating. How were these huge concrete structures built, and in such a short time? After all, they are 50 metres high, with walls almost four metres thick. The answer, of course, is simple: thousands of forced labourers using know-how derived from the Nazis' construction of Germany's motorways *(Autobahnen)*.

There is currently no on-site visitor information concerning the Augarten towers – but the basic facts are well known. From 1942 onwards, when the tide of war turned against Germany, civil engineer Friedrich Tamms (1904-1980) was commissioned to design a series of *Flaktürme* to protect Berlin, Hamburg, and Vienna. Three pairs of towers forming a defensive triangle were erected around each city, each pair comprising a heavily-armed attack tower supported by a smaller communications tower.

Even during the summer months the forbidding cylindrical Augarten attack tower throws a cold shadow avoided by park-goers (see page 2 frontispiece). Some evenings it provides a bizarre backdrop for outdoor cinema, the entranced audience unaware that after a successful war the Nazis planned to clad the tower in black marble, with the names of fallen troops inscribed in gold.

Elsewhere in the city historical details are also sparse. The Riesenrad, for example, the Prater's iconic Ferris wheel, provides a superb overview of the Augarten but the aerial photos in each gondola fail to identify the *Flaktürme*. Like post-war postcards of Vienna, in which the towers were deliberately painted out, it is an example of amnesia in a city that long struggled with its wartime image.

Looking back up at the Augarten tower a great crack is visible down one side. Some historians are of the opinion that it was the result of a failed attempt by the liberating Red Army to destroy the tower, in much the same way they had part-toppled one in Berlin. But ask around in surrounding Leopoldstadt and the story takes on a home-grown slant: daring local schoolchildren broke into the abandoned tower and detonated an abandoned weapons dump achieving what the Russians had failed to do!

It's a stiff walk of almost three and a half kilometres to Arenbergpark in Landstrasse (3rd District), where the next pair of *Flaktürme* stand. No mysteries here

An abandoned anti-aircraft tower in the Augarten

and neither tower appears damaged (see back cover). This, and the fact that the formidably thick walls guarantee a stable temperature, explains why one of them has been used since 1995 as an art depot by the city's Museum of Applied Arts (MAK).

By design it's the same distance again to the final pair of towers, where a surprise awaits. Through an ingenious programme of adaptive reuse the former communications tower in Esterházypark (6th District) has been transformed into the Haus des Meeres, a hugely popular aquarium containing sharks and giant turtles with a miniature rainforest bolted onto one side. Here surprisingly there's an exhibition on the tower's wartime role and a café installed on the roof offering a superb vista over the surroundings. The outside of the tower even doubles as a climbing wall. A museum of torture (*Foltermuseum*) occupies a suitably stygian Second World War bunker directly beneath the tower.

For more Second World War history visit the Museum of Military History (*Heeresgeschichtliches Museum*) in the Arsenal (3rd District), the Third Man Museum (*Dritte Mann Museum*) at Pressgasse 25 (4th District) and the concrete air raid shelter in Arne-Carlsson-Park at Währingerstrasse 43 (9th District), which contains the Museum of Liberation Vienna (*Befreiungsmuseum Wien*), tours of which are available by appointment.

Other places of interest nearby: 58, 59

64 Home of the Waltz King

By 1863, when Johann Strauss the Younger (1825–99) came to live at Praterstrasse 54 (2nd District), he was already a household name. The address suited him it being on a grand thoroughfare that sliced through the cosmopolitan district of Leopoldstadt, from the edge of the 1st District out to the Prater. His father, Johann Strauss the Elder (1804–49), composer of *The Radetzky March*, was long dead and so too the painful rivalry between the two of them. Strauss would surpass his father's fame, taking the mantle of Waltz King and touring Europe, Russia and even America.

A 19th-century silhouette picture of Johann Strauss the Younger in full flight

It was in the apartment on Praterstrasse, now an excellent small museum, that he composed Vienna's unofficial anthem *An der Schönen blauen Donau* (*The Blue Danube Waltz, opus 314*). Originally scored for the Vienna Male Voice Choir, it was performed as such to a nonplussed audience in 1867 in the former Diana Rooms at Obere Donaustrasse 95. However, shortly afterwards it was performed in Paris with an orchestra and immediately became a worldwide favourite. Today, the piece always features in the Vienna Philharmonic Orchestra's popular televised New Year's Day concert from the Golden Hall of the Musikverein.

Strauss finally left Praterstrasse in 1878 and died in 1899 having composed several hundred waltzes, including *Geschichten aus dem Wienerwald* (*Tales from the Vienna Woods*), and operettas, notably *Die Fledermaus* (*The Bat*). His last home at Johann-Strauss-Gasse 4 in Wieden was unfortunately destroyed in the

Music from The Blue Danube Waltz on a wall near Strauss's last home in Wieden

Second World War (see no. 47) although on the wall of an apartment at number 10 can be seen the opening bars of his famous *Blue Danube Waltz*.

Over the years Praterstrasse has been home to numerous scholars, artists and doctors. Film music pioneer Max Steiner (1888–1971), for example, was born at number 72 and worked at the nearby Volksprater before moving to Broadway and Hollywood. His 300 film credits include *Casablanca*, *Gone With the Wind*, *King Kong* and *Treasure of the Sierra Madre*. Note the Venetian-style *Dogenhof* next-door at number 70, based on the *Cá d'Oro* palace on Venice's Grand Canal (see no. 66). Number 44 was the surgery of Alfred Adler, the founder of Individual Psychology, whilst at number 31 was the former Carltheater, where Johann Nestroy (1801–62) was dramatist and director (his statue is outside number 19). At number 22 is the modest room where novelist, dramatist and 1981 Nobel Prize winner Elias Canetti (1905–94) spent his school days, whilst number 16 is the birthplace of novelist and playwright Arthur Schnitzler (1862–1931),. His *Traumnovelle* (Dream Story) set in *fin de siècle* Vienna, was used by Stanley Kubrick as the basis for his last film *Eyes Wide Shut*, starring Tom Cruise and Nicole Kidman.

In the summer of 1850, Johann Strauss the Younger organised a Grand Viennese Festival in the well-to-do suburb of Döbling (19th District). The venue was the Casino Zögernitz, a Biedermeier-style concert hall and meeting place opened in 1837. The festivities included a ball, fireworks and the specially-written *Johannis-Käferln Waltz* evoking the glow worms that can sometimes still be seen there today.

Other places of interest nearby: 65, 66

65 Memories of Mazzes Island

2nd District (Leopoldstadt), the former Greater Leopoldstadt Temple (Leopoldstädter Tempel) at Tempelgasse 3–5; take U-1 to Nestroyplatz

Vienna's 2nd district of Leopoldstadt, on the other side of the Danube Canal from the 1st District, has always been a point of disembarkation for those arriving from lands to the north and east. It was on low-lying marshy ground here, subject to regular flooding, that in 1625 Emperor Ferdinand II (1619–37) established a walled Jewish

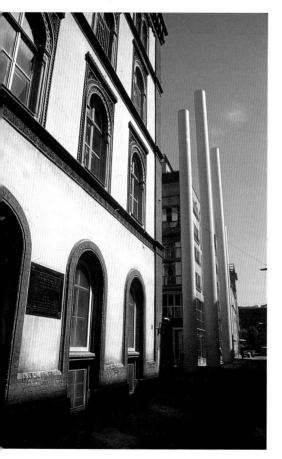

ghetto known as the *Unterer Werd*. From an Old German expression meaning Lower Island, the area is encompassed by today's Taborstrasse, Obere Augartenstrasse, Malzgasse, Schiffgasse and Krummbaumgasse. It replaced the original medieval Jewish ghetto of the 1st District (see no. 9) and soon began to flourish. However, in 1699, with the Catholic Counter Reformation in full swing, Emperor Leopold I (1658–1705) banished the ghetto's 3000 Jews and resettled the area with his own artisans. He was egged on by both Christian Viennese burghers, as well as his bigoted Spanish wife Margarita Teresa, who blamed her numerous

Mighty columns marking the former site and size of the Great Temple synagogue on Tempelgasse

miscarriages on the Jews. Leopold re-named the area Leopoldstadt and replaced the area's original synagogue at Grosse Pfarrgasse 15 with his own church, the self-styled Leopoldkirche.

Needless to say the expulsion weakened both imperial and city finances and in time the Jews filtered back to the 2nd District, encouraged by the enlightened Emperor Joseph II's Edict of Tolerance (*Toleranzpatent*) (1781) permitting them to establish communities

Pavement memorials in Jewish Leopoldstadt

outside the 1st District (see no. 59). They arrived from Bohemia and Moravia (now the Czech Republic), Galicia (now part of Poland and Ukraine) and Hungary, opening shops and coffee houses in the area's warren of back streets. Eventually, successful middle class Jews were occupying large houses on Praterstrasse and the area gained the nickname of "Mazzes Island", after the unleavened Passover bread made in local Jewish bakeries.

After the 1848 Revolution Jews were allowed to choose their place of residence and full legal emancipation followed in 1867 under Emperor Franz Joseph I (1848–1916). As a result, a huge influx of Jews arrived from the east and their self-assurance was expressed in grandiose buildings such as the Temple of the Sephardic Jews in Zircusgasse (1837) and Leopold Förster's Great Temple on Tempelgasse (1858). In 1938 both structures were destroyed by the Nazis (see nos. 14 and 59), although one wing of the Great Temple remains, together with four huge white columns erected in 1997 to give an impression of its former dimensions. A colourful mosaic on a wall at the end of the road reinforces the impression of what was once Vienna's largest synagogue.

After the First World War, the number of Jews peaked at 200,000 (10% of Vienna's population) of which half lived in Leopoldstadt, the well-to-do having moved out to the 1st and 9th Districts. The contribution of Viennese Jewry at this time to politics, business, science and the arts was enormous, with names such as Freud, Schnitzler,

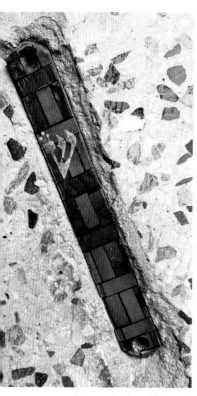
A doorway Torah scroll (Mezuzah)

Wittgenstein, Canetti, Schönberg and Mahler amongst them. Since the turn of the century, however, anti-Semitism had been on the rise again, notably under Dr. Karl Lueger (1844-1910), city mayor and founder of the Christian Social Party, the Jews this time being made scapegoat for declining economic fortunes.

Following the 1938 annexation (*Anschluss*) of Austria by Nazi Germany most of Vienna's 185,000 Jews were exiled or exterminated, their religious buildings defiled and their businesses "Aryanised", in other words expropriated. Many of the Jews who were deported left from the former Aspangbahnhof railway station in Landstrasse, now called the Platz der Opfer der Deportation in their memory.

The sensitive and informed visitor should spare a thought for the lost Jews of Vienna, especially when sipping a coffee in the Café Mozart, buying a sandwich at an Anker bakery, drinking an Ottakringer beer, purchasing medicine at the Engel Apotheke or riding on the Ferris wheel (*Riesenrad*) since all were once Jewish enterprises, most of whose original owners did not survive the war.

Thankfully, Jewish life is today reasserting itself yet again with a modest population of c.7000, a dozen synagogues across the city and Leopoldstadt once more the focus of the indomitable Jewish spirit. Little wonder, however, that their presence is low key, with prayer rooms and Kosher shops (e.g. the Ohel bakery at Lillienbrunngasse 18 and Daniel Hager's butcher's shop at Grosse Stadtgutgasse 7) marked only by modest signs and tiny prayer scrolls (*Mezuzah*) nailed diagonally to the doorframe. Security guards are always to be found outside their synagogues and schools following a terrorist attack on the main synagogue on Seitenstettengasse (1st District) in 1981. The most obvious sign of a Jewish presence is the myriad pavement memorials recalling individuals lost in the Holocaust (www.steinedererinnerung.net).

Other places of interest nearby: 64, 66

66 All the Fun of the Fair

2nd District (Leopoldstadt), the Volksprater and Prater-museum at Praterstern; take U-1 to Praterstern (note: the Pratermuseum will close in May 2023 and reopen in 2024 at nearby Strasse des 1. Mai)

The word Prater (from the Latin *Pratum* meaning 'meadow') was first coined in 1403 to describe a Danube island north of Freudenau. In 1560 it was purchased by Emperor Maximilian II (1564-1576) for use as an imperial hunting ground. To keep poachers away, access was restricted until 1766, when the enlightened Emperor Joseph II (1765-1790) declared the area open for public enjoyment.

The chestnut-lined Hauptallee has long provided the Prater with its main axis. At one end stands the Lusthaus, a former hunting lodge now used as a restaurant; at the other is the Volksprater, the fairground established after the emperor permitted the setting up of bowling alleys, food stalls, and puppet booths. One of the puppets, the Punch-like Hanswurst, gave rise to the alternative name, Wurstelprater.

Hunting continued in the Prater until 1920 but by then the Volksprater had long been centre stage. Although much of it was destroyed during the Second World War, the original fairground still lives on in the fascinating *Pratermuseum*. On the walls hang posters advertising Lionel the Lion Man and exotic creature shows, and all around are fragments of rides and sideshows long since dismantled. The nostalgic photos reveal a lost world of moustachioed strong men, tattooed ladies, human torsos, Siamese Twins and giants, as well as the little people employed to inhabit the miniature town of Liliputstadt.

The museum also recalls the 1873 World Exhibition held on the nearby showground. The 26,000 exhibitors and their many visitors were housed inside a colossal Rotunda in which all manner of wonders natural and man-made were displayed. By way of entertainment the

The Riesenrad Ferris wheel in the Volksprater

An original wooden Helter Skelter in the Volksprater

Volksprater staged an attraction called *Venedig in Wien*, featuring full-size Venetian canals along which gondolas drifted past Italianate palazzi. It was one of the world's very first real theme parks. The fabulous Venetian-style Dogenhof outside the fairground at Praterstrasse 70 dates from the same period. Unfortunately little else remains of the exhibition although an impressive mirror by local glassmakers J. & L. Lobmeyr, which was displayed in the Rotunda, can still be found in their glittering late-19th century store at Kärntnerstrasse 26 (1st District), which also boasts its own 2nd-floor glass museum. The site of the World Exhibition today is occupied by the ultra-modern architecture of the Campus WU and the development area Viertel Zwei.

The Pratermuseum also contains a model of the *Riesenrad*, the British-built Ferris wheel erected in 1897 and made famous by Orson Welles in *The Third Man*. The model includes the original complement of thirty cabins, half of which were not replaced on the real thing after it was weakened by fire during the Second World War. The wheel's owner, Eduard Steiner, died in Auschwitz.

The stately *Riesenrad* is hardly a white knuckle ride. For that try the world's oldest extant ghost train dating back to the 1930s or the vintage wooden Helter Skelter. Until recently children could enjoy a carousel using real ponies that thundered around to the sound of a pipe organ. With the ponies now departed but with the organ still in place, the building has become the Café Ponykarussell. Of course the modern rides make the old ones seem tame, especially the recently installed chain carousel, which transports its passengers to a dizzying 117 metres above the ground. The obligatory visit to the Schweizerhaus for beer and pork knuckle is best made afterwards!

Alongside the Pratermuseum is a planetarium, and behind that is something very unusual. Surrounded by barbed wire there stands a spherical wooden house. It was originally constructed in Lower Austria by the artist Edwin Lipburger and removed here in 1984 after the Austrian authorities refused to grant him a building permit. Lipburger was so affronted that he declared the structure an independent nation calling it the Republic of Kugelmugel (Spherical Hill). As Head of State he refused to pay Austrian taxes and insisted on issuing his own stamps. Eventually only a pardon by the Austrian president saved him from going to jail.

Younger fairground fans will find plenty more to please them at the Circus and Clown Museum at nearby Ilgplatz 7, with its colourful posters, magic props and live performances. Older fans should enjoy the Magic Set Museum (*Zauberkasten Museum*) at Schönbrunner Strasse 262 (12th District).

More modest than the Volksprater but still of historic interest is Vienna's other fairground known as the Böhmischer Prater on Laaer-Berg-strasse in the 10th district of Favoriten. Founded in the 1880s and named after the

The Venetian-style Dogenhof on Praterstrasse

Bohemian migrants who came here to work in the local brick-works, it is home to several historic fairground rides as well as the Otto Geissler collection of street organs. In the time of Emperor Joseph II (1765–90) the rising ground here was used as a lookout point (known more recently as *Monte Laa*) and indeed it still provides a good vista of Vienna today.

One stop farther east on the U-1 (alight station Vorgartenstrasse) is Mexikoplatz. According to an inscribed stone the name acknowledges the little-known fact that it was only Mexico (together with the Soviet Union) that lodged an international protest against Hitler's annexation of Austria with Germany in 1938 (beyond the square is the Reichsbrücke across which Hitler's troops retreated in April 1945 in the face of the Red Army). Mexikoplatz is dominated by the striking red-tiled towers of the Church of St. Francis of Assisi, constructed to mark the Golden Jubilee of Emperor Franz Joseph I (1848–1916) in 1898. In the same year the Emperor's wife Elisabeth (Sisi) (1837–98) was assassinated whilst boarding a steamer on Lake Geneva. A chapel to her memory in the left transept is based on the Palatine chapel of Aix-la-Chapelle Cathedral and is given a Byzantine flourish by the use of gold mosaics.

Other places of interest nearby: 64, 65

67 A Day at the Races

2nd District (Leopoldstadt), the Krieau Harness Race Track (Trabrennbahn Krieau); take U-2 to Krieau

Not far from the famous Volksprater in Leopoldstadt, between the chestnut-lined Hauptallee and the Danube, is the Krieau Harness Race Track (*Trabrennbahn Krieau*). Opened in 1878 it is the second oldest harness race track in Europe after the Moscow Hippodrome. The unusual name is derived from Kriegsau ('war meadow') recalling a time when ownership of this former river island was contested between Vienna and Klosterneuburg.

Visiting the Krieau today is like stepping back in time. Much of its original fabric is still standing, including the timber-framed headquarters of the Viennese Harness Racing Club (*Wiener Trabrennverein*) and a five-storey Jugendstil observation tower straight out of Jules Verne. Together with a matching grandstand it was erected in 1913 to a design by students of the architect Otto Wagner and was the first such structure to be constructed from reinforced concrete and steel.

The original president of the club was Hungarian nobleman Count Kálmán Hunyady de Kéthely. He did much to popularise the sport and after his death in 1901 a race was established at the Krieau in his honour. Together with the Österreichisches Traber-Derby established in 1886, it remains a major event in the European harness racing calendar.

The track itself is a thousand metres long and paved with sand. It is wide enough to accommodate eight two-wheeled trotting buggies known as Sulkies. They race twice a month between September and June, with the track hosting live concerts and outdoor cinema the rest of the year.

Alongside the Krieau and almost hidden by trees are the Prateateliers. These imposing artists' studios were constructed for the World Exhibition of 1873, when a significant chunk of the Prater was transformed from a royal hunting preserve into a world class cultural and entertainment facility (see no. 66).

Farther along the Hauptallee, just beyond the *Lusthaus* (itself a former imperial hunting lodge), is another historic race track. Like the Krieau, the Freudenau Horse Racing Track (Galopprennbahn Freudenau) occupies land that was once riparian forest. It is even older though having been inaugurated in 1839.

Again much historic fabric remains, notably an ornate cast iron grandstand of 1858 unveiled by Emperor Franz Joseph I. Designed by the Ringstrasse architect Carl von Hasenauer in the emperor's beloved Historicist style, it can be glimpsed momentarily from the Ostautobahn, where it crosses the Danube Canal on the way into Vienna. The elegant green dome tops out the emperor's personal loggia added in 1870.

Austria's first Derby took place at Freudenau in 1868. Racing continued unabated thereafter until the Second World War, when Allied bombing devastated the track. Reconstruction was carried out with help from the British and in 1967 the renewed race course was acquired by the Republic of Austria.

Twenty years later, however, the Viennese Horse Racing Club (Wiener Galopprennverein) ceased their activities at Freudenau, and the writing was on the wall for the old

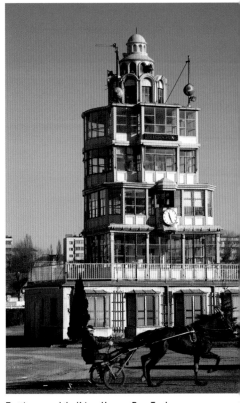

Trotting around the Krieau Harness Race Track

track. Despite being sold to another management company, racing events moved away to the plush new Magna Racino track in Lower Austria. With its last race run the track at Freudenau was forced into reinventing itself for a very different audience. Where horses once churned up the turf private picnics now take place, couples get married in the emperor's loggia, and film crews recreate bygone race days purely for cinemagoers.

68 Napoleon Attacks!

22nd District (Donaustadt), Napoleon's Headquarters (*Napoleons Hauptquartier*); take U-1 to Kaisermühlen VIC and then Bus 91 A to Ölhafen, turn left off Lobgrundstrasse and follow signs from Napoleonstrasse

The first half of Austrian Emperor Franz II (I)'s reign (1792–1806) was dominated by Napoleon's declaration of war on Europe. Following Habsburg military defeats in 1797 and 1800, French troops were only kept out of Vienna by ceding territories to them in Italy and the Netherlands. However, on November 13th 1805 Napoleon eventually entered the city and occupied the Schönbrunn palace, where his golden eagles still adorn the main gates. To cap it all, in 1806 he established the Confederation of the Rhine (*Rheinbund*) forcing the emperor to relinquish his title of Holy Roman Emperor, a Habsburg hereditary title since 1438, thereby downgrading him to Emperor Franz I (1804–35) of Austria.

Stone obelisk marking the site of Napoleon's headquarters in the Lobau

In time the Austrian army regrouped under the Emperor's brother Archduke Karl and proclaimed a War of Liberation. As a result, in spring 1809, Napoleon again marched on Vienna and reoccupied the Schönbrunn. Ten days later, however, he suffered his first major defeat, at the Battle of Aspern in the dense river forests of the Lobau, on the east bank of the Danube. Austrian troops had strategically withdrawn here before launching a surprise attack in which 20,000 French troops were killed, making a hero of Archduke Karl in the process. His equestrian statue can be seen in the Heldenplatz (Heroes' Square), together with that of Prince Eugene of Savoy (1663–1736), ironically a Frenchman, who had routed the Turks a century before.

It makes for a fascinating walk to explore what remains of the unspoilt wooded region of the Lobau, the sound of musket fire replaced today with birdsong. Signposted off Napoleonstrasse can be found the former locations of Napoleon's headquarters (*Hauptquartier*), powder magazine (*Pulvermagazin*) and cemetery (*Franzosenfriedhof*), each marked by an inscribed

The lion of Aspern

stone obelisk. In Aspern itself, at Asperner Heldenplatz 9, there is a museum devoted to the battle, as well as a magnificent stone lion by sculptor Anton Dominik Fernkorn (1813-1878). It commemorates the 50th anniversary of the battle and the 23,000 Austrian troops who died. Additionally, at Haidgasse 8 in Leopoldstadt is the *Zum Sieg* (The Victory) tavern, whose name recalls the battle, whilst at Praterstrasse 19 in the same district there is a building with an 1809-era cannonball embedded in it.

Bloodied but unbowed Napoleon soundly defeated the Austrians six weeks later at the Battle of Wagram. As a result, Austrian Chancellor Prince Clemens von Metternich adopted a policy of rapprochement, including the marriage of the Emperor's daughter Archduchess Maria Louisa to Napoleon. Vienna thus escaped further trouble and in 1814 became the setting for the Congress of Vienna following Napoleon's defeat at the Battle of Leipzig. As a result, Austria regained much of its lost territory and enjoyed thirty three years of peace in the ensuing *Biedermeier* period (shattered ultimately by the 1848 Revolution; see no. 15).

Left behind in Vienna was the French emperor's only son, Franz Karl Joseph (known as *L'Aiglon* or the eaglet), languishing in the Schloss Schönbrunn, his only companion a crested lark that can be seen preserved in the bedroom where he died. The poor child's eagle-adorned cradle and carriage (*phaeton*) are also still in Vienna in the Hofburg's Schatzkammer and Schönbrunn's Wagenburg respectively.

This stunning mosaic of Da Vinci's Last Supper hangs in the Minoritenkirche

Also connected with Napoleon is an Italian mosaic copy of Da Vinci's *Last Supper* in the Minoritenkirche on Minoritenplatz (1st District), which he commissioned in Milan as a replacement for the original that he intended to remove to Paris. Weighing 20 tons it was unfinished at the time of his abdication and bought by Habsburg Emperor Franz I (1792–1806). It was later donated by his successor, Ferdinand I (1835–1848), to Vienna's Italian congregation for display in their church, the Minoritenkirche.

Also commissioned by Napoleon, but not erected until the 1820s, was the Doric Theseustempel in the Volksgarten, intended to house Antonio Canova's statue *Theseus and the Minotaur* that can now be found in the stairwell of the Kunsthistorisches Museum. The building is a replica of the Theseion in the agora of ancient Athens.

Mosaic devotees should not miss the superb Venetian-style work at Kärntner Strasse 16 (1st District) undertaken in 1896 by Eduard Veith (and restored in the 1950s) that depicts the five continents. The oriental scenes on the right-hand side are particularly effective.

69 Cemetery of the Nameless

11th District (Simmering), the Cemetery of the Nameless *(Friedhof der Namenlosen)* at Alberner Hafen; take Tram 71 from U-Bahn Simmering (U-3) to terminus at Kaiserebers-dorfer Strasse, then Bus 76A or walk

Of Vienna's fifty-five cemeteries, both large and small, one of the most poignant must surely be the Cemetery of the Nameless *(Friedhof der Namenlosen)*. It lies on the bank of the Albern Dock beyond some large former Nazi-era grain warehouses and is protected from flooding by an earthen rampart *(Hochwasserschutzdamm)* erected in the early 1930s.

Lying just outside the city limits, the cemetery is somewhat difficult to find and is consequently little visited. Another reason that few visitors are encountered is that of the 104 corpses laid to rest here between 1900 and 1940, the majority are those of unidentified people, assumed to have drowned in the river nearby. Their corpses were washed ashore by the current at the confluence of the Danube

Unknown graves in the Cemetery of the Nameless at the Albern docks

Mourners at the Cemetery of the Nameless in bygone days

Canal and Danube proper. Forty-four persons were later identified but the final resting places of most are embellished only with a clump of mournful purple iris and a simple cross inscribed with the word *Namenlos* (Nameless). The occasional flickering candle and bunch of flowers lends a touching dignity to this melancholic place otherwise marked only by a small Chapel of the Resurrection added in 1935.

Between 1840 and 1900 the cemetery had a predecessor on the riverbank itself although its 487 bodies were never exhumed and the site has now been lost to the river forest (a signpost marks the spot).

With the construction of the nearby Albern grain dock in 1939 the river currents were themselves altered so that the Danube no longer brings its dead to the Cemetery of the Nameless. Despite this, each All Saint's Day (November 1st) sees the fishermen of Albern build a raft decorated with wreaths bearing a plaque reading "For the victims of the Danube" in German, Slovakian and Hungarian. To the tune of a band playing suitably mournful music, the raft is pushed out into the river from where it drifts slowly downstream to Bratislava, Esztergom, Budapest and beyond…

70 A City for the Dead

11th District (Simmering), the Zentralfriedhof (Central Cemetery) on Simmeringer Hauptstrasse; take Tram 71 from U-Bahn Simmering (U-3) and alight at Gate 2

November 1st is *Allerheiligen* (All Saints' Day) when Western Christians honour dead relatives who have reached Heaven. Since the Early Middle Ages they've adorned family graves with candles and flowers, bringing light and colour to cemeteries darkened by the onset of winter. On this day Vienna's Zentralfriedhof (Central Cemetery) is a remarkable sight.

During the second half of the 19th century, Vienna's burgeoning population spilled beyond its city walls. The suburban cemeteries commissioned by Emperor Joseph II (1765-1790) a century earlier became health hazards, and were cleared. In their place a single burial ground – the Zentralfriedhof – was established in the outlying district of Simmering. Fittingly, it opened for business on *Allerheiligen* 1874.

Designed to service an imperial capital of two million inhabitants, the cemetery was enormous from the start. And it needed to be since most Catholics rejected cremation in favour of a *Schöne Leich* (beautiful corpse). To avoid the horror of premature burial, customers could request a string be attached to their finger, which in the event of reawakening they could wiggle and ring a bell above ground! The writer Arthur Schnitzler opted for a stiletto blade through his heart instead.

One of Europe's largest cemeteries, the Zentralfriedhof sprawls across 240 hectares. It's so vast that it requires a separate tram stop outside each of its three main gates, and its own bus route inside the cemetery, which takes in the huge St. Charles Borromeo Cemetery Church (*Friedhofskirche zum heiligen Karl Borromäus*) completed in 1911 (see back cover). Within its perimeters there are three million burials – almost twice the city's current population – and it is teeming with wildlife, too, including a herd of deer.

The cemetery has always served the burial needs of Vienna's various faith groups. In addition to Protestants and Jews there are distinct burial areas for

A melancholic gravestone in the Zentralfriedhof in Simmering

Mormons, Buddhists, Russian Orthodox Christians, and Muslims, the latter facing towards Mecca. There are thematic groupings, too, of which the composers' graves always draw a crowd (the remains of Beethoven and Schubert were actually relocated here from cemeteries elsewhere to encourage visitors to the new cemetery). More poignant are the fields of crosses to the war dead, the floral tributes for stillborn babies, and the memorial to those who donated their bodies to medical science.

Just inside Gate 2 there are several hundred Graves of Honour (*Ehrengräber*) reserved originally for Vienna's great and good. Many are now long forgotten, which seems a pity since they include the likes of indomitable lady traveller Ida Pfeiffer, the inventor of the soup kitchen Josef Edler von Kühn, and Siegfried Marcus, who helped pioneer the automobile (see no. 71).

Elsewhere there are many more lives worth discovering: Suez Canal engineer Alois Negrelli and Margarete Schütte-Lihotzky, designer of the world's first fitted kitchen; Ludwig Köchel, who classified Mozart's work, and Ludwig Bösendorfer, piano manufacturer to the stars; actress Hedy Lamarr and physicist Ludwig Boltzmann; and one shouldn't forget the grave of Dominik Bauer, the cemetery's very first grave digger. Also buried somewhere here, albeit in an unmarked grave, is Hitler's half-niece, Geli Raubal, who shot herself in Munich in 1931.

Any tour of the Zentralfriedhof should conclude at the Old Jewish Cemetery inside Gate 1. The graves here represent the first time the city's Jews were buried in the same cemetery as its Christians. The difference in their current condition, however, is a stark reminder of the persecution of the city's Jews during the 1930s. Most of the headstones, even those of Freud's parents, have been abandoned to nature. It's a sobering but necessary experience, and when it's over the nearby Schloss Concordia offers welcome refreshment. Occupying a former mason's workshop, this eccentric restaurant is most atmospheric during winter, when its candlelit tables mirror the myriad lanterns flickering in the cemetery opposite.

In the basement of the *Aufbahrungshalle* (laying-out hall) inside Gate 2 of the cemetery is the unique Funeral Museum (*Bestattungsmuseum*). Before Vienna's funerals were centralised in 1951, private companies vied for the lucrative business of burying people, and the museum's macabre exhibits tell the full story. They include elaborate black outfits for pall-bearers and sombre liveries for hearse-pulling horses, different coloured palls signifying the deceased's former profession, and myriad wreathes, lanterns, and torches. There is even a re-useable coffin pioneered by reform-mad Emperor Joseph II (1765–1790)!

Other places of interest nearby: 71

71 A Forgotten Motor Car Inventor

11th District (Simmering), the grave of Siegfried Marcus in the Central Cemetery (Zentralfriedhof) on Simmeringer Hauptstrasse; take Tram 71 from U-Bahn Simmering (U-3) and alight at Gate 2; the grave is inside the gate on the left

Although there are several memorials in Vienna to the memory of nineteenth century inventor Siegfried Marcus (1831–1898) his name is little known. This is odd considering that he helped invent nothing less than the motor car.

Siegfried Liepmann Marcus was born in 1831 in Mecklenburg, North Germany, where his father was a businessman and head of the local Jewish community. It was an age of rapid technological progress, and the young Marcus knew he wanted to be a part of it. As a teenager he studied at technical school in Berlin, whilst also working for the engineering firm Siemens and Halske. They were busy erecting Europe's first long-distance telegraph line, and Marcus designed a telegraph relay system for them.

In 1852 Marcus moved to Vienna, where from 1856 until his death in 1898 he worked as a self-employed inventor. Wall plaques at Mariahilferstrasse 107 and Mondscheingasse 4 (7th District) mark the former site of two of his workshops. So productive was he during this period that he lodged no less than one hundred and fifty eight patents for inventions as varied as an incandescent spirit lamp, electromechanical triggers for naval mines, the *Antigraph* used by lithographers and copper plate engravers to avoid having to draw their designs in reverse, and a whaling knife used by the Austro-Hungarian

A plaque on Mondscheingasse marks the former site of one of the workshops of Siegfried Marcus

The grave of Siegfried Marcus in the Central Cemetery (Zentralfriedhof)

North Pole Expedition of 1872. He even installed an electric bell system in the Hofburg for the Habsburgs.

High on many inventors' agendas at the time was the creation of a powered vehicle to replace the horse. The answer came in the form of the internal combustion engine in which energy generated within an enclosed cylinder through the combustion of fuel with air is brought to bear on the pistons of reciprocating engines, providing drive and thus motion. As early as the 1860s Marcus had suggested petrol as a suitable fuel for such an engine, and in 1870 he attached a petroleum two-stroke engine to a conventional wooden hand cart and tested it on Mariahilferstrasse. Although the vehicle no longer exists, documents and photographs confirm it was the world's first mobile internal combustion engine.

Marcus died in 1898 and was buried in Hütteldorf cemetery and for the next forty years Austrian school children were taught that he had invented the motor car. Following the annexation of Austria by Germany in 1938, however, Marcus's papers were destroyed by the Nazis, who were unable to accept that a Jew had made such an important discovery. The legacy of Siegfried Marcus was expunged.

Fortunately, a second prototype vehicle dating from 1888 still existed in Vienna's Technical Museum (*Technisches Museum*), where it was hastily concealed in the cellar. The museum staff were determined that history should not be re-written by the city's new occupiers. After the war, the prototype was put back on display and on the fiftieth anniversary of Marcus's death his remains were transferred to an honorary tomb (*Ehrengrab*) in Simmering's Central Cemetery (see no. 70).

Remarkably Vienna is also where in 1901 the world's first petroleum-electric hybrid automobile was invented. Financed by well-established local carriage maker Ludwig Lohner (1858-1925), its revolutionary wheel-hub motors were the brainchild of a young Ferdinand Porsche (1875-1951). Although the vehicle was soon replaced by all-petroleum vehicles, the technology reappeared in the 1960s in the Lunar Rover that was used on the Moon!

Other places of interest nearby: 70

72 Gasometer Living

11th District (Simmering), the Gasometer on Guglgasse; take U-3 to Gasometer

In 1962 in the 13th District of Hietzing Vienna's last gas street lamp was extinguished. It's still there today outside the local museum, small testimony to the great network of gas pipes laid across the city in the late nineteenth century. The gas that lit it came from the Simmering Gas Works, which in 2001 were transformed into the Gasometer, an extraordinary example of industrial adaptive reuse.

It couldn't be easier to reach the Gasometer: there's a station of the same name on the U-3. At the top of the escalator the massive former gasholders fill the skyline, appearing much as they did when they were built during the 1890s. But don't be fooled. What actually remains are only the decorative brick shells, the great telescopic tanks inside, which once rose and fell as gas was added or removed, have been dismantled.

The former Simmering Gas Works re-born as a housing and retail complex

Each of the four gasholders is 65 metres wide, so it would take some time to circumnavigate them all. Since they're identical the first one – Gasometer A – will suffice. On one side of it there remains a giant pointer that once indicated the amount of gas inside. Not surprisingly a Habsburg double-eagle is emblazoned on it, a reminder that the Austrian emperor, despite his distrust of technological innovation, needed to be acknowledged during Habsburg Vienna's rapid industrialisation.

Today, like every day, several thousand people are trailing in and out of the entrance to Gasometer A. Few of them, however, seem interested in the oversized gas valve displayed on the forecourt. It's a reminder of the technological expertise required to provide a safe and reliable source of gas to Vienna's 100,000 end-users a century ago.

Despite suffering damage during the Second World War the Simmering Gas Works continued in business until 1978, when Vienna switched from coke to natural gas. Of no further use, for the next two decades the empty gasholders were used for all-night raves and as an unusual backdrop for film crews. Austropop singer Falco made a music video here, and in 1987 the abandoned site featured in the James Bond film *The Living Daylights*.

Enough of examining the exterior, it's time to enter Gasometer A, and the transformation is astonishing. The great cylindrical space is no longer recognisable for what it once was. Instead there is a bustling circular courtyard, its perimeter lined with shops and fast-food restaurants, and in the centre a café. The whole is illuminated by a glass roof affording peace to those occupying the sleek apartments above, which cling to the inside of the brick shell.

Gasometer A was designed by Jean Nouvel, one of four high calibre architects responsible for the conversion. The work of the other three can be seen easily by following the mall, which forms an axis through the entire complex. Glancing upwards reveals how each architect has chosen to grapple with the problem of creating homes within a curving space.

Returning to the U-3 one might conclude that the Gasometer is just a novel commercial endeavour – but that would be to miss its real purpose. The brief to all four architects, as well as to the non-profit making housing associations involved, was that the housing element should remain as affordable as possible, whilst also providing the 1,500 inhabitants with an infrastructure to maximise social interaction. In this way the project was brought firmly under Vienna's historic umbrella of 'social housing', inaugurated in the 1920s as part of the city's Socialist experiment known as *Rotes Wien*

Inside Gasometer A by Jean Nouvel

(Red Vienna). That some of the Gasometer's original retail ventures subsequenly died means that its greatest contribution is the unique housing it still provides for the living.

It is interesting to note that one of the three housing associations responsible for the Gasometer complex has also been responsible for the creation of several other unusual locations in Vienna. GESIBA *(Gemeinwirtschaftliche Siedlungs- und Baustoffanstalt)* was founded originally in 1921 as the Non-Profit-Making Estates and Building Materials Association, providing cheap materials and loans to co-operatives and residents' associations during the period of Socialist Red Vienna. By the mid-1920s they were creating groundbreaking residential developments of their own, the most important of which was the unique *Werkbundsiedlung* housing estate in Hietzing (see no. 82). In the 1970s they were involved in the creation of the vast Alt-Erlaa estate in the 23rd District of Liesing, where over 3,000 apartments each with a leafy sun terrace soar upwards like a modern Hanging Gardens of Babylon.

73 The Socialist Swimming Pool

10th District (Favoriten), the Amalienbad swimming pool at Reumannplatz 23; take U-1 to Reumannplatz

The combination of long hot summers and easy access to the peaceful waters of the Old Danube (Alte Donau) (see no. 96) means that *al fresco* swimming is something of a national pastime in Vienna. Favourite spots include the historic bathing island of Gänsehäufel, with its areas reserved for certain public workers, hence signs to the Tram Drivers' Baths (*Strassenbahnerbad*), and, on the opposite shore, a memorial to celebrated Austrian marine biologist Hans Hass (1919–2013). There is also the elegant Krapfenwaldbad in the foothills of the Vienna Woods (*Wienerwald*) in the 19th district, with its Mediterranean pines, original wooden changing rooms (1914), and stupendous views back over Vienna. The Schafbergbad in the 18th district also combines bathing with lovely vistas.

For those happier under cover there is the historic Jörgerbad in the 17th district of Hernals, completed in 1912 with stained glass windows depicting goldfish, and charming wave-pattern tiling in the foyer.

That said the *pièce de resistance* of Viennese covered swimming pools must surely be the Amalienbad on Reumannplatz in Favoriten. It illustrates how Vienna's Socialist government of the 1920s could not only provide facilities for the people, but could do so in considerable style. Otto Nadel and Karl Schmalhofer, who at the time were

Art Deco elegance in the Amalienbad in Favoriten

employees of the city's architecture department, designed the building. When opened in 1926 it was one of the largest of its kind in Europe and had a capacity of 1,300 people. Amalienbad is also considered to be one of the finest architectural achievements of Socialist Red Vienna (see no. 95). The main pool is 33 metres long with a curving glass roof, which until reconstruction following bomb damage during the Second World War, could be slid open to the sky. Most significantly the interior was not left plain, rather it was embellished in the popular Art Deco style of the day. Nowhere is this more apparent than in the use of colourful mosaics, both practical and aesthetic, in the main pool, sauna and foyer, for which Amalienbad is famous. The square

Stained glass goldfish at the Jörgerbad in Hernals

in which the baths were erected is called Reumannplatz after Jakob Reumann (1853-1925), labour leader and Vienna's first Socialist Mayor, well known for his struggles with the City Council in order to improve workers' conditions.

Before the Amalienbad and Jörgerbad were built, the Viennese, most of whom lacked any domestic bathing facilities beyond a communal hallway washbasin (*Bassena*), relied on their local so-called *Tröpferlbad* (literally 'drip bath'). A feature of the city's increasingly populous 19th century suburbs, the *Tröpferlbad* contained multiple shower cubicles and lockers for storing one's clothes. An intact example in use until 1977 is preserved as part of the Wieden District Museum at Klagbaumgasse 4 (4th District).

On the subject of swimming pools it is interesting to note that the only modern pool within the 1st District is to be found in the Vienna Marriott hotel. However, lurking behind an innocent-looking doorway at Weihburggasse 20 is the much older *Zentralbad*, the first and only public baths ever built in the 1st District. It lies over a natural spring producing 200,000 litres of water a day that once flowed into a suite of beautifully tiled Moorish-style baths occupying a series of colonnaded subterranean halls. The baths function today as the Kaiserbründl gay sauna.

74 The Spinner at the Cross

10th District (Favoriten), the Spinner at the Cross monument *(Spinnerin am Kreuz)* in front of the George-Washington-Hof at junction of Triester Strasse 52 and Windtenstrasse; take Tram 65 from U-Bahn Karlsplatz (U-1/U-2/U-4)

The elaborate Gothic wayside cross known as the Spinnerin am Kreuz

One of the main thoroughfares south out of Vienna has for centuries been Triester Strasse, transporting the traveller to the former Habsburg port of Trieste on the northern Adriatic coast (where the giant insurance company *Assicurazioni Generali* was founded in 1831, according to a wall plaque at Graben 12). On the roadside at the junction with Windtenstrasse, and looking not unlike a discarded fragment from the Stephansdom, is a beautiful, 16 metre-high, late-Gothic monument. Dating to 1452 it is in actual fact a wayside cross and shrine marking the then southernmost boundary of Vienna's inner suburbs, and consequently of its safe area. It was also on this prominent spot, known as the Wienerberg, that until 1868 public executions took place. The monument's canopied sculptures include the Crucifixion and the placing of the crown of thorns on Christ's head.

In addition to these known facts there are two legends connected with the monument that are worth relating. The first relates to the monument's intriguing name: *Spinnerin am Kreuz* (Spinner at the Cross). It is said that a faithful wife spent several years here waiting for her husband's return from the Crusades, biding her time by spinning wool. In those days only a wooden post marked the spot (first mentioned as early as 1296) and the woman vowed that she would use the money raised from her labours to erect a stone cross should her husband return safely – which he eventually did! A 1920s mural illustrating the legend can be found further down the road on the opposite side. Indeed, so beloved is this Viennese tale of enduring love in the face of adversity that it decorates several other buildings, too, for example the entranceway at Opernring 4 in the 1st District.

The Stephansdom's unfinished North Tower

The second legend concerns the monument's designer, Hans Puchsbaum (1390-1454), who was architect of the Stephansdom's unfinished north, or Eagle's, tower (*Adlerturm*). Cost cutting in the face of the fast approaching first Turkish siege of 1529 explains why work on the cathedral tower stopped. Legend, however, tells us that Puchsbaum fell in love with the master stonemason's daughter, Mary, whom he would only be permitted to marry if he completed the north tower within a year. Realising quickly that this would be impossible he made a pact with the devil to help complete the work, promising in return never to utter holy names again. Needless to say when Mary appeared one day and poor Puchsbaum called her name from the scaffold where he was working it immediately gave way under him. Having inadvertently disobeyed the devil's demands he plunged to his death, leaving the tower unfinished to this day.

Farther out along Triester Strasse is the Wienerberg, where deposits of Pannonian clay marl (*Tegel*) were first extracted for brick-making during the reign of Empress Maria Theresa (1740–80). Together with workings farther east on the Laaer Berg, the area was once Europe's largest brickworks. Over 50 million cubic metres of bricks were made here, notably during the great building era of the *Gründerzeit* (Founding Period) between 1860 and 1900. This is not surprising when one realises that most of Vienna's late-19th century buildings are essentially brick boxes cleverly disguised with plasterwork moulded to resemble stone. A museum dedicated to the history of Viennese brick-making (*Wiener Ziegelmuseum*) exists as part of the Penzing District Museum at Penzinger Strasse 59 (14th District). The bricks on display are each stamped with the name of the company responsible for their manufacture.

Other places of interest nearby: 75

75 Wonderful Water Towers

10th District (Favoriten), the Water Tower (Wasserturm) at
Windtenstrasse 3 off Triester Strasse; take Tram 65 from
U-Bahn Karlsplatz (U-1/U-2/U-4). (note: the interior may be
visited on guided tours by appointment)

During the course of the 19th century Vienna witnessed the Industrial Revolution, the taming of the Danube (see no. 94), the razing of the old city walls (see no. 26) and a doubling in its population. By 1890 there were c.1.4 million inhabitants and the Favoriten pumping station was built to supply water to this burgeoning population. Designed by Franz Borkowitz (1838-1909) in 1889, it was part of a municipal scheme to bring alpine spring water to the capital from the Rax and Schneeberg mountains 75 kilometres southwest of Vienna (see no. 11). This accounts for the street name of nearby Raxstrasse.

By 1900 there were 1.7 million people in the city increasing to an all-time high of more than 2 million by 1910. The necessary creation of other more effective water facilities around the city (including a new pipeline all the way from the province of Styria) meant inevitably

The ornate Favoriten water tower

that the increasingly inadequate Favoriten pumping station would be abandoned.

Of the seven original structures that made up the station only the tower remains – but what a tower it is! Rising 67 metres into the air it can be seen from miles around (see no. 51), due in part to it being situated on high ground so that gravity could assist the water flow. Built of red brick it has an air of military strength about it and indeed as "cultural property" (according to a plaque outside) it is protected by the Hague Convention in the event of war. As so often in Vienna, the tower is wonderfully grand for a building with such a mundane purpose. Its yellow and red brick walls have stone corbels and leaded lights incorporated into them, all topped off with a roof of polychrome tiles and a church-like onion-shaped dome. Over its huge wooden doors are the words *Wasserwerk der Stadt Wien* (City of Vienna Waterworks) inscribed in gold.

This old water tower is in a park in Währing

Following its abandonment, the Favoriten water tower served variously as a storeroom and a lookout tower. Today the tower has been restored superbly and the interior, with its upward spiralling metal ramp, houses occasional temporary exhibitions. Most noteworthy is the original pumping equipment that can still be seen in its original state.

Also of interest in the context of Vienna's water supply is a charming old water tower on a hillock in Anton-Baumann-Park (18th District). Built during the late-1830s to a neo-Classical design by city architect Paul Wilhelm Eduard Sprenger (1798–1854), it formed part of an early water system commissioned by Emperor Ferdinand I (1835–48). Water taken from the Danube Canal was filtered and pumped to the tower, where gravity was used to distribute it to the growing suburbs (*Vorstädte*), including nearby Währing and Hernals.

Other places of interest nearby: 74

23rd District (Liesing), a memorial to Fridtjof Nansen in Fridtjof-Nansen-Park on Rudolf-Zeller-Gasse; take the U-6 to Alterlaa, then Bus 66A to Rudolf-Zeller-Gasse

Austria and the Arctic: other than beginning with the same letter there would seem little else to connect these two places. Yet at two separate locations in the Austrian capital can be found monuments to two highly individual characters who made their names in the frozen wastes of the Arctic Circle.

The first is the Bohemian artist Julius von Payer (1841–1915), whose simply inscribed, monumental headstone can be found close to those of the great composers in Simmering's Central Cemetery (Zentralfriedhof) (see no. 70). In 1872 he set sail with the grandly-named Austro-Hungarian North Pole Expedition aboard the three-masted schooner *Admiral Tegetthoff* under the command of Captain Karl Weyprecht (1838-1881).

The expedition's ambitious aim was to discover a navigable North East passage to the Pacific through Arctic waters north of Russia. The ship, however, became locked in ice north of Novaya Zemlya and would never see free water again. Drifting slowly northwards the crew happened upon a group of islands in the Barents Sea which they named Franz-Josefs-Land after the Austrian emperor.

It would be another two years before Weyprecht finally gave orders to abandon ship. Making use of the lifeboats, the exhausted crew eventually made landfall on the Russian coast. It was during this arduous journey that artist von Payer gained inspiration for numerous oil paintings completed on his return to Austria, notably the haunting

This bronze bust in Liesing recalls the explorer Fridtjof Nansen

Nie Zurück (No Return) that now hangs in Vienna's Museum of Military History *(Heeresgeschichtliches Museum)*. Other artefacts from the expedition can be found in the city's Natural History Museum *(Naturhistorisches Museum)*.

The second hero of the polar seas famously said, "Man wants to know, and when he ceases to do so he is no longer a man". He is the Norwegian Fridtjof Nansen (1861–1930), whose bronze head by Viennese sculptor Professor Hubert Wilfan adorns the little-known Fridtjof-Nansen-Park far out in the 23rd district of Liesing. Remembered mostly for his daring Arctic adventures, it was actually his immense body of humanitarian work that brought him the Nobel Peace Prize in 1922.

The grave of Julius von Payer in the Central Cemetery (Zentralfriedhof)

Nansen was born near Oslo and followed his mother's passion for the great outdoors by becoming an expert skier. A trip on an Arctic-bound sealing vessel in 1882 triggered an interest in the polar world as a result of which he became the first European to penetrate the interior of Greenland. He followed up his achievement with a second Arctic trip that proved ocean currents carried polar ice from east to west.

With the outbreak of the First World War Nansen became interested in international politics, and from 1920 until his death he was the Norwegian delegate to the League of Nations. In this rôle he repatriated half a million prisoners of war, including Austrians, who had fought alongside Germany and its allies. His famous "Nansen Passport" was recognised by fifty two governments enabling thousands of refugees without passports to be repatriated and resettled. These would eventually include Austrians fleeing the perils of National Socialism. The bronze memorial to Nansen in Liesing is but one of several monuments recalling the debt owed by Austria to Norway.

77 Silver Screen Vienna

23rd District (Liesing), the Rosenhügel Film Studios at Speisinger Strasse 121; take U-4 to Hietzing, then Tram 60 to Sillerplatz (note: the film halls can only be seen from the outside)

Austria's first major film production company, Wiener Kunstfilm-Industrie, was founded in 1910 by photographer Anton Kolm (1865–1922), his wife Luise, and cameraman Jacob Fleck. With international cinema dominated at the time by France, the fledgling company instead curried favour with local media and cinema owners and quickly became a pioneer in Austrian silent film.

Kolm is credited not only with producing Austria's first drama film but also its first weekly newsreel, unwittingly chronicling the last glittering years of the Austro-Hungarian monarchy. But it wasn't to last, and although Kolm's French rivals were expelled during the First World War, Wiener Kunstfilm was forced into liquidation by wealthy rival Count 'Sascha' Kolowrat (1886–1927) and his eponymous Sascha-Film.

Whilst Sascha-Film was based in the Viennese suburb of Sievering, Wiener Kunstfilm was located in Mauer, then a village on the Rosenhügel, a hill on Vienna's southern boundary. Between 1919 and 1923, Kolm re-established his company there as Vita-Film. Its 990-square metre neo-Classical Halle 1 (Stage 1), Europe's first artificially-lit studio, quickly became one of Europe's largest and most modern

Film-themed street art today adorns the huge doors of Halle 1 at the former Rosenhügel Film Studios

facilities. Before being forced out of business again, this time in 1924 by a flood of cheap American pictures, Vita-Film produced a string of films, including Austria's first silent epic, *Samson and Delila* (1922) directed by Alexander Korda (1893–1956).

In 1933, the studio was revived by Sascha-Film, now headed by industrialist Dr. Oskar Pilze (1882–1939). He added Synchron Halle 6 (Sound Stage 6), where over the next two decades many popular Viennese films starring home-grown actors Willy Forst, Paul Hörbiger, Hans Moser and Paula Wessely, were scored for full orchestra.

With the Anschluss in 1938, Rosenhügel became Wien-Film and churned out Nazi propaganda films. Finally returned to Austria in 1955, the studio enjoyed further successes, including actress Romy Schneider's three hugely popular turns as ill-fated Habsburg empress *Sisi*. Furniture and fittings from Vienna's Möbelmuseum (Furniture Museum) were used to recreate the scenes at the Habsburg court (see no. 48).

In 1965, the studio was bankrupted yet again. A stint as a television studio for the Austrian Broadcasting Corporation (ORF) followed, with *Der Bockerer* (1981) directed by veteran Austrian filmmaker Franz Antel (1913-2007) a notable success. But soon enough Rosenhügel was again under threat, this time with plans for a shopping mall. A government-backed private initiative brought respite, and in 1996 Rosenhügel was reinvented as Filmstadt Wien. When its lease with ORF ran out in 2014, the studio relocated to the newly-opened Media Quarter Marx in Landstrasse, on the site of an old abattoir, where it will remain until a new, purpose-built studio complex opens in 2024 at Hafen Wien, at the southern end of the Donaukanal.

Since then parts of the old studio complex have been swept away to make room for a series of seven apartment blocks and a supermarket. But the ghosts of Rosenhügel remain, not only in the new blocks being named after famous film studios and corporations – Atlas, Buena, Constantin, Douglas, Elios, Fox and Goldwyn – but also in Stages 1 and 6 being preserved, the former named in honour of Oskar Pilze.

Films in Vienna can today be seen in several historic cinemas. These include the Metro Kino (1951), which is operated by Austria's Film Archive in a beautiful, former 19th century theatre at Johannesgasse 4 (1st District), and the retro 1950s-styled Filmcasino at Margaretenstrasse 78 (5th District), with its mirrored façade and seductively-curved foyer. The Breitenseer Lichtspiele, which opened in 1905 in a tent before transferring in 1909 to a building at Breitenseer Strasse 21 (14th District), is the world's oldest permanently operating cinema, its 186 original wooden seats still in place.

78 Schönbrunn's Beautiful Spring

13th District (Hietzing), the Beautiful Spring *(Schöner Brunnen)* off the Obeliskenallee (to the left of the Römische Ruine) in the Schlosspark at Schloss Schönbrunn; take U-4 to Schönbrunn and enter via Meidlinger Tor

The spectacular Schlosspark of the Habsburgs' summer palace at Schönbrunn, open to the public since 1799, is a must for all interested in garden history. In amongst the formal vistas and terraces so beloved of Baroque landscape gardeners are tall, clipped hedges concealing intimate pathways and an abundance of hidden follies and oddities. Armed with the official guidebook the explorer will discover sham Roman ruins, a reproduction of Empress Maria Theresa's maze *(Irrgarten)*, an obelisk carved with scenes from Habsburg history, a great Palm House (see no. 79), and statues

Schloss Schönbrunn seen from the palace gardens

of Apollo, Hannibal and a vestal virgin, to name but a few. If there is time, a foray into the neighbouring zoo *(Tiergarten)*, the world's oldest (1752), will reveal a charming timber-framed Tyrolian farmhouse, opposite which is Crown Prince Rudolf's original wooden play hut.

However, it should not be forgotten the reason why Schönbrunn is so called. To find the answer one must escape the crowds and head to the southeastern part of the garden, between the Obeliskenallee and the Ruinenallee, where a narrow hedged walk leads to the original *Schöner Brunnen* (Beautiful Spring). Legend tells of how Emperor Maximilian II (1564–76), whilst out hunting, was impressed by the excellence of a natural spring he came across here. As a result he purchased an old mill on the nearby River Wien and converted it into a hunting lodge.

Maria Theresa's pavilion for the original Schöner Brunnen

In 1612, Emperor Matthias (1612–19) "re-discovered" the spring whilst also on a hunting foray. Such was the quality of the water emanating from the spring that by 1642 a pleasure palace (*Lustschloss*) had been built nearby for Emperor Ferdinand II's (1619–37) widow, Eleonora Gonzaga, and named *Schönbrunn* after it. Although this palace was destroyed and the well damaged during the second Turkish siege of 1683, a new imperial summer palace was soon commissioned from Baroque architect Johann Bernhard Fischer von Erlach and finished in 1713.

In the spring of 1758 a well-house was erected over the spring by court gardener Adrian van Stekhoven. Later still it fell to Empress Maria Theresa (1740–80) to modify the palace into the building we see today, now painted in its iconic mustardy yellow (*Schönbrunnergelb*) though originally coloured white or pink. It was also by her order, in 1771, that the present grotto pavilion was built over the well to a design by court architect Isidor Canevale (the monogram of the well's re-dicoverer, Emperor Matthias, can be seen on a plaque on the right-hand wall). Behind the mock stalactite and shell encrusted walls is the graceful reclining nymph *Egeria*, dispensing the sweet water from her vase into a giant scallop shell. From the time of its discovery onwards, water from the Schöner Brunnen was prized highly by the Imperial household. Indeed until an Alpine spring water supply to Vienna was instigated in the late-19th century (see no. 11), the Habsburg court drew all its water from this source. They had every drop transported to the Hofburg by mule and on long journeys even took it with them in sealed metal-lined boxes!

Other places of interest nearby: 79, 80, 83

79 The Great Palm House

13th District (Hietzing), the Palm House *(Palmenhaus)* in the Schlosspark at Schloss Schönbrunn; take U-4 to Hietzing and enter via Hietzinger Tor

A considerable part of the western side of the park at Schloss Schönbrunn, the Habsburgs' summer palace, is occupied by Vienna's famous zoo *(Tiergarten)*. It is built on the site of Emperor Franz I's (1745–65) royal menagerie established in 1752 thus making it the oldest zoo in the world.

As the husband of Empress Maria Theresa (1740–80), Franz used his wealth and power to indulge his personal interest in the natural world and to create the city's superb Natural History Museum *(Naturhistorisches Museum)* (see no. 39). He was also a keen botanist and gardener, financing expeditions to Africa and the West Indies to collect rare plant species, which were brought back species, which were brought back to Vienna.

In 1860, Emperor Franz Joseph I's (1848–1916) brother Maximilian (later and briefly Emperor of Mexico) commissioned a circumnavigation of the globe. The many resulting additions to Emperor Franz I's

The Great Palm House in the park at Schloss Schönbrunn

imperial botanical collection prompted the idea of building a great glasshouse in the Schlosspark at Schönbrunn, and the architect Franz Xaver Segenschmid (1839–1888) was commissioned to design it. After visiting notable existing glasshouses in London, Glasgow and Brussels, work on the massive wrought iron and glass structure began. Opened on 19th June 1882 by Emperor Franz Joseph himself, the Great Palm House (*Palmenhaus*) is 113 metres long with no less than 45,000 panes of glass. It is made up of three distinct pavilions, each containing plants from a different climatic zone. The 28 metre-high central pavilion is home to a temperate collection of plants that includes a pair of hundred year old palms, whilst the cold north pavilion has species that include Himalayan plants. The humid southern pavilion contains tropical rainforest plants from equatorial regions.

Although no longer the largest glasshouse in Europe, Vienna's Great Palm House is surely the most beautiful. The proportions of its convex and concave lines account for its elegant appearance in spite of the massive construction techniques employed. Unfortunately, in February 1945 three bombs fell through the roof and many of the plants froze to death. The structure was subsequently repaired and reopened in 1953 but forced to close again, this time due to serious rust damage caused by the relentless action of humidity on the ironwork. Using the very latest technology, including the installation of dirt-resistant glass, the Palm House has again been restored and is once more open to visitors eager to look inside this most graceful of greenhouses.

The only major group of exotic plants missing from the Palm House are desert plants, but these can be found in the nearby Desert House (*Wüstenhaus*). It contains an artificial cactus-filled desert landscape inhabited by exotic birds, colourful gecko lizards basking in the sun, and tiny elephant shrews scurrying around amongst the rocks and succulents. The building itself, dating from 1904, was originally used for over-wintering plants from the Great Palm House.

Just as historic as Schönbrunn's Palm House, though considerably smaller, is the former Imperial conservatory that overlooks the Burggarten behind the Hofburg's Neue Burg, once the Emperor's private garden (see no. 36). It was designed by the architect Friedrich Ohmann in 1901 in the Viennese Art Nouveau (*Jugendstil*) style and today contains a free-flying tropical butterfly collection (*Schmetterlinghaus*) as well as a very stylish, palm-filled café (*Palmenhaus*).

Other places of interest nearby: 78, 80, 83

The family history of the Habsburgs, as with that of most European
dynasties, is peppered with tales of excess and eccentricity. If this
weren't the case they would certainly not be of such interest to the
visitor today. With their sprawling empire and increasingly ornate
capital, the Habsburgs seriously indulged themselves when it came
to the matter of transport. The Imperial Carriage Museum (*Wagenburg*), for instance, housed in the former Winter Riding School at
Schloss Schönbrunn contains a red leather sedan chair embellished
with 11,000 gold-plated nails that was used solely to transport the
Archduke of Austria's hat! Comical, too, is the sausage-shaped
hunting sledge (*Wurstwagen)* of Prince Leopold of Bourbon-Salerno
(a son-in-law of Emperor Franz I), with its swivel seat that enabled
him to follow his target whilst in motion. Also on display is the
gilded scallop-shell carriage of Empress Maria Theresa (1740–80) in
which she led seven grand ladies in a *quadrille* in the splendour of
the Hofburg's Winter Riding School (*Winterreitschule*). They were
celebrating the withdrawal of Bavarian and French troops from
Bohemia. Similar in style is Maria Theresa's golden racing sleigh,
used in the courtyards of the Hofburg on snow imported specially
from the suburbs!

Most outrageous of all, however, is the gold-plated carriage used
at the coronation of Emperor Joseph II (1765–90). Weighing 4,000 kg
and tall enough to enable its occupants to stand up straight, it has
windows of bevel-edged Venetian glass and a series of painted side
panels depicting the virtues of the ruler – a veritable palace on wheels!
As if this weren't plush enough, it was pulled by eight white horses
with red velvet harnesses, topped off with ostrich feathers.

Almost as   extravagant, in the nearby Museum of Technology
(*Technisches Museum*) (see no. 83), is the luxurious saloon carriage
used by Emperor Franz Joseph I's wife Elisabeth (*Sisi*) when travelling
by rail. It was built in 1873 and fitted out with the finest upholstery,
furniture and candelabra.

On the topic of railways something else related to Habsburg travel
can be found in Hietzing, it is the so-called Hofpavillon (Court Pavilion)
that straddles the platforms of today's U-Bahn station. It was designed
in 1898–99 by the famous architect Otto Wagner (1841-1918), together

with his pupil Leopold Bauer, as well as Josef Maria Olbrich, the creator of the famous Secession building on Karlsplatz. The sole purpose of this miniature palace in the Viennese Art Nouveau (*Jugendstil*) style was to provide private access for Emperor Franz Joseph I (1848–1916) to his own imperial train (*Kaiserzug*) on Vienna's metropolitan railway (*Stadtbahn*). The railway had only recently been laid out by Wagner (see no. 46), who took the opportunity to ingratiate himself with the Emperor by building him a station for use during his summer stays at nearby Schönbrunn.

The private railway station built at Schönbrunn for the Habsburgs

The station is entered through a graceful iron canopy topped with golden crowns, below which arriving imperial carriages could find shelter. Inside is a domed octagonal waiting room on the wall of which is a specially commissioned painting depicting a bird's eye view of the new railway itself. It was intended "to shorten the seconds spent waiting by the monarch with the sight of a work of art". Incorporated into the finely crafted wood panelling can be seen designs based on the Emperor's late wife Elisabeth's favourite flower, the split-leaved Philodendron.

Unfortunately for Wagner, despite all the effort and grandeur he lavished on this little building, the Emperor only seems to have used the station at most twice, a fact which has been put down to his famous distrust of all things modern (see no. 36).

Other places of interest nearby: 78, 79, 83

81 Klimt's Last Studio

13th District (Hietzing), the Klimt Villa at Feldmühlgasse 11; take U-4 to Unter St. Veit

Gustav Klimt's *The Kiss* is the world's most famous painted embrace. Its presence in Vienna has long attracted visitors, where the familiar image has found its way onto everything from cufflinks to dog jackets. But what of the studios where the enigmatic artist conjured up such trail-blazing imagery? Until recently all were considered lost.

Klimt (1862-1918) was born in 1862, one of seven children to a Bohemian goldsmith. The family's modest home at Linzer Strasse 247 (14th District), however, has long since given way to modern buildings. After attending Vienna's University of Applied Arts (*Universität für angewandte Kunst*) Klimt commenced work as a decorative painter. Commissions included the Hermes Villa for the imperial household, as well as the newly-built Burgtheater and Kunsthistorisches Museum, all in the emperor's beloved Historicist style.

But Historicism was backwards-looking, and Vienna felt staid when compared with Paris, where Impressionism was causing a sensation. In response Klimt co-founded the Wiener Secession, which quickly established itself as a fully-fledged Viennese take on Art Nouveau. Historicism would no longer hold Vienna back in the arts.

When the Secession fell apart in 1905 Klimt continued alone to develop further the idiosyncratic styles for which he is now known. How far he had already come can be gauged by the furore caused when he unveiled a series of ceiling murals commissioned by the University of Vienna. Branded pornographic by academics, Klimt returned his fee and removed the pictures. He vowed never to work for the state again.

By this time Klimt was working in his second studio at Josefstädter Strasse 21 (8th District), where he painted *The Kiss*. He had moved there in 1892 after vacating his first studio at Sandwirtgasse 8 (6th District), in which he had been ensconced since 1883. Neither is extant today although both carry commemorative plaques, as does the house at Westbahnstrasse 36 (7th District), where Klimt lived with his mother and sisters.

In 1912 Klimt moved studio yet again, this time to a single-story garden house on Feldmühlgasse in Unter St. Veit (13th District). The property was owned by a furniture manufacturer, one Joseph Herrmann, whose daughter married the painter Felix Albrecht Harta. Through this artistic connection the property was rented to Klimt, and it was there in

The so-called Klimt Villa in Hietzing incorporating Klimt's last studio on the ground floor

February 1918 that he succumbed to a fatal stroke. He had been working simultaneously on two works, *The Bride* and *Lady with Fan*.

Klimt's friend, fellow artist and neighbour Egon Schiele (1890-1918) pleaded for the studio to be left untouched in tribute to the artist – but it wasn't to be. Within months Schiele, too, was dead. Whilst the contents of the studio fell into private hands, the building itself was assumed lost after the Herrmanns erected a villa on the site in 1923, which later sold to a well-to-do Jewish family. It was therefore a complete surprise when plans unearthed only in 1998 revealed the exciting reality that the walls of the old studio had actually been incorporated into the new building.

Both villa and studio have subsequently been renovated and turned over to the Comenius Institute, for use as a museum and cultural centre. Contemporary photographs and eyewitness accounts have helped with the work. Schiele, for example, described the reception room with its collection of East Asian art, and painter Carl Moll (1861-1945) alluded to the room where Klimt's models – "several were at his beck and call" – undressed.

Klimt himself had the studio's north-facing picture window installed, and also planted the semi-wild cottage garden, filled with shrub roses and fruit trees. He captured something of it in his *Orchard with Roses* (1912). Although long lost it is hoped one day that the garden will be re-planted. One can imagine Klimt in his trademark indigo-blue kimono nodding his head in approval.

82 A Unique Housing Estate

13th District (Hietzing), the Werkbundsiedlung Housing Estate at Woinovichgasse/Veitingergasse (off Jagdschloss-gasse); take U-4 to Hietzing and then Tram 60 to Jagdschlossgasse

Due to its close proximity to the Habsburgs' summer residence at Schönbrunn, the 13th district of Hietzing has long been a desirable address. A thematic tour can be made of the area's many fine villas built in varying styles. These include *Biedermeier* (the former home of actress and imperial mistress Katharina Schratt at Gloriettegasse 9), *Jugendstil* (Friedrich Ohmann's Villa Schopp at Gloriettegasse 21; Villa Langer at Beckgasse 30 by Jože Plečnik; and the Mietvilla at Stoessegasse 2 by Ferdinand Meissner), and Modernism (Josef Hoffman's Villa Skywa-Primavesi at Gloriettegasse 14; and the Villa Beer by Josef Frank at Wenzgasse 12). There are also five villas by Modernist architect Adolf Loos, famous for his austere designs and adherence to functionalism (Villa Scheu at Larochegasse 3, Villa Strasse at Kupelwiesergasse 28, the barrel-vaulted Villa Steiner at St-Veit-Gasse 10, Villa Rufer at Schliessmanngasse 11, and Villa Horner at Nothartgasse 7).

Modernist housing by André Lurçat at the Werkbundsiedlung housing estate in Hietzing

However, there is something else in Hietzing that will delight any explorer interested in architecture. From the tram stop at Jagdschloss-gasse it makes for a pleasant quarter hour to walk uphill passing at number 36 the old hunting lodge after which Jagdschlossgasse is named. At the top on the right is the so-called *Werkbundsiedlung*, a model housing estate of 70 houses that couldn't differ more from Hietzing's traditional villas.

Founded in Germany in 1907, the Werkbund was somewhat similar to England's Arts and Crafts Movement, though it was not opposed to reaping the financial rewards made possible by mass-production. In 1930–1932, Vienna's Socialist city council organised a Werkbund Housing Exhibition based on one held successfully in Stuttgart in 1927. A group of international Modernist architects were invited to design and build affordable, two-bedroom family homes in a restricted space. It was hoped the homes would provide an innovative alternative to the vast social housing blocks erected in Vienna during the 1920s (see no. 95). Set side-by-side, so that their qualities could be judged comparatively, the houses were the work of Vienna's own Adolf Loos, Margarete Schütte-Lihotzky and Josef Hoffmann, Frenchman André Lurçat, American Richard Neutra, and Dutchman Gerrit Rietveld, among others. Meant only to be temporary, the geometric, Bauhaus-style houses, were bought up and rented out by the city council in 1934 having proved too expensive for prospective purchasers. Remarkably they are still standing today and remain as novel-looking as ever.

Although four of the Wekbundsiedlung houses were lost in the Second World War, the rest are still lived in having been renovated in the 1980s. A small information centre at Woinovichgasse 32, designed by the exhibition's director Josef Frank, contains plans and cut-away models, as well as a fascinating panoramic photograph of the site in 1932, uncluttered by the tall trees and later buildings that have now hidden the estate from view.

By way of a complete contrast, visit the Margaretenhof housing estate, with its traditional street lanterns, cobblestones and profusion of Historicist details, at the junction of Pilgramgasse and Margaretenstrasse, in the 5th district of Margareten. The ensemble is like a period drama film set awaiting its actors.

83 The Austrian Steel Revolution

14th District (Penzing), the Technical Museum *(Technisches Museum)* at Mariahilfer Strasse 212; take U-4 to Schönbrunn and walk up through the Auer-Welsbach-Park

Anyone remotely interested in things technical, such as mining and industry, energy and transport, and even the development of musical instruments, should visit Vienna's superb Museum of Technology *(Technisches Museum)*. Amongst the thousands of fascinating objects, many of which reflect Austria's contribution to the development of modern technology, is the so-called *Marcuswagen*, an early automobile created in 1888 by Vienna-based German-Jewish inventor Siegfried Marcus (see no. 71). Exhibits relating to other important Austrian inventions abound. They include the world's first water-powered turbine

The huge Vessel 1 from VOEST's Linz factory in the Technical Museum

used to generate electricity, designed by Viktor Kaplan (1876–1934) after he had graduated from Vienna's University of Technology. In 1891, the Austrian chemist Carl Auer von Welsbach (1858–1929) invented the incandescent gas light by impregnating gas mantles with metal oxides that glow. In 1848–54, the engineer Karl Ritter von Ghega (1802–1860) built the world's first mountain railway across the Semmering Pass, and in 1821 the Austrian forestry official Josef Ressel (1793–1857), whose job it was to supply timber for shipbuilding, designed an early ship's propeller based on the Archimedes' Screw.

Although the country that lays claim to being the cradle of the European Industrial Revolution is Great Britain, notably in the development of iron and steel production, there is one process that originated in Austria. During the late-19th century, the heartland of Austria's mining and metal industries was the province of Upper Styria. It was here in 1881 that the Austrian-Alpine Coal & Mining Company was created, with its headquarters in Donawitz. Following a forced merger in 1938 with the Hermann Göring Works in Linz, the group came eventually to be known as VOEST-ALPINE AG. Assisted by investment made possible after the Second World War by the Marshall Plan, VOEST became central to Austria's nationalised industry and has to this day continued to carve out new markets for itself.

Dominating the Museum of Technology's Heavy Industry Hall is a vast metal crucible from VOEST's Linz factory. Known as Vessel 1, it was used in 1952 in the first commercial production of steel by the so-called Basic Oxygen Process (BOP). Pioeneered by VOEST, the process enables large quantities of molten pig iron to be refined quickly into steel by the high-speed injection of pure oxygen. In this way up to 300 tons of iron can be turned into steel in little more than twenty minutes. The importance of the discovery of this technique is illustrated by the fact that two thirds of the world's steel is today smelted using what is known as the Linz-Donawitz (or LD) process.

Vessel 1 was one of a pair of crucibles commissioned specially for the job from the Gutehoffnung plant at Oberhausen in Germany's Ruhr Valley. It towers over a nearby Bessemer Converter of 1866 on whose basic principles, developed in 1855 by English inventor Henry Bessemer (1813-1898), the revolutionary process was based.

An important new permanent exhibition in the Technical Museum is called Inventory Number 1938. The issue of the restitution of artworks stolen by the Nazis is an ongoing topic in Vienna but it is often forgotten that they stole everyday items, too, including cars and cameras. The exhibition redresses the balance and is the first in the German-speaking world to do so.

Other places of interest nearby: 78, 79, 80

84 The Villas of Otto Wagner

14th District (Penzing), Otto-Wagner-Villas I and II at the junction of Bujattigasse and Hüttelbergstrasse; take Tram 49 from U-Bahn Volkstheater (U-2/U-3) to terminus at Hütteldorf-Bujattigasse

The Viennese architect Otto Wagner (1841–1918) is often associated with Gustav Klimt's Secession movement of 1897, in which like-minded artists and architects rebelled against what they saw as the backwards-looking and restricting Historicist style, as typified by the buildings of the Ringstrasse. Out of the Secession grew the Viennese version of Art Nouveau (*Jugendstil*), in which both Klimt (see no. 81) and Wagner made a lasting name for themselves (see nos. 46, 80 & 85).

It is interesting, however, to note that both men learned their trade in the very Historicist school they were soon to detest. Wagner's conversion to *Jugendstil*, and in time to Modernism, can be illustrated very clearly at several sites across the city. A prime example is on the Graben where he is responsible for two closely situated buildings, namely the Historicist Graben-Hof (1876) at numbers 14–15 and the later, less formal-looking Ankerhaus (1894) at number 10. The latter is a much lighter affair, its modern iron girder construction left deliberately visible and topped off with Wagner's own stylish roof studio, occupied later by the artist Friedensreich Hundertwasser (1928-2000).

Similarly, at Rennweg 3 in the 3rd district of Landstrasse, Wagner's own townhouse (1891) seems decidedly old fashioned, despite its trademark projecting cornice, when compared with the austere Modernist façade of his last home on the first floor at Döblergasse 4 (1912) in the 7th district of Neubau, where he lived and worked until his death in 1918. The façade of the latter is broken only by minimal decoration of blue tiles and aluminium. Even Wagner's two famous apartments overlooking the Naschmarkt at Linke Wienzeile 38–40 (1899), with their mass of floral *Jugendstil* motifs, appear somewhat busy when compared to his Modernist work.

Most at odds, however, are his two villas on Hüttelbergstrasse in the 14th district of Penzing, designed at either ends of his career. Otto-Wagner-Villa I at number 26 was built in 1888 as his summer residence and takes the form of a grand Italianate villa with classical colonnaded portico. Sold in 1911 it was saved from ruin in 1972 by the *Fantastic Realism* artist Ernst Fuchs (1930-2015) who converted the building into his own private museum (Ernst-Fuchs-Privatstiftung).

Otto-Wagner-Villa I, now the Ernst Fuchs Private Foundation, at Hüttelbergstrasse 26 in Penzing

It was Fuchs who added the fertility goddess at the front, as well as the coloured cornice and fountain house nearby.

In stark contrast, next-door at number 28, is the Villa Wagner II to where Wagner moved in 1913 (not open to the public). Its austere Modernist exterior of whitewashed concrete and aluminium is relieved only by a glass mosaic over the door by Viennese Secessionist artist Koloman Moser (1868-1918) and a few blue tiles. The latter echo his Döblergasse house, as well as a sluice house (*Schützenhaus*) he designed on the Danube Canal (see no. 96).

Despite his relentless move towards Modernism, Wagner ended up being buried in a surprisingly traditional Historicist-style tomb in the cemetery at Hietzing (*Hietzinger Friedhof*), where Klimt is also buried, which he designed many years before. In architectural terms Otto Wagner had come full circle.

To discover more about Otto Wagner's work visit Wagner:Werk, a museum in the Austrian Postal Savings Bank (*Österreichische Postsparkasse*) at Georg-Coch-Platz 2 (1st District). Completed in 1912 the building is a key work of European Modernity and illustrates well his belief that the functionality of each constructive detail (witness the visible aluminium rivets on the exterior) and each internal decorative feature should result in an honest, intelligent and aesthetic structure.

85 Respite on Lemon Mountain

14th District (Penzing), the Steinhof Church *(Kirche Am Steinhof)* at Otto-Wagner-Spital, Baumgartner Höhe 1; take Bus 48A from U-Bahn Volkstheater (U-2/U-3)

The architect Otto Wagner (1841–1918) was responsible for some of Vienna's most idiosyncratic architecture, including villas (see no. 84), railway stations (see nos. 46 & 80), river weirs (see no. 96) and a savings 'bank (see no. 58). He excelled at fusing functional features with the prevailing decorative style in vogue at the time. In *fin de siècle* Vienna this was more often than not Wagner's own take on European Art Nouveau, known in the German-speaking world as *Jugendstil.*

Wagner's last commissioned work was a magnificent church, noteworthy for being Vienna's only place of worship rendered entirely in the *Jugendstil* idiom. Positioned on a high point over looking the terraced pavilions of the Baumgartner Höhe psychiatric hospital in Penzing (14th District), Wagner's Church of St. Leopold (known also as the Steinhof Church after quarries in neighbouring Ottakring) was constructed between 1904 and 1907. Since it forms but one element of the overall hospital plan, itself dictated by the geography of the Gallitzin Hill *(Gallitzinberg)* on which it is built, the church unusually faces north instead of the more usual east. With functionality never far from his thoughts, Wagner used this unorthodox aspect to maximise the natural therapeutic light flooding into the building. This made it quite unlike traditional churches whose east-west alignment so often resulted in the dark and mysterious interiors usually favoured by the Viennese.

As Vienna's first truly modern church, and possibly the world's first example of ecclesiastical functionalism, Wagner deployed not only Jugendstill design motifs including patinated copper angels and gilded wreathes but also several new construction techniques, including plasterboarded ceilings and thin marble slabs bolting onto the building's brick-built superstructure. Its striking copper dome, however, nicknamed the *Limoniberg* (Lemon Mountain) because of the way it glints in the sun, still harks back to the traditional onion-shaped towers of Baroque churches.

The interior of the church is also novel in being an open cube, rather than a long hall cluttered with columns, affording each member of the congregation a clear view. Designed first and foremost with the hospital's infirm patients in mind, Wagner ensured that the pews had no sharp edges and were laid out so as to be easy to supervise. Similarly, the floor is sloping to facilitate cleaning, and the stoups had running water to prevent spread of infection. He even designed special robes for the priests and envisaged the church as a place of worship for all creeds. The only real decoration inside this calm contemplative place is the gilded altar canopy and Kolo Moser's stained-glass windows through which daylight can stream and lift the troubled souls within.

On returning back down the hill look out for Otto Wagner's oft-overlooked Viennese Art Nouveau theatre (*Jugendstiltheater*) that also makes up part of the now-disused hospital complex.

It is worth bearing in mind too that the winter visitor to the Kirche am Steinhof may be privy to one of the wonders of the natural world. At dusk each night from late October

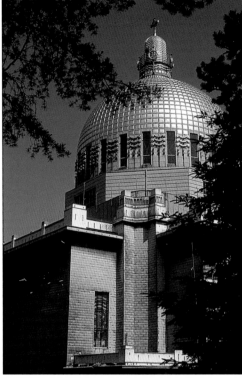

Otto Wagner's Kirche am Steinhof high on the Gallitzinberg

onwards, an estimated 140,000 rooks fly from their foraging grounds 30 kilometres away to, the tall trees of Baumgartner Höhe, where they spend the night in one of the largest rook dormitories in Europe. Each autumn they migrate from Eastern Europe to the slightly warmer climes of Central Europe, and Vienna seems to be a favourite destination.

Between 1940 and 1945, the hospital on Baumgartner Höhe was commandeered by the Nazi regime as part of its medical killing and "racial hygiene" programme. At the Am Spiegelgrund children's hospital, close to 800 children were murdered in a series of barbaric experiments designed to prepare their brains for post-mortem "research". Incredibly one of the doctors in charge, Heinrich Gross, evaded punishment and even became a leading forensic psychiatrist in post-war Vienna. Only recently has the story of Am Spielgrund come to light, with a memorial to the children on the site and their hitherto preserved brains now respectfully interred in the Central Cemetery.

86 All Change at Westbahnhof

15th District (Rudolfsheim-Fünfhaus), the Westbahnhof railway station on Neubaugürtel; take U-3 or U-6 to Westbahnhof

On 14th December 2009, the fabled Orient Express pulled into Vienna's Westbahnhof at the top of Mariahilferstrasse one last time, a victim of new high-speed trains and budget airlines. Not long afterwards the increasingly tired station terminus was dramatically overhauled. Now as much a shopping centre as a station, it contains reminders of a past both glorious and grim.

The Westbahnhof first opened in 1858 to service trains connecting Vienna with Salzburg, Bavaria, and beyond. It was a grand affair realised in Emperor Franz Joseph's preferred Historicist style, a méiange of Renaissance pavilions and Gothic turrets, with Tuscan-style arcades to afford protection in bad weather. There was statuary, too, including a Carrara marble of the wasp-waisted Empress Sisi. She used what became known as the Empress Elisabeth Railway to reach her Bavarian homeland, as well as the Habsburg retreat at Bad Ischl. The station's train shed consisted of four platforms beneath a glass-and-iron roof over a hundred metres long. It is difficult now to imagine how it must have appeared when filled with smoke and steam, porters and carts.

Many Austrian visitors to the 1873 World Exhibition, which was staged in Vienna, disembarked from trains at the Westbahnhof. Substantial numbers of international visitors did so, too, including a large contingent of English visitors, escorted personally by pioneering travel agent Thomas Cook (1808-1892).

As the railway age sped forward, so the capacity of the Westbahnhof was expanded. It was all change, however, with the arrival of Nazism, when, in common with Vienna's other main stations, the Westbahnhof began serving a darker purpose. The statue of a young Jewish boy sitting on his suitcase reminds today's travellers of the *Kindertransport* trains that departed Nazi-occupied Europe for the safety of Britain in the months before the outbreak of war. A wall plaque meanwhile recalls the one hundred and fifty Austrians transported from the station in 1938 to the concentration camp at Dachau.

Shortly before the end of the war the station was badly damaged during an air raid, its façade shattered and the roof of the engine shed collapsed. Although the line was soon cleared, it was decided to demolish the station, and in 1949 the site was levelled. It was the end of an era and only old photographs recall the grandeur that was forever lost.

The new Westbahnhof looked very different when it was unveiled in 1952. The ornate pavilions and arcades were replaced by a sleek, modernist open-plan arrivals hall illuminated by a glass facade. Beyond were eleven platforms reached by escalators, and later a direct connection was made with the city's U-Bahn network. All that survived from the old station was the marble statue of Sisi, which had unexpectedly turned up in 1982 in a council warehouse.

The new station was revamped in 2009, in line with trends seen at other European transport hubs. As Bahnhof-

This memorial at the Westbahnhof recalls the Kindertransport trains of the Second World War

City Wien West the station is now a multifunctional space offering not only transport connections but also shops, office space, catering facilities and a hotel. The opening in 2014 of Vienna's huge new Main Station (*Hauptbahnhof*) inevitably robbed the Westbahnhof of many of its international departures. Like the Westbahnhof, however, the new station also had a grand predecessor, the Südbahnhof. Built in 1869, destroyed during the war, and rebuilt in the 1950s, it too contains a memory of the old days in the form of a battered sculpture of the Lion of St. Mark (a reminder that trains departed from here to Venice). Further artefacts from the old station are displayed in a series of showcases in and around the nearby Quartier Belvedere S-Bahn station.

Many visitors arriving in Vienna at the Hauptbahnhof will proceed to the culture-rich First District, with its traditional visitor attractions. For a tour of Vienna with a difference, why not try a Shades Tour, which departs from just outside the Hauptbahnhof (www.shades-tours.com). These two-hour tours of the city are given by homeless people, shedding light not only on some less frequented corners of the city but also the complex world of homelessness itself. Taking the tour helps support the social reintegration of just a few of the city's almost 10,000 homeless people.

Other places of interest nearby: 48, 51

87 In Praise of Concrete

16th District (Ottakring), the Church of the Holy Ghost (Heilig-Geist-Kirche) at Herbststrasse 82; take Tram 9 to Gersthof from Schweglerstrasse U-Bahn (U-3)

Vienna is a sacred city and rightly proud of its very many Catholic churches. From soaring Gothic to gilded Baroque, the place boasts myriad well-documented places of worship. Concealed in its suburbs, however, lurk other more recent architectural gems that use concrete to reach the heavens.

Austria's first concrete church was unveiled in 1913 in Ottakring (16th District). The Parish Church of the Holy Ghost (*Heilig-Geist-Kirche*) at Herbststrasse 82 is the work of Slovenian architect Jože Plečnik (1872-1957), a student of renowned Viennese town planner Otto Wagner. (1841-1918). But whereas Wagner favoured clearly-defined *Jugendstil*, Plečnik pioneered an altogether more eclectic idiom.

His heavy classical frontage, for example, is deceiving since it gives onto an open space more in the tradition of early Christian basilicas. Unfettered by columns it is lit by a stained glass clerestory, which

The concrete Parish Church of the Holy Ghost in Ottakring

also illuminates an altar adorned with an aluminium dove and golden sunburst. A mosaic on the back wall illustrates the seven attributes of the Holy Ghost. The eclecticism continues in the crypt, where Klimt-like murals stand guard over a trio of grottoes. Little wonder the conservative Habsburgs decried the building as a mixture "of a temple to Venus, a Russian bath and a stable"!

By the 1930s, politics had got in the way of praise. The Christ-königskirche on Vogelweidplatz in Rudolfsheim-Fünfhaus (15th District) is a case in point. The unfussy concrete structure was consecrated in 1934 as a memorial to recently-deceased church dignitary and politician Ignaz Seipel. A member of Karl Lueger's Christian Social Party and twice Federal Chancellor, Seipel courted wealthy industrialists and paramilitary units in his quest to restore the Austrian economy. His policies resulted in the July Revolt of 1927 whereafter the Social Democrats dubbed him the "Bloody Prelate".

Back in neighbouring Ottakring, the Pfarrkirche Sandleiten on Sandleitengasse appeared around the same time. Part of a church building programme initiated by the doomed Austrofascist regime of Chancellor Engelbert Dollfuss (1892-1934) it was a riposte to the anti-clerical policies of the Social Democrats.

A further pair of concrete churches dates from the 1970s. The Kirche Maria Namen on Hasnerstrasse (16th District) was consecrated in 1974 but it was much longer in the making. The first place of worship on the site was no more than a timber warehouse pressed into service as a chapel in 1930. Only after the Second World War were plans drawn up for the austere building seen today.

Fritz Wotruba's church in Liesing

The Kirche zur Heiligsten Dreifaltigkeit on the St. Georgenberg in Liesing (23rd District) also has a secret past in that it occupies the former site of a *Wehrmacht* barracks building. Unveiled in 1976 to a design by sculptor Fritz Wotruba (1907–1975), the Wotrubakirche, as it is best known, is made up of 152 concrete blocks stacked seemingly haphazardly. Viewed a different way, however, and the startling structure illustrates the atheist Wotruba's belief that out of apparent chaos comes harmony.

Vienna's penchant for ecclesiastical concrete comes full circle with the Donaucity-Kirche in Donaustadt (22nd District). Consecrated in 2000, it takes the form of a cross-shaped box made from Styrian steel, the result of a competition to design a church that could hold its own amongst the surrounding high rises. By day portholes illuminate the interior, which then shine like a ship at night. The simple interior is clad with birch wood and features a curving skylight representing Christ's wound on the Cross.

To the rear of the church, a staircase leads down to community rooms whose stark concrete walls are enlivened by children's paintings. Parish meetings, coffee mornings, plays and exhibitions are staged here, without disturbing the sanctity of the church above.

Other places of interest nearby: 51

88 Outer Suburbs, Outer Space

16th District (Ottakring), the Kuffner Observatory (*Kuffner Sternwarte*) on Johann-Staud-Strasse 10; take U-3 to Ottakring and then Bus 46B to Ottakringer Bad

It comes as no surprise to learn that a city of learning such as Vienna has long been associated with in the study of astronomy. The Urania building, moored like a great white ship on the banks of the Danube Canal at the end of Stubenring (1st District), contains Austria's very first public astronomical observatory. Named after the Greek goddess of astronomy, it was designed in 1910 by architect Max Fabiani (1865-1962) as an adult education centre for the enlightenment of the people, a role it continues to fulfil to this day. Should the city's light and air pollution be too great or the sky overcast, however, budding astronomers can head instead to the Planetarium at the Volksprater (2nd District). Here, by means of a 2.5 ton Zeiss projector, the stars and planets of the night sky are reproduced perfectly on the inside of a 13 metre-high dome.

For those after the real thing, however, Vienna has two other observatories built on suitable highpoints free of dust and smoke in the city's northwestern suburbs. The University Observatory (*Universitätssternwarte*) lies behind the high walls of Sternwartepark on Sternwartestrasse in the 18th district of Währing (note: visitors to the grounds are warned not to stray off the path due to beehives and overhanging trees!). The grand brick building was constructed in 1880. Its porticoed entrance to shelter arriving carriages gives access to a grand staircase and long residential wing that leads to the observatory. Its main central dome contains a large refractor telescope (i.e. one whose main focussing element is a lens) seated on a 15 metre-high, structurally independent column in order to minimise vibrations. Made in Dublin, it was the largest telescope in the world when first installed. Smaller refractors terminate the building's three shorter wings, one of which is a so-called Comet Catcher.

To the southwest, on the slopes of the Gallitzinberg, is the charming Kuffner Observatory (*Kufner Sternwarte*). It was erected in 1886 as a private observatory by Moriz von Kuffner (1854-1939), a Jewish brewer whose family were responsible for reversing the declining fortunes of the famous Ottakringer Brewery. Now restored beautifully, one of the observatory's two domes has glazed plaques incorporated into it bearing the names of history's great astronomers, including

Copernicus and Galileo. It is a device repeated in the Chemical Institute on Schottentor (e.g. Bunsen and Liebig), as well as the Natural History Museum (e.g. Marco Polo and James Cook) and the Kunsthistorisches Museum (e.g. Rembrandt and Leonardo Da Vinci). Since 1946 the Kuffner Observatory has been used as an education centre, where visitors can observe the night sky using Kuffner's original telescope and other high quality instruments.

The Kuffner Astronomical Observatory in Ottakring

Also providing a good view of the night sky, as well as the surrounding area, is a fine brick-built *belvedere* tower on a hillock in Währing's Türkenschanzpark (18th District), built to celebrate the 200th anniversary of the expulsion of the Ottoman Turks, as well as the forty-year reign of Emperor Franz Joseph I (1848–1916). It is called the Paulinenwarte after the Viennese socialite Princess Pauline von Metternich, who financed the surrounding park.

Other worthwhile lookouts in Vienna include the Jubiläumswarte on the Satzberg (433 metres) next to Johann-Staud-Strasse 80 in Ottakring, and the Hubertuswarte on top of the Kaltbründlberg (508 metres) in Hietzing's Lainzer Tiergarten, a former Imperial hunting reserve where Emperor Franz Joseph I built the romantic Hermesvilla for his wife Elisabeth (*Sisi*).

Grandest of all is the fairytale Habsburgwarte, a Habsburg tower constructed in 1888 on the Hermannskogel at the edge of Döbling, which at 542 metres is the highest point within Vienna's city limits. It is possible to climb its narrow spiral stairs to the top from where a wonderful view of the surrounding Vienna Woods (*Wienerwald*) can be gained. In springtime the ground is covered with aromatic wild garlic (*Bärlauch*), which is used in seasonal Viennese cooking.

89 The Schirach Bunker

16th District (Ottakring), the Schirach-Bunker on Johann-Staud-Strasse; take Tram 46 from Thaliastrasse U-Bahn station to Ottakring U-Bahn station, then Bus 46B to Feuerwache Am Steinhof, then Bus 52B to Siedlung Kordon, then walk

Western Allied bombers first appeared in the skies over Vienna on March 17th 1944. Fifty more raids followed during which twenty percent of the city was razed to the ground. Each time the city's sirens were sounded, the instruction to do so was orchestrated from the so-called Schirach-Bunker on the Gallitzinberg, a hillside in the district of Ottakring (16th District).

Wild rumours have long surrounded the Schirach-Bunker, a ruined Second World War military command centre *(Gaugefechtsstand)*. It has been variously described as a luxuriously appointed, ten storey-deep bolt hole for Nazi grandees, a secret weapons' dump and treasury, even a home to Adolf Hitler's private collection of weaponry – but none of this is true.

In reality the Schirach-Bunker located on on Johann-Staud-Strasse was used primarily by Nazi German forces, the Wehrmacht, as a bomb-proof command and control centre *(Kommandozentrale)*, from where air raid alarms and the aerial defence of Vienna could be coordinated. Between 1942 and 1945 forced labourers were made to dig a twenty five metre long staircase into the hillside near the Jubiläumswarte, an observervation tower erected in 1889 to commemorate the fiftieth anniversary of Franz Joseph I becoming Austrian emperor (the present tower was erected in 1956). The workers then excavated a hundred metre long tunnel, at the end of which was the command centre itself: sixteen and a half metres long, five metres wide and high, and two storeys deep.

Whenever incoming Allied bomber raids were detected, a radio alert would be broadcast to the Viennese people from the first floor of the bunker: "Achtung, Achtung, hier Luftschutzsender Wien" (Attention, attention, this is air raid transmitter Vienna). The words were preceded by the seemingly innocuous but much-feared sound of a cuckoo (the more familiar sound of air raid sirens were activated as a result). The lower level of the bunker was noticeably better furnished and contained the quarters of Vienna's regional leader (Gauleiter), Baldur von Schirach (1907-1974), although in reality he only visited rarely.

A watch tower in the woods marks the site of the so-called Schirach Bunker

On 4th April 1945, with the Red Army barely three kilometres away in Hütteldorf, the Wehrmacht abandoned the Schirach-Bunker. Vienna was liberated shortly afterwards, and six months later the entrances to the bunker were sealed.

Little remains to be seen of the bunker today, and none of it can be entered by the casual visitor. There are, however, on the hillside surrounding the Jubiläumswarte, some tantalising remains: bricked-up entrances to the bunker's drainage canals, foundations of barracks, and most impressively three cylindrical guard towers, which once protected the entrance to the bunker. Fortunately the only cuckoos to be heard these days are real ones.

90   Land of the Wild Geese

17th District (Hernals), the Schwarzenbergpark on Neuwald-
egger Strasse; take U-6 to Alser Strasse then Tram 43 to
terminus at Neuwaldegg and enter via Waldegghofgasse/
Schwarzenbergallee

Tram 43 cuts like a knife across the 17th District of Hernals, from the
Gürtel out to the edge of the city. Although the journey holds little of
real interest (except for the Art Nouveau Jörgerbad and the Kalvarienberg pilgrimage church, see nos. 72 & 93) the terminus at Neuwaldegg
provides a gateway to something very special.

Just beyond the terminus is Waldegghofgasse, and half way
along there is a right turn that drops down onto Schwarzenbergallee.
This poker-straight avenue lined with mature trees is no ordinary
suburban thoroughfare. At the lower end stands the magnificent
Schloss Neuwaldegg whilst at the other end are two towering
obelisks, which form an entrance to an 80 hectare swathe of wild
woodland known as the Schwarzenbergpark. Since the late 1950s,
when the area was opened up by the City of Vienna, walkers have
come here to enjoy the untamed woodland of what was once
Europe's largest landscape garden.

Visiting the Schwarzenbergpark is an intriguing experience, because
it's now indistinguishable from the surrounding Vienna Woods. It probably looked much the same back in 1765, too, when a wealthy soldier
of fortune, Count Franz Moritz Lacy (1725–1801), purchased the land
together with Schloss Neuwaldegg. Adhering to the principles of the
then-fashionable back-to-nature movement, Lacy cleared the woodland
and imposed an entirely planned landscape. It was the first great
landscape garden in Austria, inspired by the pioneering work of English
gardening guru Lancelot "Capability" Brown.

Made up of rolling hills and sweeping vistas, Lacy Park as it was
known then was punctuated by clumps of trees, ponds and streams,
and all manner of architectural novelties. These included a Chinese
pavilion, a miniaturised Garden of Eden, and a model village or
Hameau, comprising seventeen thatched chalets (one of which is
still standing), where Lacy's guests could experience the simple
pleasures of country living.

Lacy was born in St. Petersburg, where his father, Count Peter
von Lacy (1678–1751), was a successful military commander. He was
not Russian though. English suppression and religious intolerance

had forced him and others to flee their native Ireland, selling their military skills along the way to various ruling Catholic families. Collectively they were known as the Wild Geese (*Na Géanna Fiáne*).

The grave of Count Lacy hidden in the woods of Schwarzenbergpark

Lacy Junior did likewise and settled in Austria, where he became a highly paid field marshal and statesmen for Empress Maria Theresa (1740–1780). He received her military order for services rendered during the Seven Years' War with Prussia (1756–63) and went on to become a close adviser to Emperor Joseph II (1765–90). A century later and another wild goose, Max O'Donnell (1812–1895), would save the young Emperor Franz Joseph I from an assassin's blade on the Mölkerbastei at Schottentor (see no. 56).

During Lacy's lifetime, he opened his park to the public, and it became popular with day-trippers. After his death it was acquired by the Schwarzenbergs, one of the Habsburg Empire's most powerful aristocratic families. Prince Charles of Schwarzenberg (1771- 1820) beat Napoleon at the Battle of Leipzig in 1813, so it is little wonder the park still carries his rather than Lacy's name today.

Over time, however, the park returned to its original natural state, and today only ghosts remain: an overgrown pond here, a pile of toppled stones there, and everywhere paths winding off into the leafy gloom. One of the few remaining structures is Lacy's own tomb, a miniature classical temple erected at the top of a track running up from Hohenstrasse. Surrounded by rusted railings and dense beech woods, it's a melancholy resting place, as is the nearby ruinous tomb of his favourite horse, *Timurlanka*. Looking out at the enveloping wilderness the scene inevitably evokes Percy Bysshe Shelley's *Ozymandias*: "Look on my works, ye Mighty, and despair!"

91 Fire at the Ringtheater

18th District (Währing), statues in the Pötzleinsdorfer
Schlosspark on Pötzleinsdorfer Strasse; take Tram 41
to Pötzleinsdorf

Vienna's famous Ringstrasse, the imposing nineteenth century boulevard laid out on ground occupied formerly by the city's Renaissance walls, is adorned with many iconic buildings. One of them, however, is no longer standing. The Ringtheater on Schottenring was destroyed by fire in December 1881.

The very first fire brigade in Austria was formed from Roman military veterans in 150 AD in Carnuntum, the capital of the Danube province of Pannonia. A similar force was deployed in the nearby legionnary fortress of Vindobona (modern Vienna) in 220 AD. With the fall of the Roman Empire, the art of fire prevention was lost in Central Europe until 1221, when the Babenberg Duke of Austria, Leopold VI (1198-1230), passed a law whereby fines were imposed on those whose houses caught fire, caused usually by soot-filled chimneys. With such a threat hanging over them it is little wonder that Vienna's citizens began viewing the appearance of a chimney sweep on their doorstep as a sign of good luck (see no. 5).

With the accession of the Habsburgs further fire legislation was passed, and in 1686, two years after the Great Fire of London, Vienna's first fire brigade was founded. And it was needed since most houses at the time were roofed with thatch or timber shingles. What Vienna really needed, however, was a central fire station, although it was not until 1848, when Viennese citizens stormed the Arsenal (*Bürgerliches Zeughaus*) on Am Hof, that a fire station was opened there (the Arsenal moved to a more secure location in Landstrasse). Today's fire station extends into the adjacent Baroque palace, where a museum contains a reconstruction of the firewatching post that was installed in the spire of the Stephansdom between 1534 and 1956.

Vienna's first steam-powered fire engine arrived in 1873 but still many Viennese buildings fell short in their fire prevention measures. The most notorious of these was the Ringtheater, an opera house and variety hall opened on Schottenring in 1874. The building's small footprint necessitated that the architect build narrow and high – with disastrous consequences. On December 8th 1881 a fire broke out on the stage shortly before a performance of *Les Contes d'Hoffmann*. Known thereafter as the *Ringtheaterbrand*, the fire gutted the building within a few hours killing 384 people in the process.

The cause of the fire remains a mystery although it is known that in the panic the theatre's telegraph system was not used to summon help nor were the stage water taps activated. The gas jets used to illuminate the theatre were turned off so as not to quicken the fire's spread. Plunged into darkness, the terrified theatregoers stumbled towards the main entrance on Schottenring. Here they

This statue in Pötzleinsdorfer Schlosspark once adorned the facade of the Ringtheater

became trapped, since at the time the doors of public buildings only opened inwards (the opposite is now required by law). Those that didn't succumb to the flames were quickly asphyxiated, and by 11.30pm only the shell of the building remained standing. All that could be salvaged were several statues from the façade, which today adorn the Pötzleinsdorfer Schlosspark, where they act as a poignant reminder of the tragedy.

The day after the fire, the Vienna Volunteer Rescue Society was founded and as the Berufsrettung Wien it is still in operation today. Its long and eventful history is documented in the Rescue Museum (*Rettungsmuseum*), which can be found in the Hernals Rescue Station (*Rettungsstation Hernals*) at Halirschgasse 12 (17th District).

To learn all about the history of Austrian Theatre visit the Theatre Museum (*Theatermuseum*) at Lobkowitzplatz 2 (1st District). The palatial building contains the grand Eroica Concert Hall named after Beethoven's Third Symphony and boasts a superb painted ceiling. Almost as grand is the ceiling of Vienna's charming English Theatre at Josefsgasse 12 (8th District). It is the longest-established English-language theatre in continental Europe.

92 Vienna's Via Dolorosa

17th District (Hernals), the Calvary Church (*Kalvarienberg-kirche*) on St.-Bartholomäus-Platz; take U-6 to Alserstrasse then Tram 43 to Elterleinplatz

Visitors approaching the Calvary Church (*Kalvarienbergkirche*) in Hernals (17th District) do so by way of Jörgerstrasse, a street named after a Protestant family of noble ancestry, who lost their estate here to the Chapter of St. Stephen during the Counter Reformation. In 1639, the Chapter laid out a Way of the Cross that ran from the Stephansdom in the 1st District all the way out via Schottentor to the

The Kalvarienbergkirche from the old market place in Hernals

church in Hernals – a distance exactly the same as Jerusalem's own Way of the Cross, the *Via Dolorosa*. Emperor Ferdinand III (1637–57) then laid the foundation stone of a "Holy Grave" at the church. This provided the ultimate goal for the many penitential processions that began using the route thereafter, despite the destruction of the church by the Ottomans during the second Turkish siege of Vienna in 1683 (see no. 3).

The church was rebuilt in 1709–14 at which time it was given its now famous Calvary, surely one of the most unusual in all Austria. Its most curious feature is the series of original wooden reliefs, now nearly 300 years old, which represent the seven deadly sins (Envy – dogs attacking Jesus; Pride – a strutting peacock; Covetousness – a money-grabbing raven; Gluttony – a greedy hyena; Lust – a billy goat; Anger – a lion ravaging a lamb; and Sloth – a sleeping donkey).

As the number of pilgrimages increased so the Calvary was extended in 1766–69 to accommodate them. However, in 1782 Emperor Joseph II (1765–90) dissolved the Pauline Order that had administered the Calvary, as well as its church, and all further pilgrimages were banned. In fact the reform-mad Emperor dissolved nearly one in five of Austria's monasteries believing them to be engaged in activities that did not benefit the state. Fortunately, in the years that followed pilgrimages resumed once more and the church was remodelled again, with some final modifications made to the Calvary in 1894. By this time pilgrims were making a good day out of their visit to Hernals, enjoying the hospitality of the numerous surrounding inns as well as the shopping opportunities offered by the burgeoning market in the church square in front. Either side of the building's façade there are staircases that lead up the unusual rough-hewn masonry of the ground floor to the Calvary above, symbolising the climb that Jesus made to his crucifixion site on the hill of Golgotha (hence the name *Kalvarienberg*).

Wall plaque to Franz Schubert

A plaque records that on 3rd November 1828 Schubert (1797–1828) heard his last music performed in the church, namely the *German Requiem*, written for his brother Ferdinand, who later published the work under his own name.

93 A Story of Love and Bubbles

19th District (Döbling), the Schlumberger Sektkellerei at
Heilgenstädter Strasse 39; take U-4/U-6 to Spittelau

For the last hundred years only sparkling wine made in the French Champagne region has been permitted to carry that region's name. Producers elsewhere have not been allowed to profit from one of the world's strongest brands. For the Vienna-based company Schlumberger, however, this has not been a handicap, as a visit to its extensive cellars in Döbling will demonstrate.

Robert Alwin Schlumberger (1814–1879) was the first producer of sparkling wine (German: *Sekt*) in Austria. Born in Stuttgart he was forced to give up his studies following the early death of his father. Instead he became a merchant, a job which took him to Reims in France. It was there that he found a job in the oldest Champagne cellar in France.

In 1841, during a pleasure cruise along the Rhine, Schlumberger met and fell in love with Sophie Kirchner, the daughter of a wealthy Viennese factory owner. Marriage was soon in the air but Sophie's mother firmly opposed her daughter moving to France. Instead Schlumberger relinquished his job in Reims and relocated to Vienna. The following year the pair moved to nearby Vöslau, where, with his wife's financial help, Schlumberger rented several vineyards, having identified the area as ideal for the production of sparkling wine.

Schlumberger's dream was to produce his own sparkling wine from Austrian grapes according to the French Champagne tradition (*Méthode Champenoise*). Such was his success that by the early 1860s Schlumberger Champagne was not only the preferred toast of Viennese society but also a favourite at the table of the Queen of England. For his efforts Schlumberger was ennobled by Emperor Franz Joseph I, and as a purveyor to the Habsburg court the company was permitted to use the prestigious appointment of k.u.k.-Hoflieferant.

The First World War changed everything, as a result of which the Austro-Hungarian Monarchy was dissolved and its economy left in tatters. Under the punitive terms of the Treaty of Saint-Germain-en-Laye (1919), the new Republic of Austria was disallowed from using the name Champagne. Despite this setback the Schlumberger company survived, as it did through the Second World War, too. Indeed since being acquired by the German family-owned company

Bottles of sparkling wine fermenting in the cellars of Schlumberger in Döbling

Underberg in 1973, Schlumberger has continued to produce some of the highest quality sparkling wines in Europe.

After 1919 Schlumberger was still allowed to advertise its wines as being made by the *Méthode Champenoise*. Since 1995, however, Austria's accession to the European Union prompted a further restriction, and now Schlumberger's bottles can only lay claim to the *Méthode Traditionnelle*. Whatever the name the technique is the same in so much as in-bottle secondary fermentation is used to carbonate the wine.

Schlumberger's wine cellars have long been located in Döbling, close to the Danube Canal along which the wine was originally shipped. Two and a half kilometres of brick-lined tunnels provide the constant temperature (13°C) necessary to guarantee fermentation – and storage for the 1.7 million bottles produced each year. A masterpiece of engineering, the tunnels were designed by Karl Ritter von Ghega (1802-1860), the architect behind the Semmering Railway. Each individual cellar is named after one of the disciples, with the obvious exception of Judas.

94 Döbling's Japanese Garden

19th District (Döbling), the Setagaya Japanese garden (Setagayapark) at the junction of Hohe warte and Barawitzkagasse; take U-6 to Nussdorferstrasse then Tram 37 to Barawitzkagasse (note: garden closed November–March)

The Viennese district of Döbling (19th District) has long been twinned with the Setagaya district of Tokyo, and in 1992 the partnership was celebrated by the creation of Setagayapark, a traditional Japanese garden at the junction of Hohe Warte and Barawitzkagasse. Created by renowned designer Ken Nakajima (1914-2000), the garden is close to paradise.

One needs a keen eye when visiting: from the outside Setagayapark is identified only by a bamboo door and a stone inscribed with the word *Furomon*, meaning "ageless gate". Certainly the garden that lies beyond is a timeless space and one into which Nakajima has squeezed an entire, albeit miniaturised Japanese landscape.

Setagayapark in Döbling is a classical Japanese garden

The heart of the garden is a carp-filled lake with a teahouse (*Chaniwa*) on its bank. Sometimes a peep through the window reveals ladies pursuing the delicate art of Japanese flower arranging (*Ikebana*). The view from here across the lily-strewn lake is enchanting, a three-legged *Yukimi* lantern on one side and a white gravel beach (*Suhama*) on the other, where turtles like to sunbathe.

At the far end of the lake, a gracefully-arching bridge worthy of Monet takes centre stage. Beyond it are waterfalls and a path winding uphill past maples, ornamental cherries, azaleas and magnolias. At the garden's highpoint near a stone pagoda water gurgles from a cube of stone. It is the ideal spot to pause and consider the deep Japanese love for nature and how it is enshrined in the Shinto faith (after leaving the garden be sure to track down the extraordinary former Zacherl insect powder factory at nearby Nusswaldgasse 14 constructed in the style of a mosque).

Vienna boasts several other Japanese gardens of which Takasaki-park in Favoriten is most like Setagayapark. Originally a temporary work by Kinsaku Nakane for the Vienna Garden Exhibition of 1974, it was made permanent at the behest of Vienna's Japanese community, as well as the inhabitants of the city of Takasaki. It is today a part of the Kurpark Oberlaa at Laaer-Berg-Strasse 211 (10th District).

Very different is the waterless rock garden (*Karesansui*) alongside Schönbrunn's famous *Palmenhaus*, laid out in 1913. It had become so choked with ivy by 1996 that it took a Japanese visitor to re-discover it! Used as a focus for Zen meditation the garden finds a modern counterpart in Courtyard 2 of the Old General Hospital (Altes AKH) in the 9th District, where it marks the 60th anniversary of the founding of the university's Japanese Faculty (the miniature mountains are actual stones brought from Kyoto and Kobe).

So popular has East Asian garden culture become that Vienna's horticultural college (*Berrufsschule für Gartenbau*) at Donizettiweg 29 in Kagran (22nd District) now teaches it. Since 2001 both students and visitors have been able to enjoy the so-called Asiagarten there, a teaching garden containing all the various plants and landscape features necessary for a successful Japanese garden.

Such expertise is reflected in the tiny Tora-San-Park in neighbouring Floridsdorf (21st District), which like Setagayapark is another celebration of good Austrian-Japanese relations. The name Tora-San is that of the central character in a long-running Japanese film series.

This tour finishes not far away on the Donauinsel alongside the Jedlerseer Brücke. An annual cherry tree festival has occurred here since 2002 in the so-called *Kirschenhain*, a grove of ornamental cherries given by Japan in 1996 to mark the thousand years since the founding of Austria.

Garden lovers might enjoy the Garden Museum (*Gartenbaumuseum*) at Siebeckstrasse 14, which is within walking distance of the Asia Garden in Kagran. Housed within a converted early-20th century orangery, its many fascinating exhibits encompass all facets of Austrian garden history.

Other places of interest nearby: 95

95 Building Red Vienna

19th District (Döbling), the Karl-Marx-Hof on Boschstrasse; take U-4 to Heiligenstadt

Vienna's old wine-making village of Heiligenstadt (19th District) has long been popular with visitors and locals alike. Its winding streets and pitched roofs give the place a rustic feel, especially in autumn when the vineyards are busy with grape-pickers. Beethoven came here in 1806 on the advice of his doctor in the hope that some country living might improve his hearing. His former home at Probusgasse 6 contains a lock of the composer's hair and his death mask.

Walk downhill from Heiligenstadt towards the Danube and the urban scene changes dramatically. Emerging like an island in a sea of lesser buildings is a very different sort of living space. This is the Karl-Marx-Hof, which at over one kilometre in length and spanning four tram stops holds the distinction of being the longest single residential building in the world.

The origins of this colossal structure can be found in the collapse of the Habsburg Empire at the end of the First World War. Out of this cataclysmic event the First Republic of Austria was born – but the loss of so many former territories inevitably brought severe economic hardships, widespread unemployment and even famine. Against this troubled backdrop the vote was extended to all Viennese adults, which combined with the rise of a powerful labour movement led by the country's Marxist Workers' Party resulted in a landslide electoral victory for the Social Democrats. Vienna thus became the world's first city to be governed by socialists and in 1922 it was made a separate Austrian federal province, distinct from conservative Lower Austria of which it had formerly been a part.

Despite tensions with the conservatives, who still held sway in the Austrian countryside, the new city council – dubbed *Rotes Wien* (Red Vienna) – embarked on Europe's most intensive programme of social reform. Nowhere was this more apparent than in the task of re-housing a quarter of a million workers, who at the time occupied crumbling and overcrowded nineteenth century tenements. These were replaced by some four hundred new municipal apartment complexes known as *Gemeindebauten*, which together provided almost sixty thousand new homes at an affordable rent. Basic home comforts included running water and WC, together with a hitherto unimaginable public infrastructure. Striking examples included the Reumann-Hof in Favoriten,

A tiny part of the enormously long façade of the Karl-Marx-Hof

Friedrich-Engels-Hof in Brigittenau, Sandleiten-Hof in Ottakring and Raben-Hof in Landstrasse. Red Vienna's true architectural flagship though was undoubtedly the Karl-Marx-Hof.

Constructed between 1927 and 1930 to a design by city planner Karl Ehn (1884-1959), the Karl-Marx-Hof stands on land reclaimed from the Danube. Built for a population of about five thousand, the complex comprised 1,382 apartments (each 30–60 m² in size) and communal amenities including kindergartens, clinics, shops and laundries (one of these, Wash House Number 2 at Halteraugasse 7, today contains a small museum about the building). There was also a youth centre, pharmacy, library and post office. In common with other *Gemeindebauten* the work was financed by a variety of special taxes on unearned incomes and luxuries such as champagne. Not surprisingly the finished building displayed minimal ornamentation and was named after the founding father of socialism. Its nickname, the *Ringstrasse des Proletariats*, was a cynical nod to Vienna's imperial boulevard, constructed half a century earlier as a showcase for Habsburg opulence.

Significantly the building occupies less than 20% of the total area of the Karl-Marx-Hof, the rest being made up of courtyards, gardens and playgrounds deemed vital to the occupants' well-being. Even beyond the perimeter lie rows of tiny hedged gardens known as *Schrebergärten*. Named after Daniel Gottlob Schreber (1808-1861), the 19th century German founder of the Small Garden Movement, they served as vegetable allotments during times of shortage. These days many

Entrance to a communal wash house at the Karl-Marx-Hof

have become the apartment-dweller's very own pleasure garden in miniature, replete with summerhouse, pond and tiny orchard.

Tragically, by the early thirties Vienna's socialist experiment was faltering in the face of National Socialism, global economic crises, mounting unemployment and worsening relations within federal Austria. Red Vienna had become increasingly polarised from the rest of conservative Austria and tensions climaxed in a brief three-day civil war in February 1934. Two thousand members of the socialist workers' militia (*Schutzbund*) died during fighting with superior conservative forces (*Heimwehr*), the Karl-Marx-Hof doubling as a fortress before being bombed into submission. Despite the best efforts of Chancellor Engelbert Dollfuss (1892-1934) to contain the situation, Austria had begun its inexorable slide into the hands of Nazi Germany.

Not until after the war would the flame of Red Vienna be reignited. The Social Democrats have held a majority in every election in Vienna ever since and these days the *Gemeindebauten* are inhabited by a wide range of people – no longer just the poor workers of old – who rent apartments from the municipality. About 600,000 people (approximately one third of the city's population) live this way, with many more thousands on the waiting list.

For more on the history of Austria during the time of Red Vienna visit the Haus der Geschichte Österreich in the Neue Burg on Heldenplatz (1st District). This thorough and dispassionate account of Austria's story during the 20th century covers the collapse of the Habsburg monarchy, the First Republic, Austro-Fascism, Nazism, the declaration of the Second Republic and beyond.

Other places of interest nearby: 94, 96

96 Taming of the Danube

19th District (Döbling), the Nussdorf Weir and Sluice (*Nussdorfer Wehr- und Schleusenanlage*) at Brigittenauer Sporn; take Tram D to Nussdorf

It was during the last Ice Age that layers of gravel were deposited by glacial melt water across the Vienna Basin. The River Danube, together with its numerous tributaries, gradually eroded these gravels into a series of terraces. It was on one of these terraces (the so-called City Terrace), set c.20 metres above the present level of the Danube Canal, that Bronze Age man first settled and where the Romans later built their garrison fort of Vindobona (see no. 13). Later still the streets of the medieval 1st District would also occupy this plateau, safe from the river's fickle flow, with the churches of Maria am Gestade (see no. 10) and St. Ruprecht built on its steep outer edges. Much of the surrounding land, however, remained at the mercy of the Danube, creating swampy river meadows in summer and icy marshes in winter. Bearing in mind the fact that eighty two great floods have been recorded in Vienna over 900 years, it was obvious that for the city to develop the mighty Danube would have to be tamed.

From Babenberg times the river had gradually been shifting its course northeastwards, away from the 1st District. However, the first serious attempt at river regulation in 1598 took place on a major tributary (the so-called Wiener) that still flowed right past the old city wall, where the Franz-Josefs-Kai now runs. This was in part a response to the need by city traders for a navigable waterway following the silting up of another tributary, the Salzgries. Continued flooding of low-lying areas, especially in 1787, 1830 and 1862, led to a complete channelling in 1870–75 between Nussdorf and Albern, using techniques perfected during the digging of the Suez Canal. The result was the waterway known today as the Danube Canal (*Donaukanal*). Despite its fast-flowing current and often murky appearance, the canal remarkably boasts its own swimming association (www. schwimmvereindonaukanal.org). Swimming aside, the banks of the canal are a paradise for cyclists, joggers, street artists and beach bar lovers.

Around the same time the Danube proper was also straightened enabling large modern vessels to dock safely. By 1875, this process had left several dead tributaries in the Prater (e.g. Heustadelwasser), as well as a curved arm of the original river marooned and cut off to the east. The latter, straddling Floridsdorf and Donaustadt, is known today as the

Old Danube (*Alte Donau*). Long popular with bathers (see no. 73), it is curious for being the only part of the Danube that actually appears blue (certainly when viewed from high on the Kahlenberg) – the rest being greyish green due to the current churning up lime from the riverbed.

Continued flooding in 1897, 1899 and 1954 led finally to the cutting in 1972 of a brand new channel, the New Danube, which flows parallel to the Danube proper. A by-product of this work was the creation of the Danube Island (*Donauinsel*), a 20 kilometre-long spit of land that never exceeds 400 metres in width. Needless to say, the Viennese love to use it for sunbathing, cycling and swimming, claiming it to be Europe's biggest and certainly longest urban park.

In conjunction with these major river-management projects, there have also been numerous harbours, sluices and weirs constructed over the years. Between 1878 and 1916, for example, harbours for over-wintering vessels were built at Kuchelau and Freudenau, whilst in the late-1930s docks were built at Lobau (for petroleum) and Albern (for grain). By far the most striking of these river facilities is at Nussdorf (19th District), where Otto Wagner's magnificent lion-topped weir and sluice (1894–98) controls the flow of water into the Danube Canal. As if to symbolise the might of the monarchy in taming such a river the granite structure bears the Emperor's motto *Viribus Unitis* (With United Strength).

Further down the Canal, at Obere Donaustrasse 26 (1st District), is Wagner's pretty Protection House (*Schützenhaus*) (1904–08),

A sculptured lion on Otto Wagner's Nussdorf sluice

erected in an attempt to convert the canal into a trade and winter port. Although never completed, the building's projecting cockpit remains intact, from where overhead cranes would have raised a sluice gate from the riverbed. Designed in Modernist *Jugendstil* style by Otto Wagner, it has a simple white-tiled exterior broken up by a pretty blue wave pattern and now serves as a restaurant.

More recently, where the Canal joins the Danube proper, there is the Freudenauer sluice and hydroelectric power station (*Kraftwerk Freudenau*) built in 1992–98.

Also worthy of mention here is the regulation of the 17 kilometre-long River Wien (*Wienfluss*) that drains part of the Vienna Woods and hitherto

Part of the ornate portal on the River Wien

regularly flooded the Schönbrunn Palace on its way down to the Danube Canal. Although the Romans made attempts at controlling the river, it was not until 1897 that much of it was culverted in conjunction with the building of Otto Wagner's Metropolitan Railway, which follows the same course (see no. 46). Upstream, between Auhof and Hütteldorf, retention basins with locks and spillways have been built to contain floodwaters. Downstream, after a covered section of river between the Naschmarkt and the Stadtpark U-Bahn station, the now tamed river re-emerges by means of a stunning Viennese Art Nouveau (*Jugendstil*) portal designed by Friedrich Ohmann and Joseph Hackhofer, and completed in 1906.

The walls of the U-Bahn station at Dresdner Strasse (20th District) and Floridsdorf (21st District) on the U-6 carry a fascinating series of old maps and illustrations showing the various phases of river straightening on the Danube.

Other places of interest nearby: 95

97 Freud's Secret of Dreams

19th District (Döbling), Freud monument on Bellevuehöhe; take U-4 to Heiligenstadt and then Bus 38A to Parkplatz Am Cobenzl

The father of psychoanalysis Sigmund Freud was born in Moravia (now the Czech Republic) in 1856 and died in London in 1939 having been forcibly exiled by the Nazis. He spent most of the intervening years in Vienna, where his second-floor house and practice still exists at Berggasse 19 in the 9th district of Alsergrund. Now a museum (*Sigmund-Freud-Museum*), but sadly lacking the famous couch that followed him to his new practice in London (today also a museum), Freud's Berggasse rooms still boast the great man's hat, coat and walking stick.

Freud was an inveterate walker, and smoker, and it is said that he enjoyed a brisk stroll along the nearby Ringstrasse most days. On Sundays he would don traditional Alpine walking clothes and head with his daughter Anna up in to the Vienna Woods (*Wienerwald*). It is there that an easy-to-miss monument to Freud, erected in 1977 at Bellevuehöhe (388 metres above sea level), can be found.

Alighting from the bus at Am Cobenzl car park, the visitor must follow the road back out of the car park and then turn right onto Höhenstrasse, walking down onto Himmelstrasse signposted "Häuserl am Himmel"; then turn right (this time signposted "Zur Bellevuestrasse"), and walk along an old avenue of trees, finally turning left up unmarked steps onto a track at the edge of a broad meadow. At the far end will be found a stone bearing the following inscription: "Letter to Wilhelm Fliess, Bellevue, 12th June 1900 – Do you suppose that someday a marble tablet will be placed on the house inscribed with these words: In this house on July 24th 1895 the Secret of Dreams was revealed to Dr. Sigmund Freud? At this moment I see little prospect of it." Fliess was a Berlin doctor and admirer of Freud's work. The house referred to was the Schloss Bellevue, a *Kurhotel* (equivalent to a modern wellness centre) that once stood here but which was destroyed during the Second World War. Freud was right in thinking that the building would not get its plaque but even after the Second World War there was still little official recognition of his academic achievements. Freud commented dryly on the Viennese reticence to acknowledge his work, notably when he was made University Professor of Neurology in 1902 by Emperor Franz Joseph I, saying it was as if "the role of sexuality had

Looking out across Vienna from the aptly-named Bellevuehöhe where Sigmund Freud once strolled

suddenly been officially recognised by His Majesty, the significance of dreams confirmed by the council of ministers and the necessity of psychoanalytical therapy for hysteria passed by a two-thirds majority in parliament". By contrast, today his contribution to the study of psychology is largely unquestioned, since it was Freud who pioneered the analysis of a patient's dreams as a means of unlocking coded meanings that help understand a patient's troubled mind. His book *The Interpretation of Dreams* (1900), whilst largely ignored on publication, is now considered a classic and his concepts of ego and the subconscious are taken for granted around the world. It was Freud, too, who introduced the use of "free association" now so common in the counselling of patients suffering mental illness.

A bust of Freud was eventually erected in the cloisters of the University (*Alte Universität*) on Universitätsring, alongside Vienna's other academic worthies, and he even got a park in Vienna named after him (*Sigmund-Freud-Park*), between the university and his old apartment.

Sitting on the grassy hillside at Bellevuehöhe, where Freud once walked a century ago, is the perfect place to finish this odyssey during which some of the more unusual and unsung corners of Vienna have been explored. Looking out from the woods and vineyards, across the sprawling suburbs to the 1st District and the Danube beyond, gives the satisfied explorer the opportunity to reflect on the culture, characters and contradictions encountered in this capital city at the crossroads of Europe.

Opening Times

Correct at time of going to press but may be subject to change.

Acculux Hans Kremser, 1st District, Schultergasse 3, usually Mon–Fri 10am–4pm

Alte Kunst, 1st District, Plankengasse 7, Mon–Fri 3–6pm, Sat 11am–12pm

Alte Leopoldsapotheke, 1st District, Plankengasse 6, Mon–Sat 8am–6pm

Alte Löwen Apotheke, 8th District, Josefstädter Strasse 25, Mon–Fri 8am–6pm, Sat 8am–12pm

Altmann & Kühne, 1st District, Graben 30, Mon–Fri 9am–6.30pm, Sat 10am–5pm

Amalienbad, 10th District, Reumannplatz 23, Tue & Fri 6.45–7.50am, 1–4.30pm, Wed 6.45–7.50am, 1–9pm, Thur 8–9am, Sat 8am–6.30pm, Sun 8am–5.30pm

Apotheke zum Weissen Storch, 1st District, Tuchlauben 9, Mon–Sat 8am–6pm, Sun 11am–5pm

Asia Garden of the School of Horticulture (Berufsschule für Gartenbau), 22nd District, Donizettiweg 29, Apr–Oct first Thu each month 10am–6pm

Augustinerkirche, 1st District, Augustinerstrasse 3, Mon, Wed & Fri 8am–5.30pm, Tue & Wed 8am–7.30pm, Sat & Sun 9am–7.30pm

Austrian National Library (Österreichische National Bibliothek), 1st District, Josefsplatz, Tue–Sun 10am–6pm (Thu 9pm)

Bäckerei Arthur Grimm, 1st District, Kurrentgasse 10, Mon–Fri 7am–6pm, Sat 8am–1pm

Baking Museum (Bäckermuseum), 8th District, Florianigasse 13, open by appointment

Beethoven Museum, 19th District, Probusgasse 6, Tue–Sun 10am–1pm, 2–6pm

Beethoven Pasqualatihaus, 1st District, Mölker Bastei 8, Tue–Sun 10am–1pm 2–6pm

Böhmischer Prater, 10th District, Laaer-Berg Strasse, daily 10am–9pm

Brezlg'wölb, 1st District, Ledererhof 9, daily 11.30am–12am

Büchereien–Wien Library, 7th District, Urban-Loritz-Platz, Mon–Fri 11am–7pm, Sat 11am–5pm

Burggarten, 1st District, Burgring/Opernring, daily 6am–10pm

Butterfly House (Schmetterlinghaus), 1st District, Burggarten, Apr–Oct Mon–Fri 10am–4.45pm, Sat & Sun, 10am–6.15pm, Nov–Mar 10am–3.45pm

Café Ansari, 2nd District, Praterstrasse 15, Mon–Sat 8am–11.30pm, Sun 9am–3pm

Café Bräunerhof, 1st District, Stallburggasse 2, Mon–Fri 8am–7pm, Sat 8am–6pm, Sun 10am–6pm

Café Central, 1st District, Palais Ferstel, Herrengasse 14, Mon–Sat 8am–9pm, Sun 10am–9pm

Café Diglas, 1st District, Wollzeile 10, Mon–Fri 8am–10.30pm, Sat 9am–10.30

Café Goldegg, 4th District, Argentinierstrasse 49, Mon–Fri 8am–8pm, Sat & Sun 9am–8pm

Café Hawelka, 1st District, Dorotheergasse 6, Mon–Thu 8am–12am, Fri & Sat 8am–1am, Sun 9am–8pm

Café Korb (1st District), Brandstätte 7/9, Mon–Sat 8am–12am

Café Landmann, 1st District, Universitätsring 4, daily 7.30am–10pm

Café Sperl, 6th District, Gumpendorferstrasse 11, Mon–Sat 7am–10pm, Sun 10am–8pm

Café Weimar, 9th District, Währinger Strasse 68, Mon–Fri 8am–11.30pm, Sat & Sun 8.30am–11.30pm

Cathedral of St. Nicholas (Kathedrale zur Heiligen Nikolaus), 3rd District, Jaurèsgasse 2, Mon–Fri 8am–2pm, Sat 9am–7pm, Sun 8am–6pm; Vigil Sat 5pm, Divine Liturgy Sun 10am

Chimney Sweeps' Museum (Rauchfangkehrermuseum), Wieden District Museum, 4th District, Klagbaumgasse 4, Sun 10am–12pm, Tue 9–11am

Circus and Clown Museum (Circus- und Clownmuseum), 2nd District, Ilgplatz 7, Sun 10am–1pm

Church of the Holy Ghost (Heilig-Geist-Kirche), 16th District, Herbststrasse 82, Daily 7am–7pm; Sun Mass 7.30am, 9am, 10.30am

Clock Museum (Uhrenmuseum), 1st District, Schulhof 2, Tue–Sun 10am–6pm

Coffeemuseum (Kaffeemuseum), 5th District, Österreichisches Gesellschafts- und Wirtschaftsmuseum, Vogelsang- gasse 36, Mon–Fri 9am–2pm

Collection of Historical Musical Instruments (Sammlung für Musikinstrumente), 1st District, Heldenplatz, Neue Burg, Thu–Tue 10am–6pm (Tue 9pm)

Confiserie Zum Sussen Eck, 9th District, Währinger Strasse 65, Mon 2–7pm, Tue–Fri 10am–7pm

Crime Museum (Kriminalmuseum), 2nd District, Grosse Sperlgasse 24, Thu–Sun 10am–5pm

Daniel Hager, 2nd District, Grosse Stadtgutgasse 7, Mon 11am–5pm, Tue–Thu 8am–5pm, Fri 8am–12pm

Das Rote Wien–Waschsalon, 19th District, Karl-Marx-Hof, Waschsalon Nr. 2, Halteraugasse 7, Thu 1–6pm, Sun 12pm–4pm

Demel, 1st District, Kohlmarkt 14, daily 10am–7pm

Deutschordenskirche (1st District), Singerstrasse 7, 7am–7pm

Documentation Centre of Austrian Resistance (DÖW), 1st District, Old Town Hall, Wipplingerstrasse 8, Mon–Wed 9am–5pm (Thu 7pm)

Dom Museum, 1st District, Stephansplatz 6, Wed–Sun 10am–6pm (Thu 8pm)

Donaucity-Kirche, 21st District, Donau-City-Strasse 2, daily 8.30am–6pm

Dorotheum, 1st District, Dorotheergasse 17, Mon–Sat 10am–5pm

Engelapotheke, 1st District, Bognergasse 9, Mon–Fri 8am–6pm, Sat 8am–12pm

Ephesos Museum, 1st District, Heldenplatz, Tue–Sun 10am–6pm (Thu 10am–9pm)

Esperanto Museum, 1st District, Palais Mollard, Herrengasse 9, Tue 10am–6pm (Thu 9pm)

Esterházykeller, 1st District, Haarhof 1, Tue–Fri 4–11pm, Sat & Sun 11am–11pm

Favoriten Wasserturm, 10th District, Windtenstrasse 3, May–Oct guided tours only by appointment tel. +43 (0)1 599 59–31079

Fire Brigade Museum (Feuerwehrmuseum), 1st District, Am Hof 7/10, Tue 2–5pm, Sun 9–12pm

Figlmüller, 1st District, Wollzeile 5, daily 11am–10.30pm

Fishing Museum (Fischereimuseum), 21st District, Einzingergasse 1, Sun 9am–12pm

Fleischerei Kröppel, 1st District, Postgasse 1–3, Mon–Sat 8am–6pm (Sat 12pm)

Folklore Museum Vienna (Volkskunde Museum Wien), 8th District, Laudongasse 15–19, Tue–Sun 10am–5pm

Galleria Febella, 1st District, Herrengasse 6–8, Mon–Fri 10.30am–6.30pm, Sat 10.30am–6pm

Gartenbaumuseum (Garden Museum), 22nd District, Siebeckstrasse 14, Mon–Fri 8am–3pm (first Thu each month 6pm)

Gastwirtschaft Schilling, 7th District, Burggasse 103, daily 11.30am–11pm

Glass Museum (Glasmuseum), 6th District, Mollardgasse 8/2/16, Wed 3–7pm

Globe Museum (Globenmuseum), 1st District, Palais Mollard, Herrengasse 9, daily 10am–6pm (Thu 9pm)

Haus Wittgenstein, 3rd District, Parkgasse 18, tours Mon–Fri by appointment only office@haus-wittgenstein.at

Haydn House (Haydnhaus), 6th District, Haydngasse 16, Tue–Sun 10am–1pm, 2–6pm

Heating Museum (Heizungmuseum), 12th District, Malfattigasse 4, Mon–Fri 9am–4pm by appointment only

Heimito von Doderer-Sammlung, Alsergrund District Museum, 9th District, Währinger Strasse 43, Wed 11am–1pm, 3–5pm

Hermesvilla, 13th District, Lainzer Tiergarten, Tue–Sun 10am–6pm

Hofburg inc. Imperial Apartments (Kaiserappartements), Sisi Museum & Silver Collection (Silberkammer), 1st District, Michaelertrakt, daily 9.30am–5pm (last entrance 4pm)

Hofpavillon Hietzing, 13th District, Schönbrunner Schlossstrasse, Sun 10.30–12.30pm

House of Austrian History (Haus der Geschichte Österreich), 1st District, Heldenplatz, Tue–Sun 10am–6pm (Thu 9pm)

Haus des Meeres, 6th District, Esterházypark, fritz-Grünbaum-Platz 1, daily 9am–8pm

Imperial Armoury (Hofjagd- und Rüstkammer), 1st District, Neue Burg, Heldenplatz, Tue–Sun 10am–6pm (Thu 9pm)

Imperial Treasury (Kaiserliche Schatzkammer), 1st District, Hofburg, Schweizerhof, Wed–Mon 9am–5.30pm

J. & L. Lobmeyr, 1st District, Kärntnerstrasse 26, Mon–Sat 10am–6pm

Jewish Museum Vienna (Jüdisches Museum Wien), 1st District, Dorotheergasse 11, Sun–Fri 10am–6pm

Joh. Springers Erben (8th District), Josefsgasse 10, Mon–Fri 9am–6pm

Johann Strauss Wohnung, 2nd District, Praterstrasse 54, Tue–Sun 10am–1pm, 2–6pm

Judenplatz Museum, 1st District, Judenplatz 8, Sun–Thu 10am–6pm, Fri 10am–2pm

Kaisergruft, 1st District, Kapuziner Kirche (Capuchin Church), Tegetthoffstrasse 2, daily 10am–6pm

Kalvarienbergkirche, 17th District, St.-Barthomäus-Platz, daily 7am–7pm, Calvary open daily 10am – 5.30pm during Lent only (Ash Wednesday (Aschermittwoch) to Easter Monday (Ostermontag))

Karlskirche, 1st District, Karlsplatz, Mon–Sat 9–6pm, Sun 11–7pm

Klimt Villa, 13th District, Feldmühlgasse 11, Wed–Sun 10am–6pm

Knize, 1st District, Graben 13, Mon–Fri 10am–6.30pm, Sat 10am–5pm

Kuffner Sternwarte, 16th District, Johann-Staud-Strasse 10, seasonal opening times www.kuffner-sternwarte.at

Kunst Haus Wien – Museum Hundertwasser, 3rd District, Untere Weissgerberstrasse 13, daily 10am–6pm

Kunsthistorisches Museum, 1st District, Burgring 5/Maria-Theresien-Platz, Tue–Sun 10am–6pm (Thu 9pm)

Literature Museum, 1st District, Johannesgasse 6, daily 10am–6pm

Loos American Bar, 1st District, Kärntner Durchgang 10, daily 12pm–4am

Magic Set Museum (Zauberkasten Museum), 12th District, Schönbrunner Strasse 262, first Sun in the month 10am–4pm

MAK Museum of Applied Arts (Museum für angewandte Kunst), 1st District, Stubenring 5, Tue–Sun 10am–6pm (Tue 10pm)

Margarete Schütte-Lihotsky Zentrum, 8th District, Franzengasse 16/40, Tue 10am–2pm, Fri 2–6pm

Maria am Gestade, 1st District, Salvatorgasse 12, daily 7am–6pm

Market Museum (Marktamtsmuseum), 21st District, Floridsdorfer Markt 5, by appointment only

Mekhitarist Monastery (Mekhitaristenkloster), 7th District, Mechitaristengasse 4, tours by appointment tel. +43 (0)1 523 6417, sung Mass on Sundays at 11am

Melker Stiftskeller, 1st District, Schottengasse 3, Tue–Sat 5–11pm

Minoritenkirche, 1st District, Minoritenplatz 2a, daily 7.30am–7pm

Money Museum (Geldmuseum), 9th District, Otto-Wagner-Platz 3, Tue, Wed & Thu 9am–4pm, Fri 9am–1pm

Mozarthaus Vienna, 1st District, Domgasse 5, daily 10am–6pm

Möbelmuseum Wien, 6th District, Mariahilfer Strasse 88/ Andreasgasse 7, Tue–Sun 10am–5pm

Mühlbauer, 1st District, Seilergasse 10, Mon–Fri 10am–6.30pm, Sat 10am–6pm

Museum of Liberation Vienna (Befreiungsmuseum Wien), 9th District, Arne-Carlsson-Park, Währingerstrasse 43, visits by appointment only tel. +43 (0)676 611 92-32

Museum of Medical History (Medizinisches Museum), 9th District, Josephinum, Währinger Strasse 25, Wed–Sat 10am–6pm (Thu 8pm)

Museum of Military History (Heeresgeschichtliches Museum), 3rd District, Arsenal, Objekt 18, daily 9am–5pm

Mythos Mozart, 1st District, Steffl, Kärntnerstrasse 19, Mon-Fri 10am-8pm, Sat & Sun 10am-6pm

Naschmarktmuseum, 6th District, Booth 284 near Schleifmühlgasse, Summer Sat 12–2pm

Natural History Museum (Naturhistorisches Museum), 1st District, Burgring 7/Maria–Theresien–Platz, Wed–Mon 9am–6pm (Wed 9pm)

Neidhart-Festsaal, 1st District, Tuchlauben 19, Tue–Sun 10am–1pm, 2pm–6pm

Ohel Bäckerei, 2nd District, Lillienbrunngasse 18, Mon-Thu 7am-6pm, Fri 7am-2pm, Sun 8am-3pm

Otto Wagner Pavillon, 4th District, Karlsplatz, interior currently closed

Otto-Wagner-Villa I (Ernst Fuchs Museum), 14th District, Hüttelbergstrasse 26, Tue–Sun 10am–4pm

Papyrus Museum (Papyrusmuseum), 1st District, Heldenplatz, Neue Burg, Tue–Sun 10am–6pm (Thu 9pm)

Pathologisch–Anatomische Sammlung, 9th District, Narrenturm, Altes AKH, Courtyard 13, Wed 10am–6pm, Thu & Fri 10am–3pm, Sat 12–6pm

Peace Museum (Friedensmuseum), 1st District, Blutgasse 3/1, Mon–Thu 10am–5pm

Pharmaceutical Museum (Pharmamuseum), 9th District, Währingerstrasse 14, Wed 2–5pm

Phonograph Museum (Phonomuseum), 6th District, Mollardgasse 8/2/16, Wed 3–7pm

Prater Museum, 2nd District, Oswald–Thomas–Platz 1, Fri–Sun 10am–1pm, 2–6pm (closing May 2023 & reopening 2024 at Straße des 1. Mai)

Reimer's Bonbons, 1st District, Wollzeile 26, Mon–Sat 10am–7pm, Sun 2–7pm

Remise–Transport Museum, 3rd District, Ludwig-Kössler-Platz, Sat & Sun 10am–6pm

Rescue Museum (Rettungsmuseum), 17th District, Hernals Rescue Station, Halirschgasse 12, visits by appointment only

Roman Museum (Römermuseum), 1st District, Hoher Markt 3, Tue–Sun 9am–6pm

Rudolf Scheer, 1st District, Bräunerstrasse 4, visits by appointment Mon–Fri 10am–5pm, Sat 10am–4pm www.scheer.at

Sanitärhistorisches Museum, 6th District, Mollardgasse 87, visits by appointment tel. +43 (0)1 599 1695 670

Schloss Concordia, 11th District, Simmeringer Hauptstrasse 283, Mon–Fri 12pm–11pm, Sat & Sun 11.30am–11pm

Schloss Schönbrunn inc. Imperial Carriage Museum (Wagenburg), 13th District, Apr–Oct 8.30am–5.30pm, Nov–Mar 8.30am–5pm; Schlosspark Schönbrunn daily from 6.30am; Palm House (Palm House) May–Sep 10am–6pm, Oct–Apr 10am–5pm; Desert House (Wüstenhaus) Jan–Apr, Oct–Dec 9am–5pm, May–Sep 9am–6pm

Schönbergers Caffè (formerly Naber Kaffee), 4th District, Wiedner Hauptstrasse 40, Mon–Fri 8am–6pm, Sat 9am–1pm

Schlumberger Sektkellerei, 19th District, Heiligenstädter Strasse 39, tours available by appointment Fri & Sat 11am–6pm www.schlumberger.at

Schubert Birthplace (Schubert Geburtshaus), 9th District, Nussdorfer Strasse 54, Tue–Sun 10am–1pm, 2–6pm

Schubert Death House (Schubert Sterbewohnung), 4th District, Kettenbrückengasse 6, Wed & Thu 10am–1pm, 2–6pm

Setagayapark Japanese Garden, 19th District, corner of Hohe Warte and Barawitzkagasse, daily 7am–dusk (closed Nov–Mar)

Sigmund Freud Museum, 9th District, Berggasse 19, Wed–Mon 10am–6pm

Snow Globe Museum (Schneekugelmuseum), 17th District, Schumanngasse 87, Mon–Thu 9am–3pm

Spittelau Incinerator (Mullverbrennungsanlage Spittelau), 9th District, Spittelauer Lände 45, guided tours by appointment www.wienenergie.at

St. Marx Cemetery (Sankt Marxer-Friedhof), 3rd District, Leberstrasse 6–8, Apr–Sep daily 6.30am–8pm, Oct–Mar daily 6.30am–6.30pm

St. Michael's Church (Michaelerkirche), 1st District, Michaelerplatz, daily 7am–10pm,, crypt guided tours Fri & Sat 10am & 12pm (German only)

St. Stephen's Cathedral (Stephansdom), 1st District, Stephansplatz, Mon–Sat 9am–11am, 1 – 4.30pm, Sun 10am – 4.30pm, Sun 7am–10pm; catacombs guided tours Mon–Sat 10am, 11am, 11.30am, 1.30, 2.30pm, 3.30pm & 4.30pm, Sun 1.30–4.30pm, Sun 1.30pm, 2.30pm, 3.30pm & 4.30pm; North Tower (Pummerin) daily 9am – 5.30pm, South Tower daily 9am – 5.30pm

Stadtapotheke zu Goldenen Hirschen, 1st District, Kohlmarkt 11, Mon–Sat 8am–6pm, Sat 8am–12pm

Steinhof Church (Kirche am Steinhof), 14th District, Baumgartner Höhe 1, Otto-Wagner-Spital, Sat 4–5pm, Sun 12pm–4pm

Takasaki Park, 10th District, Kurpark Oberlaa, Laaer-Berg-Strasse 211, daily 6am–10pm

Technical Museum (Technisches Museum), 14th District, Mariahilfer Strasse 212, Mon– Fri 9am–6pm, Sat & Sun 10am–6pm

Theatre Museum (Theatermuseum), 1st District, Lobkowitzplatz 2, Wed–Mon 10am–6pm

Third Man Museum (Dritte Mann Museum), 4th District, Pressgasse 25, Sat 2–6pm, tel. +43 (0)1 676 475 7818 72 for appointments at other times

Torture Museum (Foltermuseum), 6th District, Esterházypark, Mon–Fri 10am–6pm, Sat & Sun 11am–6pm

Tostmann Trachten, 1st District, Schottengasse 3a, Mon–Fri 10am–6.30pm, Sat 10am–5pm

Treasury of the Order of the Teutonic Knights (Schatzkammer des Deutschen Ordens), 1st District, Singerstrasse 7 (Staircase 1, 1st floor), Mon–Sat 1–3pm (Tue & Thu 5pm)

Vienna Shoe Museum (Wiener Schuhmuseum), 8th District, Florianigasse 66, 2nd Tue each month 4–7pm

Vienna Brick Museum (Wiener Ziegelmuseum), Penzing District Museum, 14th District, Penzinger Strasse 59, first & third Sun each month 10–12pm (closed Jul & Aug)

Viticulture Museum (Weinbaumuseum), Döbling District Museum, 19th District, Döblinger Hauptstrasse 96, Wed 9.30–11.30am, Sat 3–5pm

Virgilkapelle (St. Virgil's Chapel,) 1st District, U–Bahn station Stephansplatz, Tue–Sun 10am–6pm

Volksprater, 2nd District, Riesenradplatz 2, daily 11am–10pm; Café Ponykarussell, Karl-Kolarik-Weg 1, Prater 86a, daily 9am–6pm

Votivkirche, 9th District, Rooseveltplatz, Tue–Fri 11am–5pm, Sat & Sun 11am–7pm

Wagner:Werk Museum, 1st District, Georg-Koch-Platz 2, Mon-Thu 10am-6pm, Fri 1-8pm

Weltmuseum Wien, 1st District, Heldenplatz, Neue Burg, Thu–Tue 10am–6pm (Tue 9pm)

Westlicht Camera Museum (Westlicht Kameramuseum), 7th District, Westbahnstrasse 40, Tue–Fri 2–7pm (Thu 9pm), Sat & Sun 11am–7pm

Wien Museum, 1st District, Karlsplatz, closed for renovation, reopening late 2023

Wilhelm Jungmann & Neffe, 1st District, Albertinaplatz 3, Mon–Fri 10am–6.30pm, Sat 10am–6pm

Wotrubakirche, 23rd District, Georgenberg, Maurer Lange Gasse 137, Sat 2–6pm, Sun 9am–4.30pm

Zentralfriedhof (Central Cemetery), 11th District, Simmeringer Hauptstrasse, daily Apr–Sep 7am–7pm, Mar & Oct 7am–6pm, Nov–Feb 8am–5pm; Bestattungsmuseum (Funeral Museum), Gate 2, Mon–Fri 9am–4.30pm

Zwölfapostelkeller, 1st District, Sonnenfelsgasse 3 daily 11am–11pm

Further Reading

GUIDEBOOKS

Visible Cities – Vienna (Annabel Barber), Somerset Ltd., 2002

The Rough Guide to Vienna (Rob Humphreys), Penguin Books, 2011

PastFinder: Vom Kaiserreich bis zum Staatsvertrag (Robert Kuhn), PastFinder Ltd., 2010

Lonely Planet Vienna (Catherine Le Nevez, Marc Di Duca & Kerry Walker), Lonely Planet Publications, 2020

In Search of Vienna: Walking Tours of the City (Henriette Mandl), Christian Brandstätter Verlag, 1995

Jewish Vienna (Kevin Mitrega), Mandelbaum Verlag, 2004

Vienna for the Music Lover (David L. Nelson), Christian Brandstätter Verlag, 2006

Wanderung rund um Wien (Fritz Peterka), Bergverlag Rudolf Rother Gmbh, 1995

Vienna: A Doctor's Guide (15 Walking Tours through Vienna's Medical History), (Wolfgang Regal & Michael Nanut), Springer, 2007

Wallpaper Guide Vienna (Lukas Schaller), Phaidon Press, 2020

Gustav Klimt und Wien: Spaziergänge zu den Orten seines Wirkens (Monika Sommer & Alexandra Steiner-Strauss), Metroverlag, 2012

Vienna City Guide (Käthe Springer and Manfred Horvath), Christian Brandstätter Verlag, 2002

Eyewitness Travel Guide Vienna (Various), Dorling Kindersley, 2019

Green Guide Vienna (Various), Michelin Travel Publications, 2002

Time Out Vienna (Various), Time Out Guides Ltd, 2015

Looking for Wolfgang Amadeus Mozart (Walter M. Weiss), Christian Brandstätter Verlag, 1997

SECRET AND HIDDEN VIENNA

Unbekanntes Wien: Verborgenes Schönheit & Schimmernde Pracht (Isabella Ackerl & Harald Jahn), Pichler Verlag, 2013

Mystisches Wien – Verborgene Schätze, Versunkene Welten, Orte der Nacht (Robert Bouchal & Johannes Sachslehner), Pichler Verlag, 2004

111 Places to Visit in Vienna that you Shouldn't Miss (Peter Eickhoff), Emons Verlag, 2016

Weird Vienna: A Hilarious City Guide (Harald Havas), Metroverlag, 2015

Secret Vienna (Michaela Lindinger), Jonglez, 2018

Geheimnisvolle Unterwelt von Wien: Keller, Labyrinthe, Fremde Welten (Gabriele Lukacs & Robert Bouchal), Pichler Verlag, 2011

HISTORY

Danube Encounters (Hellmut Andics), Jugend und Volk Verlagsgesellschaft m. b. H., 1976

The Hare with the Amber Eyes (Edmund de Waal), Vintage, 2011

Vienna: A Cultural and Literary History (Nicholas Parsons), Signal Books, 2008

Fin de Siècle Vienna: Politics and Culture (Carl E. Schorske), Randon House, 1980

The Last Waltz: The Strauss Dynasty and Vienna (John Suchet), Elliott and Thompson, 2015

The Habsburg Monarchy, 1809 –1918 (A. J. P. Taylor), Penguin Books, 1964

Discovering Vienna through Legends (Hannelore Tik), Hannelore Tik, 2000

The Habsburgs: Embodying Empire (Andrew Wheatcroft), Penguin 1996

I Belong to Vienna: A Jewish Family's Story of Exile and Return (Anna Goldenburg), New Vessel Press, 2020

ART AND ARCHITECTURE

Architecture in Vienna 1850–1930: Historicism, Jugendstil, New Realism (Bertha Blaschke & Luise Lipschitz), Springer-Verlag, 2003

Vienna: A Guide to Recent Architecture (Ingrid Helsing Almaas), Ellipsis/Könemann, 2001

Jugendstil in Wien (János Kalmár & Andreas Lehne), Pichler Verlag, 1998

A Short History of Art in Vienna (Martina Pippal), C. H. Beck, 2002

Album of Socialist Vienna (Hans Riemer), Wiener Volksbuchhandlung Julius Deutsch & Co., 1947

Flaktürme – Berlin, Hamburg, Wien (Hans Sakkers), Fortress Books, 1998

Jugendstil: Otto Wagner's Footprints in Vienna (M. P. A Scheaffer), Pichler Verlag, 1998

Denkmal – Wiener Stadtgeschichten vom Walzerkönig bis zur Spinnerin am Kreuz (Matthias Settele), Deuticke, 1996

CHURCHES, CEMETERIES AND MUSEUMS

New Insights into the Kunsthistorisches Museum Vienna (Philipp Blom & Veronica Buckley), Christian Brandstätter Verlag, 2016

Graves of Honour at the Central Cemetery in Vienna (Robert Budig, Gertrude Enderle- Burcel and Peter Enderle), Compress Verlag, 1998

St. Stephan's Cathedral in Vienna 2nd rev. ed. (Reinhard H. Gruber), Church Office of St. Stephan's Cathedral, 2001

Gustav Klimt – Last Studio (Gustav Klimt Memorial Society), Zeitschrift der Österreichischen Gesellschaft für Denkmal- und Ortsbildpflege in Verbindung mit dem Verein Gedenkstätte Gustav Klimt, 2000

The Kunsthistorisches Museum Vienna Guide (ed. by Martina Haja), Kunsthistorisches Museum/Christian Brandstätter Verlag, 1988

Stephansplatz and the Virgilkapelle (Dr. Ortolf Harl), City of Vienna Museums Publications, undated

The Neidhart Frescoes ca.1400 The Oldest Secular Mural Paintings in Vienna (Eva-Maria Höhle, Renata Kassal-Mikula, Oskar Pausch & Richard Perger), Museums of the City of Vienna, undated

The Park at Schönbrunn Palace (Elfried Iby), Schloss Schönbrunn Kultur- und Betriebs ges.m.b.H, 2001

The Treasury of the Teutonic Order (Wolfgang Krones), Office of the Hochmeister of the Teutonic Order – Museum and Treasury, 2000

Kunsthistorisches Museum Vienna Wagenburg (Carriage Collection) at Schönbrunn Palace (Georg Kugler), Kunsthistorisches Museum, 1999

The Kunsthistorisches Museum Vienna – The Imperial and Ecclesiastical Treasury (Manfred Leithe-Jasper & Rudolf Distelberger), Scala Publishers/Verlag C. H. Beck, 1998

Vienna by MAK – Applied Arts/ Contemporary Art (ed. by Peter Noever), Prestel Verlag, 2002

Imperial Furniture Collection Pocket Guide (Eva B. Ottilinger), Schloss Schönbrunn Kulturund Betriebsges.m.b.H, 2000

The Treasures of Montezuma – Fantasy & Reality (Ferdinand Anders), Wilfried Seipel/Museum für Völkerkunde, 2001

TMW – Technisches Museum Wien (ed. by Gabriele Zuna-Kratky), Prestel Verlag, 2002

FOOD AND DRINK

Das Wiener Kaffeehaus (Christian Brandstätter), Christian Brandstätter Verlag, 2020

Die Heurigen von Wien (Wolfram Siebeck), Wilhelm Heyne Verlag, 1997

Cultural History of Viennese Cuisine (Thomas Stiegler), Der Leiermann, 2019

The Cooking of Vienna's Empire (Joseph Wechsberg and Fred Lyon), Time Life Books, 1979

ILLUSTRATED BOOKS

Vienna: Portrait of a City (Christian Brandstätter), Taschen, 2019

Vienna – Strolling through an Unknown City (Ernst Hausner), Edition Wien/Pichler Verlag, 1996

Wien (Ernst Hausner), Jugend und Volk Verlagsgesellschaft m.b.H., 1988

Wien (Vienna) – mit den Augen des Adlers (Alfred Havlicek & Horst Friedrich Mayer), Pichler Verlag, 2002

This Pearl Vienna – A Book of Pictures Taken from Vienna's Most Dreadful Time (Hans Riemer), Jugend und Volk G.M.B.H., 1946

FICTION AND TRAVEL WRITING

Old Masters: A Comedy (Thomas Bernhard), Penguin Classics, 2020

The Strudlhof Steps: The Depth of the Years (Heimito von Doderer), trans. Vincent Kling, NYRB Classics, 2021

The Hotel New Hampshire (John Irving), Black Swan, 1982

The Radetzky March (Joseph Roth), Granta Books, 2003

The World of Yesterday: Memoirs of a European (Stefan Zweig), Pushkin Press, 2014

WEBSITES

www.vienna.info/en (Official Vienna Tourist Board site)

www.wien.gv.at (Official City of Vienna site)

www.secretvienna.org (Vienna tours, events and activities)

www.wienguide.at (Vienna walking tours)

www.metropole.at (English-language news, advice and culture)

www.thelocal.at (Austria English-language news)

www.wienerlinien.at (Vienna's public transport system)

www.spottedbylocals.com/vienna (Useful and entertaining Blog)

Acknowledgements

First and foremost I would like to thank my original Viennese publisher, Christian Brand-stätter Verlag, for realising the first edition of this book and thereby launching the Only In Guides series. In this respect I am especially indebted to commissioning editor Elisabeth Stein, who first took an interest in my work.

For kind permission to take photographs, as well as arranging for access and the provision of information, the following people are very gratefully acknowledged: Antiquarische Fundgrube (Fuchsthallergasse), Dr. Georg Becker (Klimt Villa), Raoul Brunner (Amalienbad), Büchereien Wien, Prof. James Dickinson, Elisabeth Edhofer (Austrian National Library), Mag. Helga Farukuoye (Internationales Esperanto Museum), Dr. Franz Grieshofer & Dr. Margot Schiller (Österreichisches Museum für Volkskunde), Haas-Haus, Elisabeth-Joe Harriet, Mag. Josefa Haselböck & Wolfgang Smejkal (Hofmobil-iendepot), Mag. Benedikt Haupt (Kunsthistorisches Museum), Father Vahan Hovagimian (Mekhitaristenkloster), Michael Hugh-Bloch (Alte Leopoldsapotheke), Daniel Kennedy, Gabriele & Michael Kornherr (Confiserie zum süßen Eck), Hofrat Franz Kraljic (Schatz-kammer des Deutschen Ordens), Helmut Lackner (Technisches Museum), Frau Ledl (Bestattungsmuseum), Alexander Marwan & Marion Schuller (Michaelerkirche), Jan Mokre (Globenmuseum), Stefan Müller (Virgilkapelle), Dorothea Nahler & Prof. Bernd Lötsch (Naturhistorisches Museum), Claudia Österreicher (Wien Museum, Neidhart Fresken, Pratermuseum & Virgilkapelle), Guy & Sheila Perlaki (Shakespeare & Company Booksellers), Benjamin von Radom, Cornelia Römer (Papyrus-Collection), Walter Schmidt (Palais Coburg Residenz), Ingrid Scholz-Strasser (Freud Museum), Christian Schreitl & Angela-Jacqueline Rakuscha (Hofpavillon Hietzing), Steinmetz Gastro, Gerhard Strassgschwandtner & Karin Höfler (Third Man Museum), Brigitte Timmermann (Vienna Walks and Talks), Celine Wawruschka, Wiener Würstelstand Kupfschmiedgasse, and Dr. Günther Woratsch & Julius Reiter (Landesgericht für Strafsachen). Thanks also go to my old friend Simon Laffoley for his photo editing skills, and all the gang at Caffè a Casa.

Last but by no means least special thanks to my wife Roswitha Reisinger for encouraging and facilitating my move to Vienna, and to my late father Trevor, not only for proofreading and correcting my original hand-written manuscript but also for inspiring me to track down unusual locations in the first place. Thank you both for making it all so rewarding!

Film posters at the Third Man Museum (*Dritte Mann Museum*) (see no. 2)

5th Revised Edition published by The Urban Explorer, 2023
A division of Duncan J. D. Smith, contact@duncanjdsmith.com
www.onlyinguides.com, www.duncanjdsmith.com

Graphic design: Stefan Fuhrer
Typesetting and picture editing: Atelier 21 and Ekke Wolf
Revision typesetting and picture editing: Luke Griffin/Griffix Design
Maps: APA, Vienna. Printed and bound in Dubai by Oriental Press

All papers used by The Urban Explorer are natural, recyclable
products made from wood grown in sustainable, well-
managed forests.

ISBN 978-3-9505392-2-6

Also available, an *Only in Vienna*
smartphone audio tour recorded
live in the 1st District. For further
details visit www.onlyinguides.com
and www.hearonymus.com.